Globalization and the Future of the Welfare State

Globalization
and the Future of the
Welfare State

EDITED BY

Miguel Glatzer and
Dietrich Rueschemeyer

University of Pittsburgh Press

Published by the University of Pittsburgh Press, Pittsburgh, Pa., 15260
Copyright © 2005, University of Pittsburgh Press
Manufactured in the United States of America
Printed on acid-free paper

10   9   8   7   6   5   4   3   2   1

Library of Congress Cataloging-in-Publication Data

Globalization and the future of the welfare state / edited by Miguel Glatzer and Dietrich
Rueschemeyer.
    p. cm.
 Includes bibliographical references and index.
 ISBN 0-8229-5861-9 (alk. paper)
 1. Social policy. 2. Welfare state. 3. Globalization—Social aspects. I. Glatzer, Miguel. II.
Rueschemeyer, Dietrich.
 HN18.3.G55 2005
  361.6'1—dc22   2004025527

Contents

Tables and Figures

Tables

Figures

Acknowledgments

We would like to express our gratitude to the Thomas J. Watson Institute for International Studies at Brown University and its director, Tom Biersteker, for support of this research. We are also grateful to the Luso-American Development Foundation (FLAD) for its encouragement of this project and its general financial support of Glatzer's research in Portugal and writing at Brown. The Watson Institute provided a wonderful home for a two-year working group on economic globalization and social policy that met during the Asian financial crisis and the ensuing debate on the international economic system. During the conference that resulted from this project, the Watson Institute and its staff proved to be great hosts once again, while Brown's Wayland Collegium provided critical supportive funds. Rueschemeyer enjoyed the comfort and stimulation provided by the Swedish Collegium for Advanced Study in the Social Sciences while working on the conclusion. Among the participants in the working group and attendees at the conference, we wish to acknowledge the rich contributions of Edward Broadbent, Robert Kaufman, James Mahoney, Paul Pierson, Kenneth Shadlen, Guy Standing, and Robert Wade. We also wish to thank Patrick Heller, Joan Nelson, Elmar Rieger, and anonymous reviewers for their incisive comments and positive criticism, and we thank Mathias Vom Hau for creating the index. Finally, we are most grateful to the contributors to this volume, for their multiple insights and their lively discussion. Their contributions extend far beyond the chapters.

Globalization and the Future of the Welfare State

1

An Introduction to the Problem

MIGUEL GLATZER AND DIETRICH RUESCHEMEYER

In the last quarter of the twentieth century, and in particular in its last decade, the global political economy has been profoundly transformed. Democratic governance has prevailed in many countries, at least in the formal sense of repeated democratic elections and accountability of the state to elected representatives. At the same time, more economies have opened themselves to international trade and capital flows, while internally they have adopted a stronger market orientation. These two developments seem closely interrelated. In fact, many see them as two sides of the same coin, as in such formulas as "democratic capitalism" or "capitalist democracy," which have become common currency in public discourse. How do policies of social welfare relate to these twin transformations of democratization and increasing economic globalization? Can one expect a third transformation to join the first two, adding a growing social welfare component to democratization and liberalization of economies?

Such an expectation is not necessarily a Panglossian fantasy. It can point to at least three broad arguments. First, social welfare policies are indeed correlated with economic growth, so much so that some see the main explanation of their development in the "logic of industrialism"—in sustained economic growth and the attendant social transformations.[1] Second, the classic welfare states of Europe flourished in countries that were wide open to the world economy, and even the most comprehensive European welfare states, the Scandinavian social democracies, represent a qualified version of market-oriented capitalism, not its negation.[2] Third, welfare state policies have historically been associated with the trajectory of democratization; it is in fact reasonable to see social democracy as a deepening of a "formal" democracy that is confined to equal rights in the political sphere.[3]

Yet despite these broadly plausible arguments, there are good reasons to be skeptical of the prospect of a global triple convergence toward democratization, economic globalization on liberal terms, and social welfare provision. Among the richest countries, there are large differences between comprehensive, generous, and universal welfare provisions in some countries and means-tested and rather meager provisions for the worst-off strata in others. The logic of industrialism or of modernization does not explain these differences, though it indicates a favorable and perhaps necessary condition for public welfare provisions of any kind. Democratization may similarly present only an opening for the development of strong social welfare provisions, but not lead with any regularity to that outcome.[4] And economic globalization on liberal terms is seen by many as the major development hostile to social welfare policy. The inquiry of this project focuses on this last issue—how economic globalization affects welfare state policies.

In order to explore this question, we compare policy developments in several mid-income countries and regions against the background of developments in the comprehensive welfare states in northwestern Europe. These countries and regions include Russia, east-central Europe, Iberia, Latin America, and Korea. We look at mid-income countries and regions because they are rich enough to be able to engage in social policies aiming at social security, while their economies are at the same time plausible candidates for inclusion in the more intense international economic integration we call globalization. We chose a far-flung interregional comparison as a strategy because this maximizes variation in the conditions of interest. Exploring diverse cases in some depth is most suitable for an exploration that goes beyond the very intensively studied classic welfare states. We do not, however, dismiss cross-national statistical research. In fact, the volume opens with a cross-national statistical analysis of the impact of economic openness on mid-income political economies.[5]

Two Views of Globalization

"Globalization spells the end of social welfare states." This is the most extreme but also quite common view in current public discussion. While many bemoan this prediction, others rejoice in the imminent triumph of the market and the downfall of state-sponsored paternalism. Both sides, however, take for granted that the ever-widening global markets for goods, services, and, especially, capital undercut social welfare provisions. This volume explores the impact of different facets of globalization on national social policy in a more complex way, and it comes to conclusions that contradict the simplistic views still prevalent in much of the current discussion.

The prevailing view portrays globalization as two-sided. On the one hand, it is seen as a marvelous opportunity to increase wealth and well-being worldwide. Using well-established arguments about the benefits of free trade, advocates of economic openness argue that globalization improves economic efficiency by increasing specialization, choice, and competition. In addition, they make a political argument. Once countries open their economies, they face salutary pressures to increase transparency in the market, reduce distortions, curtail economically costly behavior, and advance productivity-enhancing policies. In this view, globalization leads to improved government performance. It penalizes bad government by reducing growth rates. Similarly, it rewards good governments—those that provide productivity-enhancing policies and transparency in economic rules—with improved economic performance.

Yet this neoliberal conceptualization of good governance implies another side of the impact of globalization. Economic globalization strengthens the role of markets and it diminishes the chances of political interventions that are guided by criteria other than profit maximization. It constrains the range of action for states. These constraints lead to the claim upon which our inquiry focuses: economic globalization undermines existing welfare states and obstructs new developments in social policy. Generous social provisions, this view holds, become an increasing burden and a drag on national performance in international competition. Even rich countries can no longer afford the economic burden of bountiful systems of social security. This claim is not uncontested. An alternative view holds that, on the contrary, economic globalization and social welfare policy mutually support each other. And this position can point to a number of critical empirical facts. As already noted, Sweden, Denmark, and the Netherlands, to name but three of the more comprehensive welfare states, have had economies open to trade for well over fifty years. In fact, their social and economic models have long been premised on the importance of exports. Overall, the major development of the European welfare states was concurrent with the shift toward openness that followed the Second World War.[6] In cross-national statistical research it was found—first in Europe (Cameron 1978), then across a large number of countries around the world (Garrett 1998; Rodrik 1997)—that foreign trade (measured in relation to total production) is positively related to social expenditure. This substantial and stable correlation is only a correlation, but it does stand in the way of simplistic "burden and drag" arguments. And so does the fact that year after year Germany has large export surpluses in spite of the fact that the wage-and-compensation packages of German workers are among the very highest in the world.

Explanations of the correlation found by Cameron, Rodrik, and Garrett typically rely on the concept of risk. Both Peter Katzenstein (1985) and John Ruggie (1982) use the concept of "embedded liberalism," in which provisions of social security, along with other rules and regulations, reduce the social risk produced by a commitment to a liberal international trading order. The churning of markets and competition in the tradables sector is made politically sustainable by a welfare and security system that reduces the social impact of risk. Domestic welfare states facilitate liberal international trading orders and reduce the potential for backlashes.

This alternative view holds, then, that the involvement in the international economy instigates social security measures because the internal dislocations created by involvement in international markets have to be compensated if continued international involvement is to be politically viable. That idea has a long history. Karl Polanyi (1957/1944) pointed to the tension between social stability and international openness of the economy in his seminal study of the "great transformation" of competitive global capitalism. Extending Polanyi through the postwar period, Rieger and Leibfried (2003) argue that globalization in advanced postwar societies was made possible by the welfare state.

Current versions of this position often go beyond the claim that social security makes economic openness sustainable. The social democratic governments of Europe embrace economic openness as a means to create the wealth that underpins generous welfare states. Participation in the global economy is valued by both sides in this debate for much the same reasons: it enhances productivity, it pressures public policy toward greater effectiveness, and it makes goods, services, and capital available at lower costs.

The discussion on globalization and the future of welfare states, then, is informed by two broad, competing hypotheses, which have been called the efficiency and the compensation hypotheses. Are these competing claims really contradictory, or could they be compatible with each other, valid under certain and not other conditions? In order to begin answering that question, it is useful to look into the causal mechanisms, the more specific hypotheses that are claimed by each of the master hypotheses.

The compensation hypothesis points to the dislocations and tensions that are created by involvement in a market that is beyond the control of most national governments. It assumes that—more often than not, but not inevitably—compensatory policies will come forth. Beyond pointing to politics as a likely response to dislocation, tension, and conflict, however, this view leaves open how problems are anticipated or made politically visible once they do occur; how strong the political forces are that respond to them; which policies will be proposed, enacted, and implemented; and even whether any responses come forth at all.

We can identify another causal mechanism, which grew in importance as modern welfare states became economically successful, when we realize that social welfare provisions are not just luxuries one can afford nor conditions that make economic openness feasible, but that they constitute conditions that enable and enhance productivity. This is obvious for education and training programs, but it also holds for the provision of health care and for measures that enable women to work outside the house, as well as for a variety of measures that reduce inequalities by class and gender in the access to enabling institutions. Recent work on cross-class coalitions and business support of the welfare state (Swenson 2002; Mares 2001; Martin 2000) casts serious doubt on earlier views in which business was assumed to be uniformly hostile to welfare provision. Nonetheless, the question remains open of when and how different forces and parties act on the insight that social welfare can enhance productivity.

It is clear that the compensation hypothesis leaves a good deal of detailed causal issues open. To a large extent, this is the case because it points to interactions of external forces with a variety of domestic factors that favor or hinder social policy developments and that shape the particular form social welfare provisions take.

The efficiency hypothesis claims that economic globalization places strong downward pressures on social welfare policy through a variety of mechanisms. The first argument, as already mentioned, is that trade competition puts pressure on social expenditures that increase costs and leave products less competitive in international markets. The decline of transportation costs and the spread of technology have given rise to low-wage competitors in the developing world. Globalization thus unleashes downward spirals of social provision as countries compete with one another not through the upgrading of skills and infrastructure (which, after all, takes time and resources to bear fruit), but rather through the lowering of tax rates and social benefits.

Yet the claim that international trade competition inevitably favors countries with low wages and low social provisions and thus exerts severe downward pressures on social well-being cannot be sustained without heavy qualifications. Although there is some evidence for low-wage competition in the third world leading to the loss of jobs in particular sectors of the advanced industrialized economies, wage-level comparisons ignore the crucial measure, which is productivity. To put it differently, what counts are not wage costs per hour, but rather their share in the costs per unit of production. And whether the high wages are mostly individual payments or contributions to collective entitlement systems is irrelevant for the price and quality competitiveness of production. For these reasons the high-skill, high-wage, and high social welfare policies of countries like Sweden, Germany, and France remain clearly feasible in the current world economy.

However, at similar levels of productivity, countries and regions can engage in competitive underbidding, and they may not only succeed in gaining a larger share of trade but may also—in the longer run—attract more outside investment by constraining wages and public social provisions. This has long been a concern among the North American states, where union busting as well as tax breaks and other benefits are often important tools in the competition to lure large corporate investments. The current attractiveness of the United States and Britain for international capital investments may rest on similar grounds. Such social underbidding, however, works only if it goes along with strong conditions for productivity. Targets with higher levels of productivity will remain immune to such competition. In the long run, then, success in international trade requires a continuous upgrading of productivity. This applies also to middle- and lower-income countries, as there is always a lower-wage competitor.

Increased capital mobility may have a greater impact on social welfare policies than increasing trade competition. Overall, it enlarges the power of capital vis-à-vis both labor and national governments. Because capital is now footloose, finding it easy to invest in other locations, it carries with it the power to exit. Unless labor and national governments acquiesce to its demands, investment is likely to occur elsewhere.

There are also a number of specific ways in which greater capital mobility is claimed to rein in the space for governmental action, including the room for policies of social welfare. Thus, capital mobility is said to put constraints on macroeconomic demand management in a single country;[7] it is also likely to impose limitations on divergent levels of taxation and, consequently, on public expenditure; and it is expected to homogenize interest rates internationally, thus eliminating lowered interest rates for special purposes as a domestic policy instrument. Yet on current empirical evidence, some qualifications seem warranted: the evidence on the homogenization of global capital markets and consequently of interest rates is far from clear-cut; levels of taxation still differ dramatically across countries, though there have been major adjustments in the highest rates of income taxation, and there continue to be great differences in the patterns and amounts of public expenditures (Swank 1998; Ganghof 2001).

Many see the spread of neoliberal economic policy ideas as another causal mechanism that undercuts social welfare policies. This acquires special importance when these ideas are advanced with the leverage of creditors. Under such circumstances, changing social policy (almost always in a downward direction) becomes a condition for the restructuring of debt.

In the attempt to assess the two master hypotheses, it is important to keep in mind the whole range of factors that affect social welfare policy. Efficiency considerations in international competition and political moves to compensate for the dislocations created by international market developments do not exhaust this range of relevant conditions.

The literature on the rise of welfare states points to such other factors as the level of economic development; new needs created by changes in family and household patterns; changing age structures of the population; and the capacity of government to take on complex tasks of planning, information gathering, taxation, administration, and service provision. This research has also revealed how welfare state policies build on inherited social patterns established in the past. Thus, state-society relations that may have established an earlier service orientation of the state will shape later social policy, and the same is true of the earlier role of the state vis-à-vis the economy and resultant patterns in the relations between state, capital, labor, and other socioeconomic groupings. Finally, one line of reasoning has acquired a special salience in the analysis of welfare state development; this assigns overwhelming importance to the balance of class power when explaining major differences in the social welfare policies of economically advanced countries.[8]

While our discussion focuses on the consequences of external economic relations for social policy, it is quite clear that these interact with the domestic factors that have been the object of most research on welfare states. The development of social policy cannot be understood in isolation from the most important domestic factors. For example, the balance of power among social and political organizations representing dominant and subordinate classes will be a major determinant of how a country responds to dislocations imposed by the workings of international markets. And the ways in which an existing system of social security is grounded in popular expectations and institutional structures will make it more or less resistant to attempts to reduce social provisions due to international pressures as well as endogenous difficulties.

Our Strategy of Inquiry

Our project explores both of the alternative conceptions about the relation between economic openness and social welfare policy. We anticipate that there is a great deal of variation in the degree to which globalization places pressures on, or provides opportunities for, the development of social policy in middle-income countries. For this set of political economies, neither the efficiency nor the compensation theory, we expect, will hold all the time. Rather, the relationship between globalization and the provision of welfare depends crucially on the strength of various domestic forces; on the ways in which state, economy, and society are interrelated; on the patterns of established social provisions; and on the particular place of a national economy in the international economic system.

Our main strategy for this exploration is a cross-regional comparison of developments over a substantial period of time. This allows us to examine a wide range of conditions along three lines of interest—the place of a country in the international economic environment, its social policy history and the underlying domestic forces and institutional patterns, and the impact of economic openness on social welfare provisions.

We open this book with a chapter that explores the two master hypotheses in cross-national statistical fashion. We are convinced, however, that the intensive exploration of national trajectories under very different conditions can yield important insights of its own. The two methodological approaches complement each other in important ways. Causal tracing in particular case histories may throw light into the often opaque results of sheer correlational analysis, while a wide-ranging quantitative analysis prevents generalizations from one or a few cases that may be misleading even if they are based on very detailed and careful analysis.

We will look at developments in middle-income countries in five different regions of the world. We begin, however, with an examination of how globalization has affected highly developed and well-institutionalized welfare states. The well-studied features of the classic European cases—their insertion into the global economy, their institutions and political forces, and the trajectories of their social policy developments—will serve as a comparative baseline for the examination of the much less studied cases of the middle-income countries.

Overall, the experience of northwestern Europe is strongly at odds with the view that globalization undermines the welfare state. This region of the world contains both the most developed welfare states and exhibits the highest degree of integration into the world economy. The high level of social spending does not predate economic openness but rather developed during the liberal trade regime instituted after World War II, and this dramatic expansion of public social provision went together with very high rates of economic growth. On balance, then, the northwestern European welfare state is not only compatible with globalization but has even thrived because of it.

If certain forms of economic globalization, such as the increase in capital mobility, do indeed constrain social policy, social provisions, once established, tend to enjoy broad-based support in society. This puts a political premium on maintaining social welfare systems and makes retrenchment of social spending politically difficult.

The welfare states of northwestern Europe certainly face pressure for change. But, as Paul Pierson (1998), among others, has argued, the main sources of pressure are domestic, not international. Technological change, the transformation of gender roles, and, above all, the aging of the population entail far greater constraints than international openness. Even where globalization does exert downward pressure, politics generally acts as a counterweight.

The main body of our analysis focuses on middle-income countries in five regions: Latin America, southern Europe, east-central Europe, the Russian confederation, and East Asia. These countries offer particularly strong insights into the nexus between economic openness and the viability of social welfare policies. Many have levels of GDP per capita at which the older welfare states embarked on social policy development. At the same time, these countries are now—through various pathways—candidates for inclusion in a more open global economic architecture. Unlike northwestern Europe, where economies have long been open, most of these middle-income countries have only recently opened their borders wide to the global economy. Many of the Latin American and southern European cases emerged late from policies of economic autarchy and import substitution industrialization. Trade in the formerly Communist countries of Eastern Europe was, of course, highly managed and largely restricted to the COMECON members. For the East Asian cases globalization is also new. Although these countries' dragonlike growth rates have been predicated on exports, their domestic economies remained highly protected against trade competition. And until recently capital flows were very restricted.

Although all of the middle-income countries we examine are now formally democracies, the quality of that democracy varies greatly. In particular, they differ in their internal balance of power, a feature that figures prominently in explanations of the rise of the European welfare state. The question thus arises: does the same logic that allowed the northwestern European states to develop their welfare states as they became more integrated into the international economy following World War II also apply to middle-income countries opening their economies today? Alternatively, is there something different, either about the international economy and a country's place in it, or about the domestic politics of these middle-income countries, that precludes a trajectory similar to that of northwestern Europe?

Social policy developments in these countries and regions are not only compared to the comprehensive northwestern European welfare states, though the features of welfare state development in Europe inform the theoretical framework we developed for the examination of the different cases. It is equally instructive to compare the different regions one to the other. They differ in important ways from one another and at the same time display significant internal variations. While all of them have opened up to the global economy, policies of social protection face very different problems in each of the countries involved.

A comparative analysis of these regions, then, yields results that are significant in two ways. First, it gives factual insights into and a deeper understanding of social policy developments in these countries of medium wealth located largely outside the power centers of the world. Second, and perhaps more important, interregional and intraregional variations can be exploited for inferences about the impact of different facets of globalization on national social policy as they interact with different domestic conditions.

To anticipate the broad results of this inquiry into the impact of globalization on welfare policies, it challenges the stark neoliberal view that economic openness uniformly reduces social welfare measures to a minimum or even renders welfare state policies impossible altogether. Different regions and different countries within regions illustrate important contrasts—in the impact of globalization, in the political responses, and in the economic structures and past policies that shape the political options.

A Theoretical Framework

Before introducing the structure of the volume and the contribution of individual chapters, we will spell out the theoretical framework developed for the volume as a whole. Following a brief delineation of what we mean by social welfare policy, this framework consists of three parts: (1) a conceptual clarification of what is meant by globalization, which also includes an initial assessment of possible and likely consequences of its various aspects, (2) a preliminary identification of the characteristic features of the northwestern European welfare states that made them relatively immune to possibly corrosive effects of globalization, and (3) the specification of a counterpart list of conditions that may make other countries more vulnerable.

Social welfare policy is a concept that has been variously defined. For this largely exploratory study, we want to keep it a broad and encompassing concept. We do not, however, impose this broad meaning on all country inquiries; in certain cases it may be too wide a lens. Many narrower definitions focus on transfer programs that protect against the economic risks of illness, disability, unemployment, old age, and insufficient income for other reasons. Broader definitions include public provision of health-enhancing measures, education, and institutions that enable both men and women to join the labor force. And yet broader conceptions include government action to secure employment opportunities for all who seek employment and policies that seek to limit economic inequality.

Conceptualizing Globalization

Globalization is an overused and overly broad concept that is obviously in need of differentiation. We restrict our analysis to economic forms of globalization and distinguish among five aspects:

- Expanding international trade in goods and services
- Expanding international capital flows
- An increasing internationalization of production through transnational corporations and global commodity chains
- A growing role of international organizations such as the World Trade Organization, the World Bank, and the International Monetary Fund
- A greater transnational flow of economic ideas

By specifying these elements of globalization we give the term analytic precision. Considering them separately makes it possible to identify different causal mechanisms through which globalization may affect welfare state policies.

Current trends toward globalization have to be seen in a historical and comparative perspective. As Robert Wade (1996) and others have shown, today's economic interdependence is historically not altogether unprecedented. Furthermore, the international flows of capital and goods and services are largely concentrated in north-north exchanges, and if one neglects certain borders (for example, the national borders within the European Union), the picture of international economic interdependence becomes substantially more modest. Yet neither of these qualifications is meant to negate the existence of a powerful reality. Even for the economies of the established welfare states, cross-border trade and international capital flows have never been as large. And although trade and capital flows in middle-income countries represent only a small proportion of trade and capital flows worldwide, these often loom large for the national economies involved.

Many have seen economic globalization as a trend that marginalizes states. Yet economic interdependence—whether at the national or international level—requires the underpinnings of legal guarantees and regulations. The bulk of this required institutional infrastructure for economic globalization is still provided by national states—either directly or indirectly—through bilateral and multilateral cooperation. That means that surges in such interdependence are not simply inexorable processes immune to collective decision making, but are based on political decisions. This is important to emphasize against simplistic ideas that see globalization as an autonomous development that makes national states obsolete. Of course, national states vary dramatically in power, and there is no question that the current surge of globalization is shaped disproportionately by the United States; but other governments, including those of a number of middle- and low-income countries, did participate in advancing economic interdependence. That said, however, it is equally important to recognize that the new role of transnational corporations and the growth of multilateral institutions at the center of today's global economy are indeed changing the balance of power in the international political economy.

The international exchange of goods and services is in principle an important instrument of specialization, choice, and enhanced productivity. The ancient claim of classic economic theory is fundamentally right: If different countries and regions specialize in production in which they have a comparative advantage, consumers in all of them will be better off. An almost equally old qualification holds that this is a static view and that some insulation of "infant industries" from international competition may permit new productive capacities to be developed to the point where the comparative advantage of a country is moved to a higher level. This qualification is valid as well, though there is no guarantee that such protection will actually lead to an upgrading in efficiency rather than result in a rental haven for inefficient and wasteful production. International competition in goods and services among countries with very different systems of labor rights and social security can harm the more generous systems of social provision unless these are associated with compensating productivity advantages. Even if all things go well, the dynamics of market-driven industrial change create not only winners but losers as well. These dynamics exacerbate existing social risks and create new ones. In the classic conception of welfare state advocates, openness to international markets for goods and services increases productivity as well as risk, rendering social welfare measures both desirable and feasible.

Most economists embrace greater mobility of capital across international boundaries as another important enhancement of productivity. Other things being equal, economically worthwhile projects have a better chance to attract capital investments, even if they are located in countries or regions with a weak capacity for savings. For them, attracting capital becomes less costly. For capital owners, including pension funds, investments become more profitable. Yet there are two problematic aspects of greater capital mobility. The first is the potential volatility of capital inflows and outflows, which can leave in sudden ruin economic developments that were built up in years. The speedy recovery of many (though not all) East Asian countries from the financial crisis of 1997-1998 must not conceal the fact that these countries suffered a blow that was comparable only to the impact of the Great Depression on economic and social life in Europe and the United States.

The other problematic side of dramatic increases in capital mobility is a matter of power. As noted earlier, owners of mobile capital gain a significant power advantage over labor and governments, which can be turned against generous social welfare provisions and used as leverage against unwanted taxation. (And there is some evidence that this leverage is actually used.) True, they may prefer not to exercise their exit option because of the productivity advantages often associated with these provisions as well as with good government; but the shift in power is real nevertheless. Greater capital mobility may, in particular, constrain a political use of capital that is guided by criteria other than profit, and it may limit other tools of economic and social governance as well.

Transnational corporations and stable production chains linking locations in different countries raise some of the same issues as expanding international trade and increased capital mobility: deepening international division of labor, the spread of technology, the potential for enhanced productivity versus the charge (and often the reality) that the export of production is driven by the chance to exploit weak labor in poor countries. What sets transnational business firms and coordinated production chains apart is their corporate character and the power international companies often derive from their market position. What in the textbook of international trade is the impersonal functioning of the market mechanism here takes on the shape of identifiable actors with considerable power of command, often enhanced by market dominance. Transnational companies may hold great power over significant parts of a country's economy and labor force as well as the government, though the residual power of even weak and inefficient states dealing with them is often too radically discounted. The relation among transnational companies and their host countries and countries of origin—and thus the impact transnational companies can have on national policy—seems highly contingent on varying economic and institutional factors.

At the multilateral level, the surge of economic interdependence after the Second World War found its institutional embodiment in the international financial and trade organizations initiated by the Bretton Woods agreements—the IMF and the World Bank, as well as the GATT, which turned later into the WTO. These are supplemented by regional organizations.

International organizations deserve special attention because they are in effect an embryonic supranational state structure without democratic control and legitimation. At the same time, they pursue a particular conception of the right economic order and back this pursuit by legal decisions as well as the granting or withholding of credit. The credit decisions of the international financial institutions (IFIs) gain further significance as many private banks take their cue from actions of these multilateral institutions. The U.S. government has a disproportionate influence on the orientation of the IFIs. Polemic against the "Washington consensus" may stereotype the content of that orientation and exaggerate its stability over time, but this rhetoric identifies the American influence quite accurately.

As the institutional embodiment of globalization, the IMF, World Bank, and the WTO have become focal points in the discussion about globalization. Many argue not against economic globalization per se, but against the particular form of globalization for which the IFIs stand. Their conception of globalization has come under attack for having a monetarist bent; for penalizing deficit spending, often at the cost of investment in skills, health and infrastructure; for not taking environmental concerns into consideration; and for exposing countries to damaging and unnecessary volatility by pressuring them to liberalize capital mobility. More immediately relevant to our inquiry is the critique that their conception of globalization pays little or no attention to labor rights and social security provisions. In contradistinction to this model of globalization, it is argued, stand other models that do pay more attention to social welfare rights. These include the development models proposed by the United Nations Development Program and the International Labor Organization.

The IMF comes under particular attack from the foes of globalization. However, the functions that the IMF plays are vital and necessary to any conception of a working global market. International lending, a lynchpin of a global market, would collapse if nothing were done to repair balance of payment difficulties and if borrowers who find themselves overexposed were free not to repay. It is also necessary to combine bailouts with conditions lest a premium is put on further unrealistic lending and borrowing. But the content of these conditions is subject to debate. To what extent do they protect lenders more than borrowers, and in what measure are the conditions inspired by political preferences that are not required in a more neutral perspective? Furthermore, the causes of the need for assistance make a difference; mistakes and mismanagement in economic policy are different from exogenous shocks such as the contagion effects of financial crises or the temporary decline of commodity prices.

The transnational flow of economic ideas is clearly intertwined with the other features of globalization, especially with the growing importance of transnational corporations, with the relations of political, economic, and cultural dominance and subordination, and with the role of multilateral institutions, some of which— such as the OECD—focus their efforts on the production of economic knowledge and advice. Keynes may have overstated the case when he claimed that "the ideas of economists and political philosophers, both when they are right and when they are wrong, are more powerful than is commonly assumed"; but there is little doubt that a major component in the current surge of economic interdependence is a "triumph of neoclassical economics in the developing world," as Biersteker puts it.[9] Though it is possible to point to a number of conditions that favored neoliberal ideas, the genesis of their current hegemony is far less well understood than the conditions and bases of social democratic ideas that became the basis for social welfare policies during the last century.

Mature Welfare States

An analysis of northwestern Europe's experience informs the theoretical design of our inquiry into the effects of globalization on social welfare policy. The welfare states of northwestern Europe have proved to be largely immune to the negative effects of globalization. Indeed, many have argued for a positive correlation between the degree of economic openness of this region and its high levels of social protection. It is true that this relative immunity is not guaranteed to extend into the future. But the past record is valuable as a point of reference. Previous research on northwestern Europe suggests a list of features relevant to these polities' insulation from the negative impact of economic globalization. This list of factors follows.

A prolonged and high integration into the world market. European economies turned toward openness following the end of Second World War. In large measure an attempt to avoid future war through the creation of economic interdependence, this turn toward openness was represented politically in the creation of the European Coal and Steel Community (ECSC), the Common Market, the European Union (which grew out of it), as well as the European Free Trade Association (EFTA). But economic openness was by no means limited to Europe. As trade and economic integration rose, after the low levels imposed by the protectionist policies and embargoes of the Great Depression and the Second World War, the systems of social provisions grew and matured.

Success and "orthodoxy" in fiscal and international trade policy. Most comprehensive welfare states developed in countries that managed fiscal and trade policy well. Balance of payments deficits were rare, and, more recently, budget deficits have been reduced. This has two important consequences. First, the end of Keynesianism, which is generally seen as a consequence of globalization, has a much smaller impact on the viability of these countries' welfare states than is commonly assumed. Although the concept of the Keynesian welfare state captures important features of the postwar political economy of Europe, the concept describes two linked but fundamentally distinct sets of policies. The welfare state is not ineluctably tied to a Keynesian macroeconomic framework, as the stability and in some cases expansion of the welfare state since the adoption of a monetarist framework attests. This is not to argue that the end of Keynesianism was unproblematic for the welfare state. Certainly, many argue that the unemployment problem that has beleaguered Europe has been largely aggravated, if not caused, by an overly restrictive monetary policy.[10] Nonetheless, the demise of Keynesianism has been much less inimical to the welfare state than predicted. The second consequence of orthodoxy is that it makes it unnecessary for a country to go to the IMF for conditional help and it reduces a country's vulnerability to speculative attacks on its currency.

High productivity economies supported by the welfare state. Generous social benefits are an integral part of the highly skilled and highly productive economies of northwestern Europe. These high tax regimes promote increases in productivity in two important ways. First, the high cost of labor and taxation forces employers to invest in high-productivity employment. Second, the welfare state directly provides, and is accompanied by, policies that produce a highly skilled labor supply.

A balance of class power, political constellations, and coalition opportunities favorable for social policy. The mature welfare states of Scandinavia and continental Europe have strong labor or social democratic parties, along with Christian Democratic parties that support social solidarity, even if with different emphases. By contrast, liberal or free-market parties remain weak in these countries. Left-wing parties that are pro-welfare but anticapitalist and against economic integration are weak, but have been able to keep issues of social equity high on the agenda. Strong union movements, with relatively high degrees of unionization and politically supported extensions of collective bargaining results to whole industries, provide an important underpinning for social welfare-oriented politics.

Popular expectations based on past experience—the "naturalization" of social provisions. Once provided, social benefits are popular and hard to remove. The relative failure in the 1980s of Thatcher and Reagan in dismantling the welfare state represents clear evidence of the difficulty in ending these programs (Pierson 1996). In the 1990s the collapse of multiple French and Italian governments following popular demonstrations over social security reforms further reinforces this conclusion (Levy 1999). Because of their peculiarities, the cases of Australia and New Zealand, where serious erosion of social provisions did take place, are likely to remain exceptions (Schwartz 2000).[11] Where provided on a universal basis, as is often the case in northwestern Europe, social programs enjoy very broad support and are all the harder to remove or even to modify significantly. From one point of view this appears as a rigidity inherent in comprehensive systems of social security; from another it indicates that welfare states create and re-create their own very strong political foundations.

Grounding of welfare state measures in established institutional structures. Welfare states exhibit great continuity not only because they are popular. They are also deeply embedded in a multitude of institutional structures, ranging from public bureaucracies to private interest groups, service organizations, churches, and universities. Analytically separate from the aggregation of individual interest as measured in surveys probing the welfare state's popularity, this grounding in institutions significantly helps to account for the welfare state's durability. These institutions shape underlying preferences, affect interests, provide constituencies, increase the number of stakeholders, influence the policy process, and transmit values across generations.

State capacity for policy innovation and adaptation. The rise of a highly skilled and professionalized welfare state civil service, along with considerable monitoring by and dialogue with academic experts and nongovernmental organizations in civil society, make it possible for the state to design and implement new policy and to evaluate old ones. One of the hallmarks of the European welfare states is that they have not remained static, but have adapted to new social and economic challenges. The provision of daycare, the shift from a passive to an active labor market policy, the array of policies targeting social exclusion, and the introduction of long-term care provisions in Germany all constitute examples of the welfare state's responsiveness to new and evolving social risks. Increasing international contact and international research allow for transnational policy learning and adoption.

Secure political standing in interstate relations and immunity from the prescriptions of international financial institutions (IFIs). The combination of wealth, prestige, good governance, and the successful managing of the external account provides these countries with considerable autonomy from IFIs and an influence in international relations that is frequently out of proportion to their economic and military power. Since they do not need to go to the IMF, these countries are not subject to the conditionality of its loans.

Overall, these countries have developed successful varieties of capitalism that represent alternatives to the dominant neoliberal thinking. Even though the latter has had considerable political appeal, the countries' politics are marked more by continuity and adaptability than by a search for radical change.

Social Welfare Development in Middle-Income Countries

The favorable conditions found in northwestern Europe can be inverted to arrive at features of a country's place in the international scene, of its domestic social forces and institutions, and its trajectory of economic and social policy, all of which create openings for a stronger impact of globalization. In the other regions under study we expected to find one or more of these features. Yet we did not assume that variation in any one of these dimensions would by itself lead to a strong negative impact of economic openness on social policy.[12] We consider both the previous and the following list as theoretically meaningful orienting devices, not as definitive hypotheses about the impact of economic globalization on the chances of social welfare policy.

New or unsuccessful integration into the world economy. The disruption produced by opening a previously protected market to world trade is obviously larger than that experienced by a country with a long history of trade. For example, wrenching change was produced in each of the following cases: abandonment of policies of import substitution industrialization, the opening of the economies of Australia and New Zealand beyond the privileged relationship with the United Kingdom, or the opening of Communist economies to both the market economy and international openness.

Past dependence on credit beyond repayment capacity; "conditionalities" for credit restructuring. Many of the middle-income countries have experienced debt and balance of payments problems, leading frequently to IMF intervention. This not only entailed a loss of policy-making autonomy, but enhanced the influence of policy inclinations that gave little weight to socially weaker interests. In Latin America, the problems of debt restructuring, which arguably strongly favored lenders over borrowers, were particularly severe, resulting in the "lost decade" of the 1980s. The severity and duration of credit problems and the degree to which IMF conditionalities are adhered to, however, vary greatly.

Competition on the basis of low skill/low wage production. Without the virtuous circle of a high-productivity and high-wage economy, many middle-income countries compete on cost. Without concomitant improvements in productivity, welfare state measures may be viewed as burdens that reduce a country's competitiveness.

Less supportive domestic balance of class power and political constellations. A smaller industrial working class, weak and competing unions, or unions tied by arrangements of patronage to conservative political parties reduce the political power of the workers' movement. In marked contrast to the rise of the European welfare state in the 1950s and 1960s, the power of organized labor in today's middle-income countries is substantially reduced by large informal sectors, high unemployment rates, divided labor movements, and neoliberal economic reform.

Problems in the functioning of new democracies and authoritarian legacies. The relationship between constitutional structure and the prospects of social policy is complex. Authoritarian governments may engage in welfare policy in order to prevent a push for democracy under left-wing auspices (as in Imperial Germany). But their legacies often constrain welfare state development.

These legacies are of two principal kinds. The first concerns the heritage of a weak civil society. Poor educational structures, impaired unions, restrictions on freedom of the press, and suspicion of reformist or pro-poor politics as leftist or proto-Communist, occur to different extents in different countries, limiting the mobilization of progressive groups and the political salience of social issues. A frequent second legacy is the economic record. Although authoritarian governments often rested their claims to legitimacy on a combination of order and economic growth, their exit from power often comes at a time of either recession or the exhaustion of their economic model. Thus, the transition to democracy often occurs at times of economic strain, providing few windows of opportunity for welfare state development. Dealing with debt or reducing inflation often become the main items on the economic agenda of new democratic governments, pushing issues of social reform and equity down the ladder.

Many of the new democratic regimes are themselves highly imperfect. Personal politics, weak legislative bodies, and overconcentration of authority in the executive branch characterize a high number of these new democracies. Deadlock between parliament and the president can lead to policy paralysis (Russia). Alternatively, an overly strong executive can overcome parliamentary reservations and implement far-reaching neoliberal reforms (Argentina). In either case, social policy development is hampered or blocked (see O'Donnell 1994; Huber, Rueschemeyer, and Stephens 1997).

Initial forms of welfare provision creating segmented beneficiary constituencies and inhibiting future developments in a low-provision environment. Previously established social benefits in many middle-income countries are not comprehensive, but limited to particular segments of the population. Typically, social protections have covered the military, civil servants, and skilled workers in critical parts of the economy or with the capacity to unionize. Especially in countries with high degrees of inequality, the extension of social benefits to the numerous poor is likely to hurt current middle- or lower-middle-class beneficiaries. These current beneficiaries could then experience a combination of increased taxes and reduced benefits. Under such conditions, extending the welfare state to provide broader or universal coverage is likely to be politically difficult.

A high-provision past that cannot be sustained in a radically changed economic and political order. Virtually all of the former Communist countries inherited comprehensive and egalitarian systems of social provision. Though often modest in the individual allocations, the commitments of the system as a whole were too high to be sustained under current conditions. This is especially true given the contraction in their economies induced by the bankruptcy of the old system and the disruptions of the transition to the market. Past commitments to employment security and enterprise-based social provisions are not compatible with a market economy. Economic contraction and problems in tax collection have reduced the ability of governments to fund Western-style systems of social protection. Even aside from the problems of transition, under the new circumstances of political pluralism and a market-based economic order, these countries are now too poor to recreate a similar comprehensive system of social provision.

Popular expectations that are too low or too high. A disorganized civil society or an electorate disillusioned with political promises and the quality of government services is likely not to demand social programs. For considerable sections of the population the very existence of such programs might be unimaginable; other groups might feel that these programs are unobtainable, and that expecting these programs, or pressing for them, is futile. On the other hand, expectations based on the "naturalization" of the social provisions experienced under Communism lead to demands that cannot be fulfilled under new circumstances, and this can result in the stalemate that blocked Russian social policy development for a decade.

Absence of an established institutional welfare structure or one that ill fits with radical transformations in politics and the economy. The network of institutions that anchor the welfare state and give it permanence are often either missing or weak. Thus, public bureaucracies involved in the implementation of social policies might be poorly developed or have their strength sapped by inflation or the contracting out of services. Unions that might once have played a key role in social policy might lose members or policy relevance, either due to the rise of competing unions or to a generalized decline in membership. The party system in many cases is recent or unstable, increasing the flux in the electoral base of individual parties and their policy agendas. In former Communist countries, many of the institutions that supported social policy delivery have withered. Large firms, the vehicle for many social protections and services, have come under severe pressure, and many either live a semifictitious existence or have gone bankrupt.

Weak state capacity for implementation, innovation, and adaptation of policies. States often lack the technical expertise to evaluate and design effective policies. More critically, their ability to implement policy is weak. Tax collection is deficient, the average educational level of government workers is wanting, productivity in the public sector is low, the territorial penetration of state institutions is uneven, and courts are slow. Poor institutions of governance thus stymie the delivery of even well-designed policy. Adequately funding and reforming the public sector to allow it to provide good schools, health care, and social services constitute serious and long-term challenges.

Weak international leverage; different forms of political-cultural "dependency." In the wake of failed models of economic development—be they flawed import substitution industrialization or command and control economies—states search for new models. Despite a healthy variety of capitalist models, the transnational network of economic ideas and advice is today dominated by neoliberal currents of thought. The prestige and current ascendancy of the American model in the advice of influential international organizations frames the debate on the design of social policy in many middle-income countries. Other models, such as the northwestern European, fade in importance, at least outside of Europe.

With this conceptual and theoretical framework we approached the cross-regional analysis. To repeat, we consider these three sets of specifications on globalization, mature welfare states, and middle-income countries as theoretically meaningful orienting devices, not as definitive claims about the impact of economic globalization on the chances of social welfare policy. This goes especially for the last list of features that may make the political economies of middle-income countries more vulnerable to globalization. In many cases, we expected to find one or more of these features, but we did not assume that variation in any one of these dimensions would lead to a strong negative impact of economic openness on social policy.

The Chapters to Follow

Geoffrey Garrett and David Nickerson open the volume with a quantitative analysis of the relationship between globalization and social spending in middle-income countries. They show that the relationship between openness and public spending is far from uniform. Adding to the earlier findings of Cameron (1978) and Rodrik (1997), they show that in middle-income countries the positive correlation between openness and public spending holds for capital mobility as well, and that democracy mediates the relationship and is significantly associated with increases in public spending.

John Stephens discusses the overall success of the northwestern European welfare state in the face of globalization. He shows how trade has long been an integral facet of the political economies of these welfare states, but argues that the shift toward greater capital mobility—instituted in the 1990s—holds the potential for disruption.

Evelyne Huber argues that there have been distinctly different policy reactions to globalization in Latin America. Although the adoption of neoliberal policies has received the most attention, some countries, such as Costa Rica and to a lesser extent Uruguay, have maintained a social democratic approach to globalization. Domestic politics plays a central role in explaining these different policy trajectories.

Miguel Glatzer presents Portugal and Spain as the clearest instances of the possibility for welfare state development in the face of globalization. These countries emerged from dictatorship and relative economic autarchy to embrace a triple transition to democracy, economic openness, and welfare state building. Although not yet at the level of their richer northern European counterparts, the Iberian welfare states have become an impressive institutional edifice, providing universal coverage for the full array of risks. They are well grounded in politics and society.

Mitchell Orenstein and Martine Haas discuss the impact of globalization on the social protection policies of east-central Europe. Keeping domestic causes of the downturn in social provision analytically separate from external ones, they highlight the difficulties of moving from a centrally planned to a market economy. After considerable initial variation in domestic politics they observe a partial convergence in social policies, guided by advice from international institutions.

Linda Cook examines the impact of globalization on Russia. Despite the overall calamitous state of social policy, she finds important variation across policy areas, clearly demonstrating the role played by political processes and institutions in determining the effects of international advice.

Ho Keun Song and Kyung Zoon Hong chart the trajectory of Korean social policy, paying special attention to the last ten years. Underdeveloped in comparative terms, the Korean welfare state faces conflicting pressures. On the one hand, democratization and demographic factors have led to calls for greater social spending. On the other hand, the recent Asian financial crisis had contradictory effects; it increased pressures to reduce social charges and worker protections, but it also engendered expansions of support for the unemployed and the poor. Although Korea's spectacular history of growth has been linked to its export success, the Korean domestic market remained highly protected until recently. This degree of protection, along with historically strict capital controls, may account for why globalization has until recently exerted only a muted effect in promoting welfare state growth.

The book closes with concluding reflections by the editors that return to the two competing master hypotheses. In our examination of the different causal mechanisms associated with each of these, we focus in particular on the diversity of risks to which social welfare policies respond. The concluding essay above all seeks to integrate hypotheses about the impact of external factors on social welfare policies with the rich work on the genesis of the classic welfare states that saw them rooted primarily in domestic conditions.

2

Globalization, Democratization, and Government Spending in Middle-Income Countries

GEOFFREY GARRETT AND DAVID NICKERSON

Research on the relationship between integration into international markets and the welfare state has a long and distinguished history. There are three major findings in the literature. First, countries that are more exposed to trade tend to have larger public economies, allowing governments to compensate those who are adversely affected by international competition (and maintaining political support for openness [Ruggie 1982]). The original result was for the rich countries of the Organisation for Economic Co-operation and Development (OECD) (Cameron 1978), but more recently Rodrik (1998) has shown that the positive trade-spending nexus holds for the developing world as well. Second, it has been argued that this relationship is stronger in more democratic regimes where the political incentives are greater for governments to mitigate market-generated inequalities of income and risk (Adsera and Boix 2001). Finally, many analysts suspect that increasing capital mobility in recent years has put downward pressure on the public economy (see, for example, Rodrik 1997), but exploratory empirical work has not confirmed this conjecture (Garrett 2001b; Garrett and Mitchell 2001; Quinn and Inclan 1997; Swank 1998).

In this essay, we explore the globalization-government spending relationship in middle-income countries, which we consider to be particularly interesting from the standpoint of broader debates about national autonomy in the global economy.[1] The dynamics in middle-income countries are likely to be different from those in the OECD for at least two reasons. First, integration into international markets has tended to increase more rapidly in middle-income countries in recent decades. Second, transitions to democracy in the past two decades have given political power to would-be globalization losers in political systems that may not be sufficiently stable to withstand the conflict this might generate. On the other hand, political economic dynamics are also likely to be different from those in low-income countries with largely autocratic regimes, where government spending is often used as a way to feather the nests of public officials and their cronies rather than redistributing wealth and risk broadly throughout society.

Our analysis yields three central findings. First, irrespective of how one measures the *level* of exposure of national economies to international markets (that is, not only trade, but also flows of foreign direct investment and policy restrictions on the capital account), more integrated middle-income countries tend to have larger public economies. The relationship found is much stronger for foreign direct investment (FDI) and restrictions on capital movements, but the results are consistent with the Cameron-Rodrik thesis and hold quite broadly across the middle-income countries.

Second, government spending has risen less quickly in middle-income countries in which the increase in capital mobility has been most dramatic between the 1980s and the 1990s. This is consistent with popular perceptions about the constraining effects of financial integration.

Finally, in countries in which political regimes became more democratic over these two decades, heightened international market integration of all sorts was associated with faster growth in government spending. Thus, there has been a virtuous circle in middle-income countries among globalization, democratization, and bigger government. Integration into international markets has promoted economic development in middle-income countries (Garrett 2001a); this development has made successful transitions to democracy possible (Przeworski et al. 2000), and newly democratic governments have used the public economy to broadly redistribute the fruits of openness throughout society.[2]

The remainder of this chapter is divided into four major sections. The first section briefly reprises the contending theoretical arguments about the effects of globalization on the public economy. The next section describes overtime and cross-national variations in market integration and government spending in middle-income countries. The fourth section presents our regression analysis. We summarize our results and discuss their implications by way of conclusion in the last section.

Efficiency, Compensation, and Globalization

There are two basic positions in the globalization and government spending debate. The conventional wisdom about globalization constraints on the public economy can be called the "efficiency" hypothesis because it highlights competitiveness pressures and threats of exit by mobile asset holders. The "compensation" hypothesis, in contrast, emphasizes the domestic dislocations generated by globalization and the incentives for government interventions in the economy that these generate.[3]

The Efficiency Hypothesis

The fundamental tenet of the efficiency hypothesis is that government spending—beyond minimal market friendly measures such as defense and securing property rights and other fundamental public goods—reduces the competitiveness of national producers in international goods and services markets. There is no market for, and hence no market constraints on, publicly provided services. Income transfer programs and social services distort labor markets and bias intertemporal investment decisions. Moreover, government spending must be funded, often by borrowing in the short term, and ultimately by higher taxes. Taxes on income and wealth directly erode the bottom lines of asset holders and distort their investment decisions, and the more progressive a tax system, the greater the distortions. Borrowing results in higher real interest rates that further depress investment. If this also leads to an appreciation in the real exchange rate, the competitiveness of national producers is decreased.

According to the efficiency hypothesis, therefore, there is a zero-sum quality to the relationship between trade and the size of government. It does not matter whether one considers trade liberalization as the inevitable product of exogenous technological innovations in transportation and communication or as the conscious choice of governments to reap the benefits of trade (scale economies, comparative advantage, and the like).[4] Either way, exposure to trade should curtail government spending.

This logic is thought to be even more powerful with respect to capital mobility, particularly financial capital. Traders operating twenty-four hours a day can instantly move massive amounts of money around the globe in ceaseless efforts to increase returns on their investments. For many, the potential for massive capital flight has rendered international financial markets the ultimate arbiters of government policy. The logic underpinning this view is straightforward. Governments are held ransom by mobile capital, the price is high, and punishment for noncompliance is swift. If the policies and institutions approved by the financial markets are not found in a country, money will hemorrhage unless and until they are. In turn, financial capital is usually thought to disapprove of all government policies that distort markets, and excessive government spending is among the most prominent villains.

In sum, the efficiency hypothesis contends that government spending should have been subjected to powerful lowest common denominator pressures as a result of the increasingly global scale of markets in recent decades. From the Depression until the 1970s, it may have been possible for governments to expand the public economy at little cost, because this was a period of relative closure in the international economy. In the contemporary era of global markets, however, the trade-off between efficiency and welfare is harsh and direct, and governments have no choice but to shrink the state.

The Compensation Hypothesis

The efficiency perspective's focus on the economic costs of government spending overlooks the possibility that there are political incentives to expand the public economy in response to globalization and that these may outweigh the constraints imposed by market integration. Globalization may well benefit all segments of society in the long run through the more efficient allocation of production and investment. But the short-term political effects of globalization are likely to be very different. Expanding the scope of markets can be expected to have two effects that would heighten citizen support for government spending—increasing inequality and increasing economic insecurity.

The effect of trade is likely to be more pronounced on inequality than insecurity in the OECD, with the converse more likely to obtain for much of the developing world. In accordance with Hecksher-Ohlin models, expanding trade will reduce demand (and hence employment opportunities and incomes) for relatively scarce factors of production (labor in the north, capital in the south) while increasing demand for abundant factors. This should result in increasing inequality in the OECD but more equality (as labor benefits from market integration) in developing countries (Wood 1994). In contrast, trade patterns are not particularly volatile in the OECD and are characterized by very high levels of intra-industry and intra-firm trade. As a result, trade growth is unlikely to increase economic insecurity much in the advanced industrial democracies. But given more specialized patterns of trade in the developing world, volatility—and hence economic insecurity—should be more widespread in these countries (Rodrik 1997).

There is less work on the domestic effects of capital mobility. One reasonable premise, however, is that rising capital mobility should substantially increase both inequality and insecurity in the OECD, and that these effects should be even more apparent in less developed countries. The primary beneficiaries of financial market integration are the owners of liquid assets and those in the finance sector—or more specifically, large financial houses in the wealthiest OECD countries. It is less clear that these benefits trickle down to other segments of society, or across national borders. Moreover, unexpected and massive volatility comes hand in hand with financial globalization—as the headline crises of the 1990s attest. The societal insecurities associated with this volatility are likely to be large and are more pronounced in countries with greater short-term international liabilities (that is, the less developed countries, or LDCs).

Democracy

Adsera and Boix (2001) argue that the compensation hypothesis is likely to hold in more democratic political regimes, whereas the efficiency dynamic is more likely to dominate policy choice in autocratic regimes. The reasoning behind this argument is straightforward. Democratic leaders have a greater incentive to address the political demands of broad swathes of society, and in particular those of rank-and-file workers whose electoral support is likely to be essential to their continuing political success. Making sure that capital performs its "public function" of investing is just as important, perhaps more important, for democrats than for autocrats, but there are good reasons for capital to support a somewhat redistributive democratic government. This is Ruggie's (1982) compromise of "embedded liberalism," in which democratic redistribution of income and risk is a small price to pay for broad public support for openness.

This logic is likely to be even stronger in democratizing regimes. Pent-up citizen demands for redistributive government are likely to be high, and newly established democratic governments are likely to be particularly sensitive to meeting these demands. In turn, economic actors know that public sentiment for supporting market losers could well be channeled into protectionism, and building up a large public economy is a way to avoid this outcome.

It should be noted that we are not directly concerned with inequality of income or wealth. Even closed economies may decide to redistribute wealth from the rich to the poor (or vice versa) and such redistributive pressures will always be present. Rather, what concerns us is redistribution from groups that are benefiting from globalization to groups who are suffering. Quite often the declining groups will not be the poorest of the poor since they were operating in what was once a profitable niche in the economy. In fact, in order to express a meaningful political voice and receive compensation, a group must have some resources a government cares about (for example, money or people). Inequality is certainly important and plays a role in how compensation is provided, but it is not our immediate concern in this analysis.

Over-time Trends and Cross-National Variations

Government Spending

The two broadest available measures of the size of the public sector are total central government spending and consumption expenditures for general government. Total central government spending comprises all types of central government activity, but it does not capture expenditures by state and local governments. Most middle-income countries are quite centralized, but there are important exceptions—notably Argentina and Brazil (in which more than 40 percent of public spending occurs at the state and local level [Garrett and Rodden 2001]). The consumption-spending variable, in contrast, takes into account all levels of government. But this only measures the purchase of goods and services by government. One can argue that much of this spending redistributes wealth and risk. Public health and education are obvious examples, but all forms of public employment are likely to disproportionately benefit the less well off and the lower skilled.

It must be noted, however, that the general government consumption measure does not take into account some facets of government that are central to conventional conceptions of the welfare state—most notably income transfer programs such as pensions and sickness and unemployment benefits. Income transfer payments are typically a much smaller portion of government spending in middle-income countries than in the OECD, but again there are some important exceptions—particularly in transition countries. Latvia, Belarus, and Bulgaria all devote roughly 12 percent of GDP to social security and welfare transfer programs.

In essence we are using size of government, as measured by total central government expenditures and general government consumption, as a rough proxy for compensation to groups that lose out from globalization. Since each measure captures a slightly different facet of welfare effort, we report results using both measures. It could be argued, of course, that we should measure compensation more narrowly—say using unemployment benefits and pensions or education and health spending. We use the broader size of government measures for two reasons. First, the data for disaggregated expenditures is not as widely available. Our goal was to analyze government responses to globalization for as wide a range of middle-income countries as possible and not only those that are covered by the IMF's *Government Finance Statistics*.

Second and more important, governments can and do compensate sectors of the economy in ways that are not easily captured in a single class of expenditures. For example, Esping-Andersen (1990) considers the corporatist and Christian Democratic welfare states of the Benelux countries and the social democratic welfare states of Scandinavia equally redistributive. But the Christian Democratic model relies on income transfer programs that are mostly run by central governments, whereas the Scandinavian systems are characterized by the generous provision of public services (education, health, and daycare) that are often decentralized. Neither is inherently "better" in terms of compensation, and it would seem imprudent to use a narrow definition of welfare effort that might exclude important redistributive programs.

Figure 2.1 plots over time trends in our two broad measures of the public sector, based on (unweighted) averages of spending relative to GDP for all middle-income countries for which the data are available. Although the scale of general government consumption is considerably lower than that for total central government spending (a ratio of almost 1:2) and although general government consumption has been more volatile, the overall trends in the two variables are quite similar. Government spending in middle-income countries increased quite rapidly in the 1970s, stabilized or somewhat declined in the 1980s, and then rose again appreciably in the 1990s. On both variables, for example, government spending in 1998 was a larger fraction of GDP than at any other time in the preceding three decades. The overall growth in spending for the 1973–1998 period was about 50 percent (from 20 to 30 percent of GDP) with respect to total central government spending; the growth in general government consumption was more modest, from about 13.5 to 16 percent of GDP (roughly 20 percent). Finally, one should remember that average GDP per capita in the middle-income countries increased by more than 50 percent in real terms from the early seventies to the late 1990s. Thus, the rate of growth in real government spending was much higher than it would seem from these plots normalized to GDP.

These averages for all middle-income countries, however, conceal important variations among different types of countries in this grouping. Figure 2.2 plots averages with respect to general government consumption for four groups of middle-income countries—the transition economies of the former Eastern bloc, Latin America, oil exporters, and other middle-income countries. General government consumption more than doubled as a portion of GDP among oil exporters from 1973 to 1990—a graphic example of Wagner's law that society's demands for government spending increase with higher levels of per capita income. With the

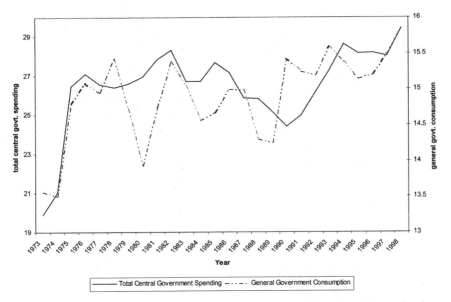

Fig. 2.1. Government spending relative to GDP (%), 1973–1998. Data from International Monetary Fund, 1998, *Government Finance Statistics*, 1971–1998 [computer file]; World Bank 1999b.

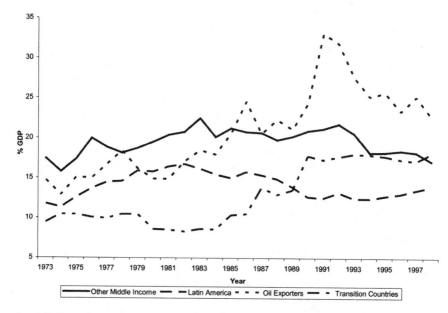

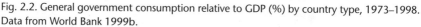

Fig. 2.2. General government consumption relative to GDP (%) by country type, 1973–1998. Data from World Bank 1999b.

onset of the Gulf War, however, this trend was reversed. Nonetheless, average general government consumption was still higher at the end of the 1990s among oil exporters than any other type of middle-income country.

General government consumption also appears to have increased by more than 50 percent during the 1980s in the transition economies, but then was flat in the 1990s, even though the massive economic dislocations in this period should have greatly increased demand for government compensation. But one should be suspicious about official statistics from the Communist period. Finally, government consumption in Latin America and the remaining middle-income countries, in contrast, was quite stable over the whole sample period. And in the 1990s, the Latin American countries spent less on government consumption than any of the other groupings.

Figure 2.3 plots over time variations in central government spending by country type. The trends in these data are different from those for general government consumption in several ways. First, government spending during the Gulf War dominated the oil exporters' line. Second, total government spending roughly fell to half in Latin American countries in the middle of the 1980s—in response to the debt crisis—but then increased by about one-third in the 1990s (not returning, however, to the portions of GDP in the 1970s). Third, total government spending declined quite steadily in the transition economies from the late 1970s to the late 1990s, with the largest drop occurring immediately after the end of Communism.

Let us now turn to differences in public spending across middle-income coun-

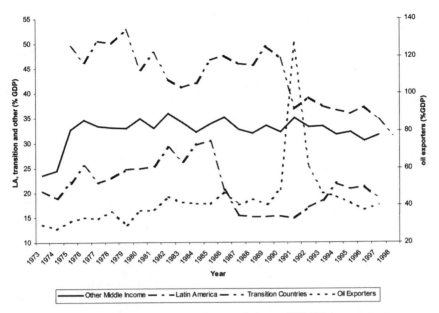

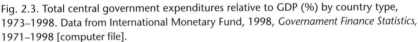

Fig. 2.3. Total central government expenditures relative to GDP (%) by country type, 1973–1998. Data from International Monetary Fund, 1998, *Government Finance Statistics*, 1971–1998 [computer file].

tries in the 1990s (table 2.1). The most important thing to note here is that there are large variations in patterns of government spending within each of our country groupings. Consider first the transition economies. Government spending in the 1990s was far higher, for example, in Croatia, the Czech Republic, and Poland than in Albania and Russia.[5] Latin America, Argentina, and Mexico both have very small public economies, whereas Brazil's (and Costa Rica's) is much larger. Government spending in Chile, the darling of market reformers, fell somewhere in between these two extremes. In the remaining middle-income countries, government spending is highest in Botswana (the one country in Sub-Saharan Africa that seems to have escaped the development trap) and Oman and lowest in some of the East and Southeast Asian newly industrialized countries (NICs)—notably South Korea, the Philippines, and Thailand.

What explains these over-time and cross-national variations in government spending? We begin by presenting data on market integration and political regimes, then move on to analyzing their relationships with government spending.

Market Integration

We use three different measures of integration into international markets. Total trade (the sum of exports and imports as a percent of GDP) is the simplest and most widely analyzed aspect of market integration. Figure 2.4 presents

Table 2.1 Government Spending in the 1990s

	General government consumption	Total central government spending		General government consumption	Total central government spending
Transition					
Albania	15.1	29.8	El Salvador	9.2	
Belarus	20.5	35.7	Guatemala	5.7	
Bulgaria	16.5	42.4	Jamaica	14.8	
Croatia	26.1	41.6	Mexico	9.9	15.5
Czech Republic	21	36.1	Panama	16.1	25.2
Estonia	19.9	30.2	Paraguay	8.5	12
Georgia	8.4	9.2	Peru	7.6	15.9
Hungary	11.2	49.9	Puerto Rico	14.3	
Kazakhstan	13.1		Trinidad and Tobago	12.1	28.1
Latvia	18.1	31.1	Uruguay	13.3	31
Lithuania	17.8	26.2	Venezuela	7.7	19.4
Macedonia, FYR	18.1		*Other*		
Poland	18.6	39.7	Botswana	26.4	35.4
Romania	13.2	33.5	Egypt, Arab Republic	10.5	33.6
Russian Federation	15.2	26.6	Jordan	24.7	33.5
Slovak Republic	22.5		Korea, Republic of	10.4	16.7
Ukraine	20.4		Lebanon	16.3	34.3
Uzbekistan	22.2		Libya		
Oil Exporters			Malaysia	12.4	25.2
Algeria	16.6	31.5	Mauritius	11.9	22.6
Gabon	14	25.3	Mayotte		
Iran, Islamic Republic	14.2	23.5	Morocco	17	31.1
Saudi Arabia	29.8		Namibia	31	37.2
Latin America			Oman	33.4	38.6
Argentina	9.5	13.8	Papua New Guinea	20.1	32.7
Bolivia	13.1	21	Philippines	11.1	18.9
Brazil	18.3	31.9	South Africa	19.7	30.6
Chile	9.9	20.8	Sri Lanka	10	27.4
Colombia	13.7	13.1	Syrian Arab Republic	13.1	24
Costa Rica	16.9	27.2	Thailand	9.9	16.2
Cuba			Tunisia	15.3	33.1
Dominican Republic	5.3	14.8	Turkey	12	23.2
Ecuador	9.9	15.1	West Bank and Gaza	20.8	

Source: Consumption from World Bank 1999b. Spending from International Monetary Fund, 1998, *Government Finance Statistics,* 1971–1998 [computer file].

unweighted average trade dependence among different groups of middle-income countries. The most important feature of this graph is perhaps the fact that trade dependence increased markedly after 1985–1986 in all types of countries—on average by about twenty points of GDP. This is wholly consistent with the view that the period from the mid 1980s and on constitutes the new era of globalization. As

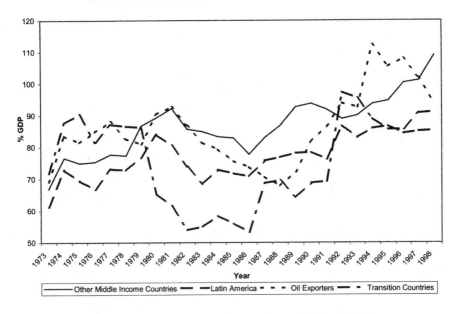

Fig. 2.4. Trade relative to GDP (%), 1973–1998. Data from World Bank 1999b.

was the case for government spending, developments in oil exporters and the transition economies were more extreme than those in Latin America and other middle-income countries, but nonetheless the directions of change are quite consistent.

Figure 2.5 plots total inflows plus outflows of foreign direct investment as a percentage of GDP for these types of countries (note that inflows overwhelm outflows in most middle-income countries). The general story in these data is quite similar to that for trade—FDI took off from the mid to late 1980s. To be sure, this was more pronounced in transition economies and among oil exporters, but annual FDI flows increased in Latin America from about 0.5 percent of GDP in the early 1980s to 2.5 percent of GDP in the latter 1990s.

Finally, figure 2.6 plots over time changes in capital mobility, using a new 0–9 scale of capital account restrictions derived from IMF data (Brune et al. 2001). As was the case for both other measures of openness, it is clear that the period from the mid-1980s and later was one of rapidly increasing integration into the international economy for middle-income countries. Unlike trade and FDI, however, the trend to capital account openness was most pronounced in Latin American countries. On average, capital accounts were more closed in these countries in the 1980s than they had been in the 1970s—almost as closed, in fact, as the transition economies were in the years before the fall of the Soviet empire. By the mid-1990s, however, Latin American countries were considerably more open than the other three groups of countries, which had converged to very similar policy positions on the capital account.

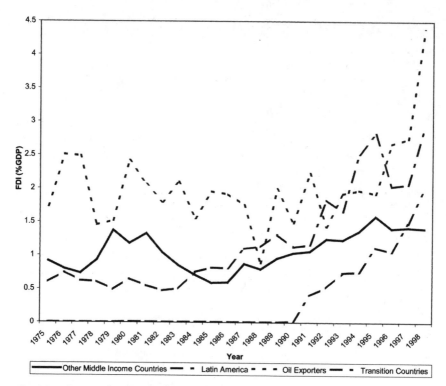

Fig. 2.5. Inflows and outflows of foreign direct investment/GDP (%), 1975–1998. Data from World Bank 1999b.

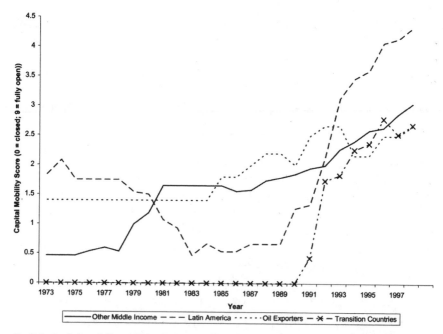

Fig 2.6. Capital mobility, 1973–1998. Data from Brune et al. 2001. Calculations from IMF data.

Table 2.2 focuses on differences across countries in terms of international economic integration in the 1990s. The table makes clear that there is enormous heterogeneity in the extent of market integration within country groupings and among different facets of market integration. One clear association is that smaller middle-income countries tend to have more integrated economies (compare, for example, Georgia and Russia among former parts of the Soviet Union, or Brazil and Jamaica in the Latin American group)—presumably because smaller nations are more dependent on external markets to realize scale economies.

But it is also apparent that openness on one dimension does not necessarily translate into openness on other dimensions. For example, the two largest countries in Latin America, Argentina and Brazil, remain among the world's smallest traders (relative to their GDPs). But Argentina had one of the most open capital accounts for all middle-income countries in the 1990s, whereas capital mobility in Brazil was much more limited. Few countries are open on every measure like Jamaica or closed on every measure like Iran. There are a few striking cases where countries are very open by one measure and very closed under another. For instance, Panama has few capital controls and attracts significant FDI, but relies little on trade. Malaysia and Gabon have economies dependent upon FDI and trade, but restrict capital movements. Belarus and Bulgaria have closed capital markets and do not attract much FDI, but have economies highly involved in trade.

A combination of tables 2.1 and 2.2 provides a rough preliminary assessment of the efficiency and compensation hypotheses in middle-income countries. Big-spending governments in open economies like Croatia, the Czech Republic, Costa Rica, Botswana, and Oman point toward the compensation hypothesis. The same can be said for closed economies whose governments spend little on welfare in countries such as Russia, Albania, and Korea. However, there are countries such as Poland and Brazil that have large public economies despite being relatively closed—as predicted by the efficiency hypothesis. Similarly, countries like Thailand that have relatively small public expenditures in an open economy also support the efficiency hypothesis. It would be easy to choose a set of case studies to support whatever hypothesis one wants.

An alternative strategy would be to look at over-time trends in government spending and market integration. Grossly speaking, one might be willing to claim on the basis of figure 2.1 that government spending increased in the 1990s, following closely on the move to more economic integration in the later 1980s. This would seem to support the compensation view. But one could equally look more closely at the time trends in government spending and market integration—broken down by country type—and find evidence for the efficiency view. For example, spending was relatively flat in Latin America in the late 1980s and in the 1990s, even though market integration increased considerably over this period.

Table 2.2 Market Integration in the 1990s

	Trade / GDP	Capital mobility (0–9)	FDI (% GDP)
Transition			
Albania	57.4	2.3	0.5
Belarus		0.7	
Bosnia	105.0	1.9	1.3
Bulgaria	86.6	1.0	0.6
Croatia	116.5	0.6	0.1
Czech Republic	94.5	0.8	0.4
Estonia	108.0	3.1	1.3
Georgia	153.7	5.4	2.8
Hungary	70.0	6.9	
Kazakhstan	73.7	1.3	2.1
Latvia	82.6	0.3	1.6
Lithuania	106.2	7.9	2.2
Macedonia, FYR	106.3	6.1	1.2
Poland	47.5	0.3	1.0
Romania	55.7	0.3	0.4
Russian Federation	53.9	1.7	0.4
Slovak Republic	119.4	0.7	0.8
Ukraine	70.7	0.0	0.3
Uzbekistan	63.4	0.4	
Yugoslavia, FR		0.0	
Oil Exporters			
Algeria	50.8	0.8	0.0
Gabon	90.0	0.0	7.1
Iran, Islamic Rep.	39.5	0.0	0.0
Iraq		0.0	
Saudi Arabia	77.0	4.4	0.8
Latin America			
Argentina	18.4	6.3	1.5
Bolivia	48.9	4.2	1.9
Brazil	17.6	1.0	0.9
Chile	59.2	1.0	3.2
Colombia	34.8	1.8	1.0
Costa Rica	85.9	5.1	1.8
Dominican Republic	67.9	2.0	1.0
Ecuador	57.3	3.3	1.2
El Salvador	54.0	4.6	0.5
Guatemala	43.2	6.1	1.2
Jamaica	122.2	6.2	2.4
Mexico	47.5	2.3	1.2
Panama	75.9	7.2	3.5
Paraguay	86.4	3.0	0.7
Peru	25.9	4.9	1.5
Trinidad and Tobag	86.7	5.6	4.9
Uruguay	43.4	8.0	0.4
Venezuela	52.8	2.8	1.9

Table 2.2 Market Integration in the 1990s *cont'd*

	Trade / GDP	Capital mobility (0–9)	FDI (% GDP)
Others			
Botswana	87.5	1.2	2.7
Egypt, Arab Republic	52.0	3.0	0.5
Jordan	133.0	5.1	0.9
Korea, Republic of	62.9	1.0	0.8
Lebanon	81.1	6.8	
Libya		0.0	
Malaysia	176.1	1.7	3.1
Mauritius	128.1	6.6	0.5
Morocco	46.8	1.0	0.6
Namibia	114.6	2.0	1.7
Oman	87.9	6.7	
Papua New Guinea	102.1	2.1	1.5
Philippines	80.6	1.7	0.5
South Africa	43.9	1.4	0.6
Sri Lanka	76.0	1.6	0.3
Syrian Arab Republic	67.2	0.0	0.2
Thailand	84.9	2.6	1.0
Tunisia	89.4	1.0	0.9
Turkey	41.0	2.1	0.3
West Bank and Gaza	88.0		

Source: Trade and FDI from World Bank 1999b. Capital mobility from Brune et al. 2001.

One might then discount development among the transition economies and the oil exporters as sui generis, and find it is not particularly related to globalization.

Discerning tight relationships from the descriptive data is fruitless. We want to take country level differences in spending and integration seriously, as well as over-time trends in these variables among countries. We should also take into account the fact that political economic dynamics in transition economies, for example, may have been very different than those in Latin America. For these reasons we use multivariate regression analysis in the next section to allow for a more precise delineation of the relationships of primary interest.

Political Regimes

Figure 2.7 plots over-time changes in political regimes, using the common −10 (complete autocracy) to +10 (complete democracy) measure derived from the Polity III database. It is true that the middle-income countries as a whole democratized considerably during the 1973–1998 period, but this broad development conceals at least two important subtrends. On the one hand, Latin America has always been more democratic than other middle-income countries, and it democratized as a continent fairly steadily from the early 1970s to the late 1990s. On the other hand, the clearest regime shift in the data is the dramatic transition from Commu-

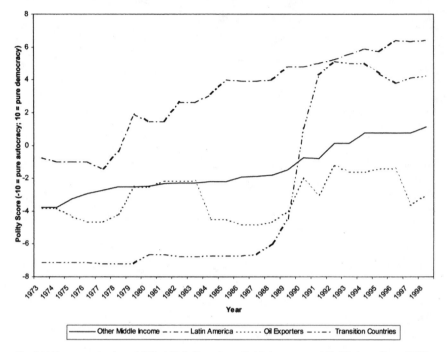

Fig 2.7. Democratization, 1973–1998. Data from Keith Jaggers and Ted Robert Gurr, 1998, *Polity III*. ftp://isere.colorado.edu/pub/datasets/polity98/polity98.asc

nism to democracy in the countries of the former Soviet bloc. In the late 1990s, these countries were on average just as democratic as those in Latin America, and considerably more democratic than other middle-income countries.

Table 2.3 presents national level data on political regimes in the 1990s. The lessons of these data are familiar. Most ex-Communist countries became quite democratic in the 1990s, with some notable exceptions such as Uzbekistan and Yugoslavia. By the 1990s, most of Latin America was also quite democratic, again with some notable exceptions (such as Cuba, and to a lesser extent Mexico and Peru). Oil exporters continued to have quite authoritarian regimes. The remaining middle-income countries were a mixed bag, ranging from wholly democratic (Mauritius and Papua New Guinea) to very authoritarian (Libya, Oman, and Syria).

Regression Analysis

In order to isolate the associations between market integration and government spending, we estimated several types of ordinary least squared (OLS) regressions (with heteroskedasticity-consistent standard errors) for all middle-income countries with populations over one million. The basic form of the simplest equation was:

Table 2.3 Democracy and Democratization

	Average Polity Score in 1990s		Average Polity Score in 1990s
Transition		Cuba	−7.0
Albania	2.7	Dominican Republic	6.4
Belarus	0.8	Ecuador	8.9
Bosnia	−1.4	El Salvador	8.8
Bulgaria	8.0	Guatemala	4.7
Croatia	−0.6	Jamaica	9.3
Czech Republic	9.3	Mexico	2.7
Estonia	8.0	Panama	8.6
Hungary	10.0	Paraguay	5.3
Kazakhstan	−0.4	Peru	2.1
Latvia	8.0	Trinidad and Tobago	9.0
Lithuania	10.0	Uruguay	10.0
Macedonia	6.7	Venezuela	8.2
Poland	8.4		
Romania	6.0	*Other*	
Russian Federation	4.0	Botswana	8.0
Slovak Republic	7.4	Egypt, Arab Republic	−3.0
Ukraine	5.7	Jordan	−3.2
Uzbekistan	−8.0	Lebanon	−3.0
Yugoslavia, FR	−6.1	Korea, Republic of	9.2
		Libya	−7.0
Oil Exporters		Malaysia	4.6
Algeria	−4.1	Mauritius	10.0
Gabon	−3.0	Morocco	−4.1
Iran, Islamic Republic	−6.0	Namibia	7.7
Iraq	−8.1	Oman	−9.2
Saudi Arabia	−10.0	Papua New Guinea	10.0
		Philippines	8.8
Latin America		South Africa	7.5
Argentina	8.0	Sri Lanka	5.0
Bolivia	9.0	Syrian Arab Republic	−9.0
Brazil	8.0	Thailand	7.2
Chile	8.0	Tunisia	−3.7
Colombia	8.0	Turkey	8.8
Costa Rica	10.0		

Source: Keith Jaggers and Ted Robert Gurr, 1998, *Polity III.* ftp://isere.colorado.edu/pub/datasets/polity98/polity98.asc

$$\text{SPEND90s} = \alpha + \beta_1 \text{MI80s} + \beta_j \text{CONTROLs} + \beta_\kappa \text{DUMMIES} + \text{error} \qquad (1)$$

In this equation, the spending variables (general government consumption and total central government spending) were measured as average percentages of GDP in the 1990s (typically, 1990–1998). The three market integration terms (trade and FDI flows as a percentage of GDP, and the 0–9 index of capital account openness) are all averages for the 1980s. This specification mitigates the problems of reverse causality that might otherwise plague this analysis. That is, countries with larger public economies might subsequently choose to open their economies; we are more interested in the responses of governments to the extent of market integration (that is, viewed as a largely exogenous condition).

We included three control variables that are standard in the literature. Countries with larger populations are expected to have smaller governments (as a result of scale economies in the provision of public services). Higher dependency ratios of those under fifteen and over sixty-four to people of working age should be associated with higher levels of government spending. Finally, following Wagner's law, countries with higher GDPs per capita are expected to have larger public economies.

Our regressions also included three dummy variables that take into account the possibility that different types of middle-income countries might have different levels of government spending. We used a dummy variable for the Latin American countries because this is the largest group of countries in our sample. One might expect that the transition countries of east and central Europe might have larger public economies than other middle-income countries by virtue of their Communist histories. Finally, we also added a dummy variable for oil-exporting nations.

This baseline specification allows us to ask the following question: Was government spending in the 1990s higher or lower in countries that were more integrated into international markets with respect to trade, FDI, and capital mobility in the 1980s?

However, given that we know that the extent of market integration increased substantially between the 1980s and the 1990s, it is also worth asking a follow-up question: Did government spending increase between the 1980s and 1990s faster or slower in countries in which market integration increased more rapidly between these decades? The functional form of the estimated equation was thus:

$$\Delta\text{SPEND} = \alpha + \beta_1\Delta\text{MI} + \beta_2\Delta\text{GDPPC} + \beta_K\text{DUMMIES} + \text{error} \tag{2}$$

In this equation, the spending and market integration variables are all expressed as changes in natural logs (that is, $\ln(90س)-\ln(80s)$). This allows us to talk about the elasticity of spending with respect to market integration ("a 1 percent change in integration is associated with an x percent change in spending"). We continued to include the dummy variables for different types of middle-income countries. Dependency ratios and population only changed marginally in most countries between the 1980s and 1990s, so we excluded them from the regressions to preserve degrees of freedom.

Finally, we assessed the mediating effects of political regimes by asking the following question: How did the extent to which a country democratized between the 1980s and 1990s affect the relationship between changes in market integration and changes in spending? This equation can thus be written as:

$$\Delta SPEND = \alpha + \beta_1 \Delta MI + \beta_2 \Delta DEM + \beta_3 \Delta MI^* \Delta DEM + \beta_4 \Delta GDPPC + \beta_k DUMMIES + error \qquad (3)$$

In this equation, one can assess the combined effects of changes in political regime and changes in market integration on changes in spending by estimating spending changes on the basis of β_{1-3}, multiplied by different values of market integration and democracy.

Levels of Market Integration and Government Spending

Table 2.4 reports our baseline results concerning the impact of levels of market integration in the 1980s on levels of government spending in the 1990s. In the general government consumption equation on the full sample of middle-income countries with populations over one million (column 1), higher dependency ratios and higher GDP per capita in the 1980s were both strongly and positively associated with more spending in the 1980s. But government consumption was about four points of GDP lower in Latin America than in other middle-income countries. Latin American countries also had much lower central government spending in the 1990s, whereas spending was much higher in transition economies and a little higher among oil exporters (column 2).

For the full sample of middle-income countries (columns 1 and 2), trade had a weakly positive and statistically insignificant impact on both general government consumption and total central government spending. Given the collinearity between FDI, capital mobility, and trade we do not view this as a repudiation of the broader Cameron-Rodrik thesis. There was a somewhat stronger positive capital mobility effect, though in neither equation did the estimated parameter quite reach traditional levels of statistical significance. It is clear, however, that countries with greater average flows of foreign direct investment in the 1980s had higher levels of government spending in the 1990s. These effects were statistically significant and substantively large with respect to both general government consumption and total central government spending. An increase in average annual FDI flows of one standard deviation (1.32 percent of GDP), for example, is estimated to have increased both central government spending and government consumption by $1.32^*1.60 = 2.1$ points of GDP. Average government consumption in these countries was 15.6 percent of GDP in the 1990s; the mean for total central government spending was 27.2 percent of GDP. Thus, the positive effects of FDI on the public economy were quite significant.

We then ran the same type of regressions for the Latin American countries to ascertain whether the positive effects of market integration evident in the whole sample were also apparent for this group of countries. The broad answer is that they were, though in this case the significant positive relationships between inte-

Table 2.4 Integration into International Markets and Size of the Public Economy in the 1990s

	General government consumption	Total central government spending	General government consumption (Latin America only)	Total central government spending (Latin America only)
Population	0.20	−0.52	1.92[+]	2.54
	(1.11)	(1.88)	(1.15)	(2.62)
Dependency ratio	14.42[***]	5.04	−9.13	−39.58[+]
	(5.41)	(8.19)	(11.94)	(22.08)
Per capita GDP	1.00[**]	0.44	0.04	0.04
	(0.43)	(0.83)	(0.89)	(1.56)
Trade	0.02	0.00	0.12[*]	0.22[+]
	(0.05)	(0.06)	(0.06)	(0.16)
FDI	1.60[***]	1.60[*]	0.47	0.00
	(0.55)	(0.94)	(0.67)	(1.69)
Capital mobility	0.49[+]	0.80[+]	0.59[**]	1.20[*]
	(0.30)	(0.62)	(0.25)	(0.61)
Latin America	−4.15[**]	−8.02[**]		
	(1.88)	(3.11)		
Transition	2.30	16.89[***]		
	(3.52)	(5.25)		
Oil exporters	−0.90	2.52[+]		
	(1.39)	(2.27)		
Constant	−2.75	20.66[*]	6.77	30.77[+]
	(8.09)	(12.18)	(13.73)	(20.63)
N	39	35	18	15
R-sq	60.9%	60.2%	43.2%	56.2%

Source: All data from World Development Indicators (2000), except the dummy variables, which are from Easterly and Yu 1999.
Note: The dependent variables are average general government consumption (% GDP) and average total central government expenditures (% GDP), 1990–1998. Trade, FDI, financial integration, (the log of) population, dependency ratio, and per capital income all averages for the 1980s. Countries with population under one million are excluded.
OLS regressions with robust standard errors. *** $p < .01$; ** $.01 < p < .05$; * $p < .10$; + t-ratio > 1.0.

gration and spending were for trade and capital mobility rather than for foreign direct investment. In the general government consumption equation (column 3), an increase in trade of one standard deviation (for the Latin American countries only) is estimated to have increased spending by 29.2*0.12 = 3.5 points of GDP; an increase in the capital mobility index of one standard deviation would have increased spending by 2.36*0.58 = 1.4 points of GDP. Since average general government consumption in Latin American countries in the 1990s was 12.1 percent of GDP, these were substantial effects. For total central government spending, an increase in capital mobility among Latin American countries of one standard deviation is estimated to have increased spending by 2.36*1.20 = 2.8 percent of GDP, compared with a mean for total government spending in 1990s Latin America of 20.9 percent of GDP.

In sum, table 2.4 lends strong support to the compensation view. Countries that were more exposed to international market forces had larger public economies. This is wholly consistent with Cameron's original work on the OECD and Rodrik's more recent findings for a global sample of countries. While Cameron and Rodrik use trade as their measure of openness and we find no relationship between trade and government spending, the broader argument that more open economies have larger governments holds. It is possible that different types of economic openness receive different governmental responses, but it is also possible that trade is swamped by collinearity with the other two variables. It is important to note that the positive effects of FDI and capital mobility on government spending have not been found in studies outside the middle-income countries (Quinn [1997] is a partial exception).

Changes in Market Integration and Government Spending

These levels results, however, are subject to a potentially telling criticism. Globalization connotes for most people the notion that international market integration has increased dramatically in recent years, and our descriptive statistics confirmed that this has indeed been the case in middle-income countries. It is interesting that countries that were more integrated into international markets in the 1980s tended to have larger public sectors in the 1990s, but perhaps those in which market integration has been faster have experienced slower growth in the public economy. Garrett (2001b) and Garrett and Mitchell (2001) found evidence that this was the case both for the OECD and for a broader global sample of countries.

Table 2.5 presents our estimates of the effects of globalization—now measured as changes (in logs) in market integration between the 1980s and the 1990s—on changes (in logs) in government spending between the two decades. The basic structure of the estimated equations is similar to that for table 2.4, except that we excluded the relatively stable population and dependency ratio variables to preserve degrees of freedom. As would be expected, economies that grew more quickly between the 1980s and the 1990s experienced slower spending growth (as a percentage of GDP) because of the stickiness in spending programs. Spending growth was also considerably slower in the transition economies and among oil exporters than in other middle-income countries.

In the general government consumption equation for all middle-income countries, faster growth in trade and FDI were weakly associated with faster spending growth, but neither of these effects was statistically significant. In marked contrast, greater changes in capital mobility were associated with slower growth in general government consumption. The standard deviation in changes in capital

Table 2.5 Changes in the Size of the Public Economy in Response to Changes in Market Integration

	General government consumption	Total central government spending	General government consumption (Latin America only)	Total central government spending (Latin America only)
ΔGDP per capita	−0.55***	−0.39*	−0.68*	−0.79**
	(0.18)	(0.20)	(0.37)	(0.36)
ΔTrade	0.21⁺	−0.05	0.39⁺	−0.14
	(0.20)	(0.25)	(0.22)	(0.44)
ΔFDI	0.07⁺	0.05	0.08	0.00
	(0.06)	(0.06)	(0.13)	(0.08)
ΔCapital mobility	−0.16**	0.00	−0.21**	−0.07
	(0.07)	(0.07)	(0.09)	(0.09)
Latin America	−0.07	−0.05		
	(0.09)	(0.10)		
Transition	0.46**	−0.26⁺		
	(0.22)	(0.21)		
Oil Exporter	−0.33***	−0.16**		
	(0.12)	(0.07)		
Constant	0.24**	0.18⁺	0.18	0.34*
	(0.10)	(0.11)	(0.22)	(0.19)
N	34	30	18	15
R-sq	47.2%	21.54%	28.4%	25.67%

Source: All data from World Development Indicators (2000), except the dummy variables, which are from Easterly and Yu 1999.
Note: Change in general government consumption, total central government expenditures, per capita income, trade, and FDI all represent the differences of the natural logs of the averages from the 1980s and 1990s. Change in financial integration is the difference in the natural log of 1 plus the average of the 1980s and 1990s. Countries with populations under one million excluded. Columns 3 and 4 use only Latin American countries. OLS regressions with robust standard errors. *** $p < .01$; ** $.01 < p < .05$; * $p < .10$; ⁺ t-ratio > 1.0.

mobility was 0.62. This implies that an increase of one standard deviation in this variable would have resulted in a $0.62*-0.16 = 10$ percent decrease in general government consumption between the 1980s and the 1990s. None of the change in market integration terms had any significant effect on changes in total central government spending.

We also estimated the change equations only for the Latin American countries. Here again, the only significant relationship was the negative effect of changes in capital mobility—and its substantive effect was similar to that estimated for the whole sample.

Thus, when one moves from the analysis of levels of market integration and government spending to changes in these variables in recent decades, support emerges for the widely held view that the growth of capital mobility has significantly constrained public sector expansion.

The Mediating Effects of Democratization

Table 2.6 asks whether the effects of globalization (that is, changes in market integration) on the growth or contraction of the public economy was affected by the other important trend in the middle-income countries since 1980—democratization (changes in *Polity* scores between the 1980s and 1990s). This was accomplished by including a democratization variable (ΔDemocracy) and its multiplicative interaction with the change in market integration variables. Since this strategy necessarily introduces considerable collinearity among the regressors, we estimated the democratization-change in integration interaction separately for the three different indicators of market integration. In these equations, the multiplicative interaction term is the most important. Positive coefficients indicate that the combined effect of democratization and globalization was to increase the pace of government spending growth, whereas negative coefficients would show that the combined effect of these variables was to slow down public sector expansion.

The most striking feature of table 2.6 is that the bulk of the multiplicative interaction terms are positive and statistically significant. That is, middle-income countries that both globalized and democratized between the 1980s and the 1990s tended to experience more rapid growth in government spending over the same period, with respect both to general government consumption and total central government spending. Using a different indicator of statistical significance—the joint significance of the multiplicative term and its two constituent parts (that is, the change in market integration and change in democracy terms)—also shows that the interaction setup had important statistical effects.

The problem with such interaction specifications, however, is that their substantive effects are difficult to read directly off regression results. To facilitate interpretation, we generated a series of counterfactual estimates of growth or decline in government spending at high and low changes in market integration and democracy. We denoted high as the ninetieth percentile in the sample distribution, whereas low was set at the tenth percentile. All other variables were set at their means, and estimates of changes in spending were generated (see figures 2.8 and 2.9).

Consider first figure 2.8 for general government consumption. This clearly shows that government spending grew fastest in the high-high cells for both trade and foreign direct investment. For a hypothetical country whose change in democracy (that is, democratization) and change in trade scores were both at the ninetieth percentile, government consumption is estimated to have increased by 25 percent between the 1980s and 1990s; for the combination of high democratization and high FDI, the estimated increase in spending was over 47 percent. These estimates are considerably higher than those in the low change in market integration

Table 2.6 The Mediating Effects of Democratization

	ΔGeneral government consumption			ΔTotal central government spending		
ΔGDP	0.25⁺	−0.58***	−0.38*	−0.24⁺	−0.49**	−0.27⁺
	(0.24)	(0.16)	(0.19)	(0.18)	(0.18)	(0.18)
ΔTrade	−0.17			−0.24⁺		
	(0.22)			(0.23)		
ΔFDI		0.03			0.00	
		(0.06)			(0.05)	
ΔCapital mobility			−0.18**			−0.03
			(0.07)			(0.07)
ΔDemocracy	0.08	−0.10⁺	0.01	−0.08	−0.12**	−0.06
	(0.12)	(0.08)	(0.11)	(0.08)	(0.06)	(0.07)
ΔDem*ΔTrade	0.35⁺			0.44*		
	(0.34)			(0.25)		
ΔDem*ΔFDI		0.25***				0.16***
		(0.08)				(0.04)
ΔDem*ΔCM			0.10			0.20**
			(0.19)			(0.08)
Latin American	−0.01	−0.14*	0.04	0.00	−0.05	0.04
	(0.10)	(0.08)	(0.11)	(0.07)	(0.08)	(0.09)
Oil exporter	−0.08	−0.37***	−0.23**	−0.07	−0.16**	−0.13**
	(0.12)	(0.11)	(0.10)	(0.10)	(0.07)	(0.05)
Transition	0.25⁺	0.61⁺	0.48*	0.11⁺	−0.79***	−0.09
	(0.22)	(0.41)	(0.27)	(0.11)	(0.23)	(0.12)
Constant	−.016⁺	0.29***	0.16⁺	0.13⁺	0.27**	0.12⁺
	(0.14)	(0.10)	(0.14)	(0.11)	(0.12)	(0.12)
N	45	34	39	36	30	34
R-sq	22.0%	48.0%	40.5%	22.1%	32.8%	18.96%
Joint significance of interaction	30.2%	2.1%	3.6%	40.1%	0.2%	9.2%

Source: All data from World Development Indicators (2000), except the dummy variables, which are from Easterly and Yu 1999.
Note: The change in democracy is coded as the difference in natural logs of the average Polity score for the 1980s and 1990s.
OLS regressions with robust standard errors. *** $p < .01$; ** $.01 < p < .05$; * $p < .10$; ⁺ t-ratio > 1.0.

column, and for the combination of high change in market integration but low change in democracy.

Things were different, however, for capital mobility. The change in government spending was lower in both cells with high change in market integration than where this variable was set at the low value—consistent with the negative and significant coefficient on the change in capital mobility term in table 2.5. It is true that spending growth was more rapid in countries that democratized faster, but this did not counteract the negative effects of rapid increases in capital mobility.

Figure 2.9 shows even clearer evidence of the positive effects of simultaneous globalization and democratization on the trajectory of government spending—

| | ΔMarket Integration | |
	Low	High
Low	Trade: −1.5% FDI: −9.6% CM: +11.2%	Trade: −11.8% FDI: −5.0% CM: −19.0%
High	Trade: +0.5% FDI: −34.8% CM: +6.5%	Trade: +25.2% FDI: +47.6% CM: −0.7%

ΔDemocracy (row label)

Fig. 2.8. Change in government consumption at different levels of change in market integration and democracy. Counterfactual estimates derived from Table 2.6. All variables were set at their means except for the three indicators of market integration (trade, FDI and capital mobility) and democracy. High (low) values refer to the ninetieth (tenth) percentile in the sample distribution. The values represent percent increase or decrease in general government consumption from the average during 1980s to the average in the 1990s.

this time with respect to total central government expenditures. In this case, estimated spending growth was fastest in the three different high-high cases, that is, where the change in the democracy variable interacted separately with changes in trade, FDI, and capital mobility.

The bottom line on table 2.6 and figures 2.8 and 2.9 is thus clear. The conjuncture of globalization and democratization in middle-income countries resulted in faster public spending growth, whereas this was less apparent in countries that did not democratize as much between the 1980s and 1990s.

Conclusion

This chapter has explored the relationships among government spending, international market integration, and political regimes in middle-income countries. Our analysis yields three central findings. First, countries that are more exposed to international markets—not only in terms of exports and imports, but also foreign direct investment and policies affecting cross-border capital flows—tend to have larger public economies. Thus, in the middle-income countries at least, Dani Rodrik's recent finding of a positive relationship between trade and government spending extends to other aspects of market integration as well.

Things are quite different when one moves from levels of market integration (for example, what portion of GDP does trade constitute in different countries?) to changes in market integration (for example, how much has trade increased in the

| | ΔMarket Integration | |
	Low	High
Low	Trade: +6.1% FDI: −0.4% CM: +2.3%	Trade: −9.5% FDI: −1.8% CM: −4.7%
High	Trade: −15.3% FDI: −25.2% CM: −16.5%	Trade: +8.2% FDI: +18.9% CM: +29.2%

ΔDemocracy

Fig. 2.9. Change in total expenditures at different levels of change in market integration and change in democracy. Counterfactual estimates derived from Table 2.6. All variables were set at their means except for the three indicators of market integration (trade, FDI and capital mobility) and democracy. High (low) values refer to the ninetieth (tenth) percentile in the sample distribution. The values represent percent increase or decrease in general government consumption from the average during 1980s to the average in the 1990s.

past decade?). It is probably fair to say that the contemporary debate is implicitly more about recent changes in market integration than their levels. To take an example close to home, the American policy debate focuses on the fact that trade in the United States has increased dramatically in recent years rather than the— equally true—observation that trade remains a very small portion of U.S. GDP.

Our second major finding details the relationship between changes in market integration and changes in government spending. Countries in which restrictions on cross-border capital movements were more quickly removed from the 1980s to the 1990s experienced considerably slower growth in government spending over these two decades. This is wholly consistent with the view, even endorsed by Rodrik, that increasing capital mobility in recent years has significantly constrained the scope for public sector expansion.

Our third and final important result, however, is that democratization has significantly mediated globalization change in government spending dynamics. In countries that became more democratic between the 1980s and 1990s, increasing market integration was associated with much faster growth in government spending, but the converse was true in countries that did not democratize. This reinforces the analysis of Adsera and Boix (2001) with respect to the whole world. The consequence of democratization and globalization, the two sweeping changes in middle-income countries since 1980, has been to accelerate, rather than retard, public spending growth in these countries.

3

Economic Internationalization and Domestic Compensation
Northwestern Europe in Comparative Perspective

JOHN D. STEPHENS

In the early nineties, unemployment rose dramatically in the Nordic countries and they joined Continental Europe, which had been suffering from this malady for a decade or more. The onset of chronic unemployment in both groups of countries was followed by cutbacks, albeit modest ones, in welfare state entitlements. The dominant interpretation among academic, political, and journalistic observers is that both the rise of unemployment and retrenchment of the welfare state in the region were a direct product of "globalization," the increasing openness of the economies of the region not only vis-à-vis one another but also toward the world economy. The most common version of the globalization theme was an extension of the neoliberal "Eurosclerois" thesis, which linked unemployment and slow growth to the overly generous welfare states, rigid labor markets, and counterproductive state intervention said to be characteristic of western European economies. There is also a social democratic version of the argument, an extension of the structural dependence of the state thesis, that links the poor performance of the economies to the loss of economic policy-making autonomy of governments, and that relates retrenchment to the increased capital mobility that made governments ever more dependent on not just the need but the desires and prejudices of employers, investors, and money market managers.

Recent comparative work on the welfare state in advanced industrial democracies has begun to question both versions of the globalization thesis. Esping-Andersen (1999), Pierson (2001), Myles and Pierson (2001), and my co-authors and I (Stephens, Huber, and Ray 1999; Huber and Stephens 1998, 2001a) contest the thesis linking globalization to welfare state retrenchment, particularly the neoliberal version of it, citing other more important causes of stagnation and retrenchment such as changing demographic patterns, changing gender roles, the changes in the rates of return on capital relative to wage growth, and changing sectoral and occupational compositions of the economy. Based on analyses of pooled time series data, Garrett (1998b) and Swank (1999, 2002) go further, arguing that globalization is positively related to welfare state generosity, at least in some groups of countries. In doing so, they resurrect the thesis that economic openness generates demands for "domestic compensation" and for productivity-enhancing public goods characteristic of an earlier generation of writings on comparative political economy, particularly the work on corporatism (for example, see Cameron 1978; Katzenstein 1985).

In this chapter, I examine the relationship between globalization, economic openness in its various manifestations, and changes in social policy in both the era of welfare state expansion up to the early eighties and in the era of retrenchment since that time. The chapter is based on extensive quantitative and comparative historical research on the development and crisis of advanced welfare states conducted by Evelyne Huber and myself.[1] The quantitative analysis consists of pooled time series and cross-sectional analyses of the eighteen advanced capitalist democracies that were continuously democratic since 1945 and had populations of over one million. The comparative historical analysis focuses on seven advanced capitalist countries of northern Europe, the Nordic countries, Austria, Germany, and the Netherlands, all very open[2] and, to varying degrees, corporatist political economies, contrasting them to the historically closed economies of the Antipodes. A number of other countries (the United States, United Kingdom, France, Italy, and Switzerland) are less systematically treated but in sufficient detail to allow us to cover Esping-Andersen's (1990, 1999) three or four worlds of welfare capitalism as well as Castles's (1985; Castles and Mitchell 1993) fourth Australasian wage-earner welfare state type.

Covering the period before the early eighties is essential for the intellectual inquiry represented by this volume because it is for this period that the most far-reaching claims for a positive effect of economic openness on the welfare state and other state interventions in the economy are made (Cameron 1978, 1984; Katzenstein 1985). It is indisputable that trade openness as measured by imports plus exports divided by GDP and various measures of welfare state generosity are strongly correlated, but it is deeply disputed whether trade openness is causally related, directly or indirectly, to welfare state generosity and, if indirectly, through what mechanism. For the portability of the northern European model, it obviously matters very much whether openness has a quite direct effect on welfare state generosity or whether it is mediated by corporatist bargaining, as Katzenstein (1985) suggests, or social democratic governance, as I argued over twenty years ago (Stephens 1979).

Economic Openness and the Welfare State: The Arguments

David Cameron's classic 1978 article was the first quantitative demonstration that trade openness was strongly correlated with the "scope of the public economy" measured, in this case, as the change in total taxes as a percentage of GDP from 1960 to 1975. Cameron's article is often cited as evidence of a powerful direct effect of trade openness on the size of the public sector. Indeed, this is what his analysis shows: Compared to social democratic government, the only other significant independent variable in his final equation (p. 1254), openness shows a higher zero order correlation (.78 versus .60), a higher level of significance (3.22 versus 1.75), and a higher standardized regression coefficient (.58 versus .34). In his initial discussion of hypotheses, Cameron (1978, 1250–51) does cite literature that suggests strong direct effects. He cites Lindbeck (1975, 56; 1974, 9, 214–27), who argues that governments counter the negative effects of openness, such as imported inflation and lack of effectiveness of Keynesian policies, by direct interventions in the economy. Social insurance and the tax system are built-in stabilizers that smooth out the business cycle. Active labor market policies, unemployment compensation, subsidies to firms to retain and retrain workers, and public employment allow governments to maintain full employment and offset the negative effects of unemployment in the face of uncertainties inherent in openness. Finally, through tax concessions and direct subsidies, governments can stimulate business investment. However, while the final step of causal sequence resembles Lindbeck's argument, Cameron's own explanation of the relationship between openness and the size of the public sector was that the causal effect was entirely indirect (1256–58). Citing Ingham's (1974—see below) work on the size of the domestic economy, industrial structure, and union structure and my work (Stephens 1979) on union organization and social democratic strength, Cameron argues that openness led to industrial concentration, strong and centralized unions, and thus to leftist government and centralized bargaining which, in turn, led to increases in social expenditure and a large public economy. In fleshing out his argument, Cameron notes the explicit trade-off of union wage restraint for public sector expansion.[3] Thus, in terms of his causal explanation of social expenditure, Cameron's article is properly cited as one of the earliest comprehensive statements of the effect of social democratic corporatism on social spending and public sector size, despite the fact that the word "corporatism" is only mentioned in passing.[4] Since his data analysis contained no measures of union or bargaining centralization, he did not actually test his entire causal model.

Peter Katzenstein's 1985 book, *Small States in World Markets*, is a second seminal statement of the thesis that economic openness is causally related to social expenditure as well as to productivity and growth-enhancing state interventions in the economy. As for Cameron, corporatist bargaining is the immediate link between openness and social expenditure, but, in contrast to Cameron's argument, social democratic governance is not causally related to corporatism. In fact, he explicitly rejects my contention that social democratic governance and strong unions are preconditions for corporatism (compare Katzenstein 1985, 97–98; and Stephens 1986/1979, 121–28), rather arguing that it is the economic and political strength of labor that differentiates the two types of corporatism—"social corporatism" and "liberal corporatism." Nonetheless, relatively well-organized and centralized interest groups are a necessary feature of corporatism in Katzenstein's view. Moreover, neither corporatist tripartite bargaining nor centralized interest groups arise in a straightforward manner from economic openness. Rather, they are a product of the interaction of historical development, the economic and political crises of the 1930s and 1940s, which reveal the vulnerabilities of small size and openness, and social and political preconditions; a divided right, a moderate left, and proportional representation, which enable compromise across parties and labor market actors.

One should not be too hasty to conclude that neither Cameron nor Katzenstein argue that there is no direct effect of openness on social spending. In both of their arguments openness appears as a motivation for labor to cooperate in corporatist compromises that involve wage restraint. That is, protection is not an option for labor in an open economy because so many workers' jobs are dependent on export competitiveness. One can examine the position of labor unions and left-wing governments in closed economies with left-wing governments as counterfactual. Katzenstein is explicit on this point: labor is more likely to resort to protectionist policies in more closed economies instead of relying on the state to cushion the effects of external shocks on workers. Thus, one might hypothesize an interactive effect of openness and corporatism or left-wing government on social spending.

In closing the discussion of the theoretical arguments for positive links between openness and large welfare states and state economic intervention, it is worth underlining that they pertain only to trade openness. These authors are largely silent about capital flows, transnational production processes, and transnational organizations.

For the period of retrenchment, the neoliberal argument, typically found in analyses of European economies in the *Economist* and articles on Europe in *The New York Times*, but also in the writings of academic economists (for example, see Lindbeck 1992, 1994), takes as a given the difference in welfare state generosity at the outset of the retrenchment era.[5] That is, no attempt is made to explain why countries with generous welfare states generally delivered lower unemployment and somewhat above-average growth rates in the earlier period. The neoliberals contend that as markets for goods, capital, and, more recently, labor have become more open, all countries have been exposed to more competition, and the liabilities of generous social benefits have become more apparent as these raise the cost of production. When one adds the costs of social benefits to the market wage paid to the employee, the total wage costs make enterprises in these countries less competitive. In addition, generous social benefits, by raising the reservation wage, make it particularly difficult for enterprises at the low end of the wage market to compete. As capital markets have become more open and capital controls increasingly unworkable, capital in these countries moves elsewhere in search of lower wage costs. Thus, governments respond directly as they recognize the cost of generous social benefits and cut the benefits to regain competitiveness or, if they attempt to retain them, growth declines and unemployment rises and the resulting tax shortfalls and spiraling social expenditures force them to cut benefits in order to reduce deficits.

The social democratic version of the globalization thesis begins with the assumption that state interventions in the economy were responsible for the relatively good performance of the northwest European economies, particularly with regard to unemployment, prior to the early seventies. Increased openness subsequently deprived the government of the policy tools it used to stimulate growth and employment. Increased trade openness and the transnationalization of production mattered not because they exposed these economies to competition but because they made Keynesian demand management more difficult as economic stimulation would increase demand for imports, which would lead to balance of trade deficits and thus pressures to devalue and then the possibility of an inflationary spiral. This was the lesson often drawn from the French socialist government's first eighteen months in office in 1981–1982 (see, for example, Streeck 1995). The declining ability to control capital movements was yet more damaging as countries could no longer control both interest rates and exchange rates and could not use controlled capital markets to privilege productive business investment in the domestic economy. In addition, capital mobility increased the structural dependence of the state on capital. In the closed economy version of this argument (see, for example, Block 1977; Lindblom 1977), the state was dependent on capital to invest, but abstaining from investment had a cost for capital in the form of forgone returns on invested capital. Capital could simply invest elsewhere and thus was in a position to press governments for tax concessions and other measures to create a more favorable business climate in much the same way that businesses had played American states off against each other in an earlier era. Thus, in the social democratic version of the globalization argument, there are net welfare losses due to beggar-thy-neighbor policies of governments, a sharp contrast to the neoliberal assumption that increased openness would lead to net efficiency gains and higher aggregate growth (though, of course, losses for those countries who cling to inefficient state intervention).

In the social democratic version of the globalization thesis, the development of one transnational organization, the European Community/Union, played a central role in the globalization process. The deepening of European integration was seen alternately, or perhaps sequentially, as a cause and cure to deepening globalization. On the one hand, European integration was seen as a response to the North American and East Asian economic challenges. On the other hand, it was furthering the transfer of economic tools out of the hands of the national state. In the case of the Nordic social democrats, it was only after these tools appeared unrecoverable at the national level that the parties turned to a pro-EU position, based on the hope that EU-level control could be substituted for the lost national policy instruments.

Trade Openness and the Welfare State in the Golden Age: The Evidence

The quantitative evidence on the effects of trade openness on welfare state generosity in advanced capitalist democracies is, unfortunately, ambiguous. For the first generation of studies, cross-sectional multiple regression on the approximately eighteen advanced capitalist democracies that have been democratic since World War II, the ambiguity might appear to be the product of "too many variables, too few cases," as the number of hypothesized determinants of welfare state generosity exceeded the number of cases. The study of pooled time series analysis promised to resolve this debate, and though it did serve to decidedly narrow the terms of the debate, it did not resolve it. The reason for this, in my view, is that some of the key hypothesized determinants of welfare spending—openness, union strength, corporatism, and social democratic government—are causally interrelated; part of what Czada (1988) terms a "size complex," which David Cameron (1978) and I (1979) identified two decades ago (see table 3.1).

In the literature on social democracy, one source of social democratic strength is almost undisputed: A strong union movement, that is, one not divided by ideology or confession and with a high portion of the labor force organized, results in higher levels of support for leftist parties and, in turn, leftist parties, once in government, facilitate union organization. Union organization provides the link to the "size complex" (see table 3.1). Wallerstein (1989, 1991) argues for a close link between country size and union organization as he contends that absolute size of the dependent labor force is a primary determinant of union organization. I have argued (Stephens 1979, 1991) that economic concentration is a strong determinant of labor organization, and, following Ingham (1974), see concentration as primarily a product of the size of the domestic market. I also contend (Stephens 1979, 1991), along with Visser (1991) and Swenson (1991), that the centralization of employers' association furthers unionization. This, in turn, has been linked to economic concentration (Ingham 1974) and openness of the economy (Swenson 1991).

Table 3.1 Correlates of the "Size Complex"

	1	2	3	4	5	6	7	8	9	10	11
1. GDP in U.S. dollars	1.00										
2. Total labor force	.99	1.00									
3. Trade openness, 1960–1973	-.64	-.67	1.00								
4. Economic concentration	-.51	-.52	.59	1.00							
5. Union density	-.53	-.54	.38	.49	1.00						
6. Union centralization	-.56	-.61	.66	.67	.81	1.00					
7. Cumulative left cabinet share	-.44	-.47	.43	.46	.83	.83	1.00				
8. Degree of corporatism	-.46	-.50	.75	.49	.62	.92	.71	1.00			
9. Liberalism of capital controls	.38	.31	-.13	.01	-.44	-.40	-.35	-.11	1.00		
10. Outward direct foreign investment	.24	.24	.09	-.14	-.05	-.06	.01	.10	.11	1.00	
11. Borrowing on international capital markets	-.38	-.37	.32	.10	.27	.17	.21	.04	-.28	-.06	1.00

Data definitions and sources:
(1) GDP in U.S. dollars. Huber, Ragin, and Stephens 1997, based on OECD data.
(2) Total labor force in thousands. Huber, Ragin, and Stephens 1997, based on OECD data.
(3) Value of exports plus imports as a percentage of GDP. Huber, Ragin, and Stephens 1997, based on OECD data.
(4) Weighted average of four firm concentration ratios. Stephens 1986/1979, 118, based on Pryor 1973.
(5) Percent of the labor force organized. Huber, Ragin, and Stephens 1997, based on data from Ebbinghaus and Visser 2000.
(6) Union centralization. Alvarez, Garrett, and Lange 1991.
(7) Left cabinet, scored 1 for each year when the Left is in government alone, scored as a fraction of the Left's seats in parliament of all governing parties' seats for coalition governments, 1946 to date. Huber, Ragin, and Stephens 1997.
(8) Corporatism, four point scale. Lehmbruch 1984.
(9) Liberalism of capital controls. Quinn and Inclan 1997.
(10) Outward foreign direct investment as a percentage of GDP. Provided by Duane Swank (see Swank 1998), originally coded from IMF, *Balance of Payments Statistics,* various years.
(11) Total borrowing on international capital markets as a percentage of GDP. Provided by Duane Swank (see Swank 1998), originally coded from IMF, *Balance of Payments Statistics,* various years.

Highly centralized tripartite bargaining, or "corporatism," has also been seen as a central feature of the social democratic project as it is a precondition for wage restraint, a cornerstone in social democratic growth and full employment policy. Moreover, it facilitates "compensation" for labor, that is, the expansion of the "social wage" as a quid pro quo for wage restraint. Again there are different accounts of the social origins of corporatism. Czada (1988) and I (1979) contend that strong and centralized unions and social democratic governance are prerequisites for strong corporatism and link these in turn to economic concentration and a small domestic market (see also Western 1991). Katzenstein (1985) contends that economic openness is a precondition for the development of corporatism. Wallerstein (1991) contends that high dependence on nonagricultural exports encourages union centralization, which in turn is a precondition for corporatist tripartite bargaining. Thus, as in the case of the strength of social democracy, the origins of corporatism can, in one way or another, be traced back to small size according to all of these scholars.[6]

As one can see from the preceding paragraphs, there is an economic logic that ties these features of the "size complex" together. There are other correlates of size that are associated with social democratic dominance or corporatism or both, which are a product of historical development, some with a political logic behind them and some by accident. Katzenstein (1985) has argued that a divided right encourages the development of corporatism, and Castles (1978) has linked the presence of a divided right to the success of Scandinavian social democracy. Both authors see divisions on the right as opening up the possibility of center-left coalitions, which result in the inclusion of labor in the policy-making process.[7] As Rokkan (1970) points out, the Protestant small holding countries of Scandinavia produced agrarian parties that further divided an already divided bourgeois bloc. This facilitated the formation of red-green (that is, worker-farmer) alliances, which brought social democracy in the region to power. In the case of the Catholic or religiously divided countries of the continent, the split between the liberals and Catholics (and in the Netherlands between the religious blocs) produced similar results and a parallel possibility for social democratic-Christian Democratic pro-welfare state alliances. As Rokkan (1970) and Katzenstein (1985) point out, these structural-historical splits in the bourgeois bloc led to the development of proportional representation which, in turn, sustained the divided right.

As one can see, the elements of the size complex are all strongly correlated and some of them, particularly the key variables of interest here (openness, social democratic government, corporatism, and union organization), are extremely strongly correlated. In our analysis of pooled data with eight different indicators of welfare state effort, Evelyne Huber and I (2001a, chap. 3; see also Huber, Ragin, and Stephens 1993; Huber and Stephens 2000a) attempt, with only partial success, to tease out these relationships. Here I would like to briefly summarize our results without actually presenting all of the regressions. First, let me point out that with one exception (civilian government employment), trade openness is strongly correlated to our indicators of welfare state effort (r = .47 to .65). We do not try to claim that there is no causal relationship between openness and welfare state effort. Rather, we attempt to specify how much of this effect is direct and how much is indirect and, if indirect, through which intervening variables it operates.

The first stumbling block in sorting out these effects is that three of the four variables of central interest here—social democratic government, corporatism, and union organization—are multicollinear, which is not surprising given the high intercorrelations exhibited in table 3.1. Thus, we regressed our eight dependent variables on one of the three variables (trade openness) and twelve other independent variables. When we compared the three sets of regressions, we found it easy to argue that the resulting estimates with union organization were inferior to left cabinet or corporatism. Three cases—New Zealand and Australia with relatively high levels of union organization and low values on our dependent variables, and the Netherlands with relatively low levels of union organization and high levels of welfare state effort—go far in explaining the poorer performance of this variable. Comparing the regressions with corporatism as an independent variable with those with left cabinet, we found that left cabinet outperformed corporatism in all regressions save one, pension expenditure adjusted for the size of the aged population. As for trade openness, it was insignificant in every regression. To summarize very briefly the positive findings of the analysis: Partisanship, either social democratic cabinet share (when the dependent variable measures services only) or Christian Democratic governance (when the dependent variable measures transfers only) or both are the most powerful predictors of welfare state effort. Our measure of constitutional structure veto points (federalism, bicameralism, presidentialism, referenda), followed by women's labor force participation, are the other positive findings.[8] Thus, our results argue that the effects of openness are entirely indirect.

I should note that other analysts have gotten different results due to differing measures of the dependent and independent variables. The critical decisions in our case were to measure the dependent variable as a level and not change variable (or include a lagged dependent variable, which turns the analysis into one of annual change) and to measure the cabinet variables as cumulative cabinet share and not cabinet share in the preceding year. These two decisions went together. We decided on the level measurement of the dependent variable for a variety of reasons, including the sensitivity of the annual change variables to economic cycles and the long-term fashion in which we conceived the political effects to work themselves out (for example, long maturing programs such as pension systems which are phased in over a number of years). The measurement of the cabinet independent variable followed: Surely the level of social expenditure of, say, Sweden in 1980, depended not on the government composition in the previous year but on the cumulative composition over the previous several decades. If one measures the dependent variable as a level, the cabinet share variable as the previous year or the previous few years, and uses a time invariant measure of corporatism or one that varies little through time[9] (see, for example, Swank 2002; Kenworthy and Hicks 1999), the results generally show small partisan effects and large effects of corporatism. These specifications may or may not show direct effects of openness, but if they do appear they are small.

Our contention that partisan government along with constitutional structure are the main determinants of welfare state generosity is based as much on our comparative case studies as on the conviction that we have properly measured the dependent and independent variables. Moreover, the comparative case studies allow us to bring corporatism and openness back into the explanation since the nuances of the interactions of these factors simply cannot be captured by the quantitative analyses. We did not find that major pieces of welfare state legislation were passed as part of explicit corporatist tripartite bargains between capital, labor, and the state. These were products of the political coalitions in the sitting government along with competitive bidding against the opposition. Adjustments to programs, such as increasing child allowances or indexing benefits, were more often part of explicit deals trading wage restraint for social benefit expansion, but these were generally deals between the government and labor aimed at securing wage restraint and not tripartite deals. Moreover, this cannot be disconnected from partisanship: Such deals were most common when the Social Democrats were in power, less common when the Christian Democrats governed without social democratic coalition partners, and almost never occurred when secular center and right parties were in government alone.

As to trade openness, even if it is difficult to show that it had any direct and independent effect on social expenditure, there is no doubt that it formed part of the backdrop in which wage negotiations and social policy making occurred and that all parties—employers, unions, and the political parties—were deeply aware of the vulnerabilities of openness. Thus, the welfare states and wage bargaining systems in northwestern Europe (among our cases, the four Nordic countries, Netherlands, Germany, and Austria) were built around the interests of export sector unions and employers. The whole political economy could not work if they were not. Here, of course, we find the key to the resilience of the social protection systems of these countries which one can usefully contrast to the Australasian systems of social protection which were not built around the interest of workers and employers in competitive export sectors, as we will see below. Moreover, even if partisan government is part of the picture, there was a long-term dynamic in which unions were being compensated for wage restraint (which they knew to be an economic necessity) by public sector expansion. Furthermore, cushioning the impact of externally induced change on workers through active labor market policy, industrial policy, or generous transfers, or all three, was certainly part of the policy pattern. And finally, even if it is difficult to demonstrate that openness directly affected welfare state generosity there is no doubt that the generous welfare state was designed to be and had to be compatible with a competitive exposed sector given the dependence on exports and the low level of tariff protection of domestic producers in the exposed sector.

Before moving on to the period of retrenchment, it is necessary here further to explore some of the characteristics of the Golden Age model of the northwestern European welfare states as these are relevant to the impact of globalization on these welfare states in the era of retrenchment. As one can see from table 3.1, capital market openness, as measured by either capital flows or capital market restrictions, is not related to any of the elements of the size complex. In fact, corporatism and social democracy appear to be negatively related to the degree of capital market liberalization as measured by the Quinn-Inclan (1997) index. This can be seen more clearly in table 3.2. As Huber and I have argued elsewhere (Huber and Stephens 1998), capital controls were an essential feature of the Golden Age social democratic economic model, characteristic of Sweden, Norway, Finland, and Austria (but not Denmark), which employed supply side measures and tax policies that largely affected the supply side to stimulate economic growth and maintain full employment.[10] The supply side policies extended beyond general supply side policies such as education, infrastructure, cheap credit policies, and generalized support for R and D to selective policies such as active labor market policy, credit policies favoring industrial borrowers over consumers and speculators, regional policies, and subsidies or subsidized credit to selected industries. Tax policies heavily favored reinvestment of profits over distribution. Interest rates were kept low through credit rationing and through public sector surpluses. Accordingly, fiscal policy was generally austere: these countries usually ran budget surpluses (see column 9 of table 3.2). By contrast, in the Nordic countries, monetary policy was generally accommodating, a policy that was facilitated by the subordination of central banks to political authorities (see column 10 of table 3.2). The four Nordic countries in this period appear to fit well into the policy configuration identified by Iversen (1998) and Franzese and Hall (2000) which produces low unemployment via real wage restraint but nominal wage inflation and price inflation through accommodating monetary policy and centralized bargaining (see discussion below)

With its closer integration with Germany, Austria relied more on fiscal and less on monetary stimulation, a pattern that became more pronounced when Aus-

Table 3.2 Selected Indicators of Economic Openness and Macroeconomic Policy by Welfare State Regime Type

	1	2	3	4	5	6	7	8	9	10
	Degree of liberalization of capital controls		Trade openness		Outward direct foreign investment		Borrowing on international capital markets		Average budget surplus	Central Bank Independence
	1960–73	1990–94	1960–73	1990–94	1960–73	1990–94	1960–73	1990–94	1960–73	
Sweden	2.4	3.8	46	59	0.5	6	0.17	10.54	2.8	0.27
Norway	1.5	4	82	72	0.1	1.9	1.37	5.01	3.4	0.14
Denmark	3	4	60	65	0.2	1.6	1.01	3.91	1.8	0.47
Finland	1	3.5	45	54	0.2	1.5	0.92	9.63	2.3	0.27
Mean	*1.98*	*3.83*	*58.25*	*62.50*	*0.25*	*2.75*	*0.87*	*7.27*	*2.58*	*0.29*
Austria	2.2	3.5	53	77	0.1	0.8	0.39	4.16	0	0.58
Belgium	3	4	77	138	0.3	3	0.35	2.77	–3	0.19
Netherlands	3	4	92	99	1.3	6.6	0.41	4.01	–0.4	0.42
Germany	4	4	40	62	0.3	1.2	0.05	1.85	0.4	0.66
France	2.9	3.6	27	44	0.2	1.9	0.09	2.69	–0.3	0.28
Italy	2.9	3.6	31	39	0.3	0.7	0.42	1.91	–3.5	0.22
Switzerland	3.9	4	61	69	0	4.4	0.06	2.21	4.6	0.68
Mean	*3.13*	*3.81*	*54.43*	*75.43*	*0.36*	*2.66*	*0.25*	*2.80*	*–0.31*	*0.43*
Canada	3.75	4	40	56	0.3	0.9	1.69	4.91	–1.5	0.46
Ireland	2	3.3	78	119	0	0.7	0.73	7.15	–4.3	0.39
UK	1.9	4	41	51	1.1	4.5	0.45	4.61	–2.1	0.31
USA	3.7	4	10	22	0.6	1.4	0.1	1.81	–1.9	0.51
Mean	*2.84*	*3.83*	*42.25*	*62.00*	*0.50*	*1.88*	*0.74*	*4.62*	*–2.45*	*0.42*
Australia	2.3	3	30	37	0.2	0.9	0.35	3.7	1.3	0.31
New Zealand	1.5	3.5	46	58	0.1	6.5	0.67	4.12	NA	0.27
Japan	2	2.8	20	18	0.2	0.7	0.09	1.46	1.4	0.16
Grand Mean	*2.61*	*3.70*	*48.83*	*63.28*	*0.33*	*2.51*	*0.52*	*4.25*	*0.06*	*0.37*

Data definitions and sources:
(1–8) See Table 3.1.
(9) Total revenue—total expenditure as a percentage of GDP. Huber, Ragin, and Stephens 1997, based OECD data.
(10) Iversen 1998.

tria pegged the Schilling to the German mark at the close of the Golden Age. Austria came to rely more on measures that stimulated business investment without using direct capital controls to keep interest rates down, such as tax concessions, subsidies, and direct state ownership of banks and large industry. In Germany, the state's role was limited to providing education and training, subsidizing research and development, and ensuring macroeconomic stability. However, the German model depended indirectly on capital immobility, as it depended on "patient capital." Strong links between industry and banks enabled banks to take a longer-term view of industry needs rather than having decisions dictated by short-run profitability. The state's role in the Netherlands was even more limited and the Dutch model cannot be said to have relied on controlled financial markets and low levels of capital mobility. In fact, outward Dutch direct foreign investment was very high in this period (see table 3.2, column 5).

Thus, given that the social policy regimes in northern Europe were developed in trade open (but in most cases financially closed) economies, one might expect them to be resilient to increasing trade competition but vulnerable to increasing financial liberalization in those cases in which financial controls were important tools of economic management. The resilience of these welfare states is further enhanced by the fact that they are embedded in mutually reinforcing production regimes, that is, modes of organizing production, conducting labor market relations, and managing the macro economy (Ebbinghaus and Manow 1998; Huber and Stephens 2001a, chap. 4). These economies are what Soskice (1999) terms "coordinated market economies" in which relationships between economic actors—employers, financial institutions, suppliers, skilled workers, scientists—are based on long-term stable relationships involving trust. As Estevez-Abe, Iversen, and Soskice (2001) argue, in such systems employment protection and unemployment insurance give workers incentives to invest in firm and industry-specific skills. Moreover, the highly egalitarian nature of these societies provides an environment in which people at the bottom of the system develop good general numeracy and literacy skills (Huber and Stephens 2001a, chap. 4). The wage bargaining systems further reinforce this high skill—especially at the bottom profile—since both centralized wage bargaining or coordinated sectoral-level bargaining, which is characteristic of these systems, result in compressed wage differentials when compared to the decentralized wage bargaining systems characteristic of the liberal market economies/liberal welfare states. These systems developed in a path-dependent, mutually reinforcing fashion through time. Thus, for example, as employers faced high wages at the bottom but a high-skill profile in the workforce, they gradually, over the postwar period, shifted production out of low-wage, low-productivity, low-skill sectors to high-wage, high-productivity, high-skill sectors.

Globalization and Welfare State Retrenchment: The Evidence

In the case of welfare state expansion, Huber and I reanalyzed the pooled quantitative data to test various hypotheses about the causes of variations in welfare state generosity through time and across countries. Given the methodological conclusions we developed in the course of our analysis of the expansion period, we also became extremely skeptical of the analyses of retrenchment employing pooled data (Huber and Stephens 2001a, chaps. 2, 3, and 6). A complete recapitulation of our argument would take us too far afield, so I will make a few key points here before reviewing the results of other analyses of these data. First, to analyze retrenchment, one cannot measure the dependent variable as the level of expenditure, employment, and so on because these are products of developments over the whole postwar period and not just a result of dynamics due to the retrenchment period. Second, if one measures the dependent variables as annual change, or includes a lagged dependent variable that is the logical equivalent, economic cycles explain most of the change while partisan effects and most other theoretically interesting variables are dramatically reduced, even in the preretrenchment time period. Indeed, for the preretrenchment period, we found no significant partisan effects for this period with annual change as the dependent variable or with the lagged dependent variable, country dummy specification as favored by Beck and Katz (1996), a result that is impossible to square with the pattern of long-term change and the variation across the countries observed at the end of the time period, not to speak of the results of our comparative case studies. Third, for the retrenchment period, the expenditure and, to a lesser extent, employment variables are poorer proxies for the underlying dimensions of welfare state generosity we are interested in, namely entitlements to transfers and services, than they were for the earlier period. For the earlier period, controls for aged and unemployed portions of the variations in the recipient population were adequate controls for the size of the recipient populations. In the retrenchment period, the unemployed were often absorbed in early retirement schemes, disability insurance, labor market policies, and further education, making the unemployment control much less effective than before. Thus, it is very common to observe increases in expenditure in given periods in given countries when one knows from case study material that entitlements are actually being cut.

Others have come to different conclusions about the nature of the data, and it is worth reviewing the results of two recent prominent quantitative studies on the retrenchment period: Geoffrey Garrett's *Partisan Politics in the Global Economy* (1998b) and Duane Swank's *Global Capital, Political Institutions, and Policy Change in Developed Welfare States* (2002). Both find that measures of openness of trade and financial markets are actually positively related to their indicators of welfare state effort and that the relationship appears to be stronger in social democratic welfare states (Swank) or in countries high on "left-labor power" (Garrett). Garrett is particularly optimistic about the continued validity of the social democratic model of political economy. In my view, he has overinterpreted his results. Garrett follows Beck and Katz (1996) and includes a lagged dependent variable and country dummies in the analysis. As he recognizes at various points in the analysis, these variables explain most of the variation, and the variables he is theoretically interested in explain very little. The real finding is that there is no support for the neoliberal version of the globalization thesis. If the pressures for convergence on neoliberal policy were as dramatic as the proponents of the thesis claim, one would expect to find strong evidence that globalization was related to retrenchment, especially in left-dominated countries or, if these countries maintained their welfare states, that it would be related to declining growth. Garrett found neither.

Swank presents somewhat more nuanced findings on the effects of globalization and interprets these in the light of his examination of the case materials. His analysis of interaction terms indicates positive globalization effects on social protection at the highest levels of corporatism and negative effects at the highest levels of liberalism. In a second set of analyses, disaggregating the data by regime types, he finds little or no effect of globalization in social democratic or Christian Democratic regimes and significant negative effects in liberal regimes. After examining the case materials, Swank (2002, chaps. 4 and 5) does not claim that globalization has a positive effect in social democratic and Christian Democratic groups and instead claims that the negative effects of globalization are muted, indirect, and weak. With regard to the liberal welfare states, he partly agrees with my own interpretation of the evidence that the positive relationship between globalization and retrenchment is due to common causes—neoliberal policy reforms—but also argues for a direct causal effect of globalization on retrenchment in this group of countries. In addition, he also maintains that there is a "political logic" to globalization in which the political resources of capital are enhanced, in turn contributing to retrenchment.

Because of our methodological conclusions, we limited our data analysis to cross-sectional regression and to the single question of the durability or lack thereof of partisan effects on policy outcomes in the retrenchment era. To document the pattern of retrenchment, we examine a wide range of indicators, not only the ones analyzed in our earlier chapters but also the indicators of social rights appearing in the studies emerging from the Social Citizenship Indicators Project directed by Walter Korpi and Joakim Palme (Huber and Stephens 2001a, chap. 6). To identify the causes of social policy changes, we relied on our analysis of our nine case study countries as well as studies of other countries mentioned in the initial paragraphs of this essay (Huber and Stephens 2001a, chap. 7; Stephens,

Huber, and Ray 1999; Scharpf and Schmidt 2000). We find that rollbacks and "restructurings" in welfare state programs have been a universal phenomenon in the past two decades. We distinguish "restructuring" from rollbacks because certain programs, most significantly public pension systems, have been significantly modified in some countries in a fashion in which the benefits have not been significantly cut but contributions or taxes have been increased to make the pension systems viable.

As to actual cutbacks—reductions in social benefits and social services—our case studies indicate two different dynamics: ideologically driven cuts, which occurred in only a few cases, and unemployment driven cuts, which were pervasive. The timing and severity of the latter type of rollbacks suggest that they were largely unemployment driven. The countries where unemployment rose early (Denmark and the Netherlands) initiated cuts in the mid-1970s; the countries where unemployment rose late (Sweden, Norway, Finland) continued to expand welfare state entitlements until the late 1980s. The countries where unemployment levels remained very high for a long time (the Netherlands, for example) made deeper cuts than the countries where they remained more moderate (for example, Norway). This is not to say that all the policy changes were somehow dictated by economic constraints; perceptions and beliefs about the effectiveness of different policies in achieving certain goals did play a role. Thus, the rising hegemony of neoliberal doctrines certainly contributed to the rollbacks.

These rollbacks in most cases did no more than reduce the increase in welfare state expenditures. In fact, if we look at the aggregate data for the different welfare state types, the average annual increase in most indicators of welfare state expenditures in the seventies was higher than it had been in the Golden Age, and it continued to increase in the 1980s, though at a slower pace than in the previous two periods. Essentially, in the 1970s governments countered the deteriorating economic situation with traditional Keynesian countercyclical policies, but by the 1980s they realized that the rules of the economic game had changed and demanded new approaches. Still, the increase in claimants of benefits kept pushing up expenditures.

Retrenchments generally began with lags in adjustments of benefits to inflation and increased copayments for welfare state services, particularly health care. The data on public share of total health care expenditures reflect these economizing measures; the average annual increase in the public share was already lower in the 1970s than in the earlier period, and in the 1980s the public share declined. Increases in waiting days for benefits, decreases in the length of time for which the most generous benefits could be claimed, and decreases in replacement rates followed. Eligibility criteria for a variety of programs were stiffened, particularly for unemployment and disability benefits. In the case of pensions, cuts in benefits promised for the future but not yet enjoyed by retirees were implemented in some countries. Only rarely were entire programs abandoned or radically changed, such as the maternity and death grants and the child benefit in Britain or the universal health care system in New Zealand. Nevertheless, the accumulation of these changes meant in some cases a significant reduction of entitlements, though not a system shift.

Our data show a sharp decline in partisan effects on welfare state expansion/ retrenchment, with one important exception—public social service employment. Curtailment of entitlements, or, at best, defense of existing entitlements, was on the agenda everywhere. As Pierson argues (1996; also see Huber and Stephens 1993, 1998), the politics of retrenchment is different from the politics of welfare state expansion. The right was constrained in its ability to cut by the popularity of most of the large welfare state programs, and the Left was constrained in its ability to raise taxes to keep the programs on a sound financial basis by the economic slowdown. This is not to say that there have not been significant differences in the rhetoric of political parties with regard to desirable welfare state reforms, but simply that electoral constraints worked against radical departures from established welfare state models. In our data analysis, the only indicator we found of continued partisan effects was public employment, a result that was driven by the expansion of the public social service sector in Scandinavia that continued throughout the 1980s. As the unemployment crisis hit Scandinavia in the early nineties, the expansion of public employment ceased.

There were only a few cases of large-scale, ideologically driven cuts. The most dramatic were Thatcher in Britain, the National (conservative) government in New Zealand, and the Reagan administration in the United States. In the case of the Reagan administration the cuts were focused on cash and in kind benefits to the poor, a small but highly vulnerable minority, while Social Security was preserved by a large increase in the contributions. In any case, the United States cannot have been said to have made a "system shift" if only because it already had the least generous welfare state of any advanced industrial democracy. Only in Great Britain and New Zealand could one speak of an actual system shift from welfare state regimes that used to provide basic income security to welfare state regimes that are essentially residualist, relying heavily on means testing. We argue that the exceptional nature of these two cases can be traced to their political systems, which concentrate power (unicameral or very weakly bicameral parliamentary governments in unitary political systems) and make it possible to rule without a majority of popular support (single member districts and plurality elections that allow parties with a minority of votes to enjoy large parliamentary majorities). Thus, in both cases, the conservative governments were able to pass legislation that was deeply unpopular.

Given the crucial role that the rise in unemployment has had in stimulating welfare state retrenchment, we have to seek to understand the reasons for the dramatic increases in unemployment in the eighties and early nineties. Here we can only summarize the arguments we make elsewhere at length (Huber and Stephens 1998, 2001a, chaps. 6 and 7; Stephens 1996). Let us begin by dispensing with the standard neoliberal argument on trade openness; that is, with increased trade openness, the countries with generous welfare states and high wages were increasingly exposed to trade competition and their generous social provisions made them uncompetitive in ever more open world markets. First, increased trade openness is not a good candidate for explaining dramatic change since it has increased only modestly. As one can see from table 3.2, total trade, imports plus exports as a percentage of GDP, increased by an average of 30 percent from the 1960s to the 1990s, while the two measures of capital mobility increased more than sevenfold.

Second, as we pointed out above, the generous welfare states of northern Europe were developed in very trade open economies in which the performance of the export sector was pivotal for the economic welfare of the country. Moreover, retrenchment was unrelated to export performance. For instance, the export sectors of countries such as Sweden and Germany were performing incredibly well in the mid-nineties at precisely the same time the governments of those countries were cutting social benefits (Huber and Stephens 1998; Pierson 2001; Manow and Seils 2000).

The question, then, becomes: What caused the increases in unemployment?[11] Let us begin by observing that it was not the low level of job creation because employment growth after 1973 was as rapid as before (Glyn 1995). Rather, rising labor force participation due to the entry of women into the workforce is one proximate cause of the increase in unemployment. The inability of the Christian Democratic welfare states to absorb this increase either through an expansion of low-wage private service employment as in the liberal welfare states or through the expansion of public services as in the social democratic welfare states is one reason the unemployment problem in these countries has been particularly severe. The other proximate cause is the lower levels of growth in the post-1973 period. This in turn can be linked in part to lower levels of investment, which in turn can be linked in part to lower levels of savings, to lower levels of profit, and to higher interest rates.

At this point, globalization in the form of financial market deregulation does enter our argument. Real interest rates increased from 1.4 percent in the sixties to 5.6 percent in the early nineties (OECD 1995, 108). The deregulation of international and domestic financial markets is partly responsible for this increase in interest rates.[12] As a result of the elimination of controls on capital flows between countries, governments cannot control both the interest rate and exchange rate. If a government decides to pursue a stable exchange rate, it must accept the interest rate that is determined by international financial markets. As a result of decontrol of domestic financial markets (which was in many cases stimulated by international financial deregulation), government's ability to privilege business investors over other borrowers also became more limited. Countries that relied on financial control to target business investment were particularly hard hit as businesses moved from a situation in which real interest rates offered to them via government subsidies, tax concessions, and regulations were actually negative to a situation in which they had to pay the rates set by international markets. In addition, in the pivotal German economy, the increase in capital mobility weakened the bank-in-dustry link with capital that became less patient, less willing to wait for the long-term payoff (Manow and Seils 2000; Streeck 1997).

External financial decontrol also limits a government's ability to employ fiscal stimulation as a tool since fiscal deficits are considered risky by financial markets and either require a risk premium on interest rates or put downward pressure on foreign exchange reserves. Thus, at least a portion of the increase in unemployment can be linked to globalization in the form of deregulated capital markets.

Note that our argument fits what I have termed the "social democratic" version of the globalization thesis and not the "neoliberal" version since it emphasizes the loss of tools for economic control, which had had positive effects on economic performance in the past.[13] This squares with the fact that the era of deregulation has been one of lower growth than the earlier period, which is a problem for the neoliberals since they predict that, though there may be losers (those who continue to cling to generous welfare states and state economic intervention), market deregulation should produce higher growth rates net of all other factors. Of course, the neoliberals would simply claim that there are countervailing factors that explain the outcome, but I have yet to encounter a compelling explanation of what these factors might be from their point of view.

While I do think the evidence supports the view that financial deregulation has contributed to the rise in unemployment, it is important to recognize the importance of political decisions and conjunctural developments in explaining the current high levels of unemployment in Europe. Though it almost certainly was not a conscious decision, or at least not seen in these terms, the Christian Democratic welfare states, faced with a growing supply of (female) labor, rejected the alternatives of creating a low-wage market in private services along American lines or expanding public services (and thus raising taxes) along Nordic lines.[14]

When I mention conjunctural developments, I do not mean to imply that these developments are necessarily cyclical and transitory; rather, I want to distinguish them from secular changes that are clearly irreversible. With regard to conjunctural elements of the present employment crisis in Europe, then, one can begin with the contribution of the debt buildup of the seventies to the current high levels of interest rates. With only two exceptions, the countries included in our quantitative analysis increased expenditure faster, in most cases much faster, than revenue in the seventies and then did the reverse in the eighties, but not enough to erase the debt, and in many cases the deficits, inherited from the seventies. This legacy, plus the development of the European monetary system (EMS), the collapse of the Soviet Union, German reunification, the Maastricht accord, and the development of the EMU (Economic and Monetary Union) led, in sequence and in combination, to the extremely austere monetary and fiscal policy now prevalent in Europe (Hall 1998; Soskice 2000). With open financial markets and the European monetary system of fixed exchange rates, interest rates in European countries were determined by financial markets and, given the pivotal role of Germany in the European economy, this increasingly meant that the Bundesbank set European interest rates, imposing its traditional, nonaccommodating policies on the rest of the region. The collapse of the Soviet Union, and with it the Soviet economy, sent a negative shock to all countries with exports to the Soviet Union, a shock that was a major blow to the Finnish economy and a minor one to a number of others. The budget deficits caused by German reunification stimulated an exceptionally austere response on the part of the Bundesbank, which was then communicated to the rest of Europe.[15] The convergence criteria contained in the Maastricht accord pressed further austerity on all governments, including those not committed to becoming EMU members, such as Sweden, and even on those outside of the EU, such as Norway. Since the establishment of the monetary union, the European Central Bank has continued to respond conservatively and slowly to economic downturns, arguably aggravating the recession of the early 2000s.

In the cases of Finland, Sweden, and to a lesser extent Norway, government policy mistakes strongly contributed to—indeed, may have created—the crisis.[16] All three countries deregulated their financial markets in the eighties, which led to booms in consumer spending and skyrocketing real estate prices and to overheating of the domestic economy and wage inflation. With all three countries following a fixed exchange rate policy until the international currency crisis of fall 1992, this wage inflation translated into a rise in relative unit labor costs vis-à-vis competitors and thus declining export performance. In the bust that followed the boom, property values collapsed, which caused bank insolvency and consumer retrenchment, which in turn aggravated the deep recession. The bank bailout cost the Swedish government 5 percent of GDP and the Finnish government 7 percent of GDP, greatly adding to the deficit in both countries.

In Australia and New Zealand, a case can be made for the neoliberal version of the globalization thesis in that changes in the international economy compelled both countries to deregulate markets and fundamentally change their systems of social protection. Following Castles (1985), I classify Australia and New Zealand as a distinctive type of political economy, "wage-earner welfare states" in which social protection was delivered primarily by a compulsory arbitration system that assured the family of an adequate living standard by providing a family wage to a male breadwinner and a number of social benefits from the employer to the wage earner. It was developed early in this century in an explicit compromise in which industry received protection, and it was enabled by a transfer of resources from a highly productive primary product export sector. The formal welfare state, that is, transfers and services delivered by the state, was rather underdeveloped by European standards. This distinctive Australasian political economy became unviable as a result of long-term secular changes in commodity prices and the entry of the United Kingdom into the European Community. In both countries, the wage regulation system, which was the core of the system of social protection, was changed substantially (in New Zealand it was altered completely), and this, along with the rise in unemployment, exposed workers to much higher levels of risk of poverty than had earlier been the case. Add to this other marketizing reforms (see Castles, Gerritsen, and Vowles 1996; Schwartz 1994a, 1994b, 1998), and it becomes apparent that the political economy of the Antipodes has converged on the liberal type. Thus, in these two countries, it is accurate to say that changes in the international economy forced them to abandon policies that had protected an uncompetitive manufacturing sector.

However, there are strong differences between the two countries with regard to not only the extent of labor market deregulation but also changes in the social policy regime proper. In Australia, the Labor government attempted not only to compensate those hit hardest by the ongoing changes with targeted programs, it also introduced two universalistic policies, medical care and supplementary pensions, which make the Australian social policy regime one of the most generous in the liberal group. Thus, the formal welfare state has not only not been cut back, it has been substantially expanded. By contrast, the conservative government elected in 1990 in New Zealand and unchecked by veto points in the country's unicameral unitary system carried out deeply unpopular reforms that completely deregulated the labor market and substantially cut social benefits.

Thus, on closer examination, with regard to the welfare state proper, Australia under Labor in the 1983–1995 period is hardly a confirmation of the neoliberal globalization thesis. On the contrary, it fits much better the thesis that openness leads to domestic compensation in the form of welfare state expansion. Indeed, it fits that theory almost perfectly and explicitly. Even before Labor came to power, party leader Hawke, a former president of the Australian union confederation, ACTU (Australian Council of Trade Unions), had worked out the basic parameters of policy change with the cooperation of ACTU. The centerpiece of economic management was the Prices and Income Accord, usually referred to as simply the Accord, an agreement between the government and ACTU, in which the unions agreed to restrain wage growth and cooperate with the government's market deregulating reforms in return for government efforts to increase employment and introduce social policy changes favorable to workers. In the course of the Hawke and Keating Labor governments, the Accord was renegotiated eight times and the two big social policy initiatives mentioned above, the universal health insurance system and the earnings-related pension system, were explicit quid pro quos that the unions received in return for their cooperation. Australia in the recent period confirms the argument that the positive effect of openness on social policy expansion is contingent on the partisan composition of the government: the Liberal government elected in 1995 and narrowly reelected in 1998 and 2001 ended the Accord process and implemented social policy cuts, among other things, cutting the employers' contribution to the new pension system from 12 percent to 7 percent of payroll.

Conclusion and Discussion

I find considerable support for the thesis that trade openness leads to the expansion of the welfare state and higher social expenditure, but this effect is contingent on the partisan composition of the government. It is most likely to occur under labor or social democratic governments or coalitions of Christian Democrats and social democrats and simply does not occur when secular right parties are in government. I also find support for the view of Katzenstein (1985), Cameron (1984), and other corporatism theorists that the innovations in social policy can be considered as compensation to labor for wage restraint. However, most major program innovations did not come about as explicit quid pro quos, though this did occasionally happen as we saw in the Australian case. Such explicit exchanges were more frequent in the case of adjustments to social policy. Moreover, these exchanges were most often deals between governments and labor unions; they rarely if ever involved an explicit three-way exchange with employers.[17]

Our finding on trade openness and welfare state expansion is directly connected to our rejection of the neoliberal globalization of trade and welfare state retrenchment thesis. The generous welfare states of northwestern Europe were built in open economies around the interests of exposed sector employers and workers. They were not only compatible with export competition; to the extent that they enabled wage restraint and provided collective goods valued by employers, such as labor training, the generous social policies actually contributed to competitiveness.

We found some support for the social democratic version of the globalization and retrenchment thesis. The immediate cause of social policy retrenchment was a substantial increase in unemployment and accompanying soaring budget deficits. The decontrol of capital markets and increased capital mobility contributed to the rise in unemployment in a number of ways. First, though the world buildup of debt in the wake of the two oil shocks was the most important cause of the rise in interest rates, the decontrol of financial markets ensured that no country could set interest rates below those set by international markets without sparking a massive outflow of capital and spiraling currency devaluations. Second, the decontrol of financial markets made it much more difficult for countries to privilege business investment over other uses of capital. Both of these factors led to lower levels of investment and therefore lower growth and lower employment growth. Third, decontrol of financial markets and increased capital mobility made countercyclical demand management more difficult since international capital markets are quick to punish any government that runs substantial deficits, resulting in downward pressure on the currency and upward pressure on interest rates. Thus, it became almost impossible to apply fiscal and monetary stimulus at the same time.

Granting these difficulties, it is important to recognize the conjunctural feature of the early 1990s employment difficulties in Europe. The worldwide debt buildup, the development of the EMS and EMU, German reunification, and the collapse of the Soviet Union combined to produce the fiscal and monetary austerity characteristic of Europe in the 1990s and 2000s. The combination of policy mistakes and uncontrollable international developments go far, very far, in explaining the Scandinavian crisis of the early 1990s. The turnaround of the Scandinavian countries is a tribute to this. Budgets are balanced or in surplus in all four Scandinavian countries, interest rates have fallen, and interest differentials against the German mark have shrunk or disappeared. Unemployment has fallen to under 5 percent in Denmark and Sweden, and Norway is experiencing labor shortages in many sectors. While Finland's unemployment rate remains at 9 percent, it has been brought down from a high of 18 percent. In Sweden, the percent of the population fifteen to sixty-four years of age and employed rose from a low of 71 percent in 1997 (still high by OECD standards) to 75 percent in 2001. While the Christian Democratic welfare states as a whole face serious employment problems, in two of the three Christian Democratic cases in our study, the Netherlands and Austria, unemployment has been around 3–4 percent in the last few years, which is substantially below the European average, and is all the more significant given that they are two of the most generous welfare states in continental Europe.

The editors of this volume point to the growing influence of international organizations as one dimension of globalization, and it is obvious that the growth of EC/EU authoritative decision making has changed the environment in which these national states operate. To the extent that European integration furthered financial liberalization, it has contributed to the difficulties of at least some of these northwestern European countries. On the other hand, to the extent that European integration has served to open up opportunities for new business investment and thus contributed to growth, it has played a role in solving the problems of these welfare states. Whether these positive effects outweighed the negative is virtually impossible to say because there are no comparative cases on which to construct a counterfactual (that is, a generous social democratic or Christian Democratic welfare state unaffected by European integration). One point that is important to stress in the context of this volume is that, unlike the cases of the IMF's and World Bank's relationships with developing countries, the EU does not use its authority to impose neoliberal models of social policy (or labor market relations) on its member states. If anything, the Social Charter and the more recent efforts to fight poverty and social exclusion via the open method of coordination (OMC) aimed at harmonizing policy upward, though actual achievements of the Social Charter have so far been disappointing to Social Democrats, and it is too early to evaluate achievements via the OMC. In contrast to the EU, the OECD, through its *Jobs Study* initiative, has vigorously promoted neoliberal solutions in the areas of social policy and labor market relations, though it can provide little incentives or disincentives to national states to follow its recommendations, unlike the EU, IMF, or World Bank. While it has certainly moved the debate in a neoliberal direction, it is difficult to gauge how much influence it has actually had on social policy making. In any case, its influence on social policy has been small in comparison to, for example, the World Bank's on pension reform in Latin America (see Huber, this volume; Huber and Stephens 2000b).

I have only mentioned the editors' fourth dimension of globalization, the transnationalization of production, in passing. There is no question that a qualitative change in multinationalization of production has accompanied the European integration process, as we have witnessed a wave of foreign acquisitions and mergers as businesses have positioned themselves to take advantage of the expanded European market and to compete in the world market. Though these mergers and acquisitions have often been accompanied by streamlining of operations and thus labor force reductions, there is little evidence that the moves have been motivated by a search for lower labor costs. Rather, market entry, expansion of market share, and economies of scale have been much more central motivations. The multinationalization of production along with financial liberalization puts business in a position to play governments against one another in order to get tax concessions or general reductions in capital taxation, but so far this has not resulted in falling income from taxes on capital (Swank 1998; Ganghof 2000), though it certainly has the potential to do so in the future should capital attempt to exploit these opportunities. However, as Ganghof (2000) points out, even were this to occur, it would not have a major impact on social expenditure because taxes on capital are a small portion of total taxation.

In stressing the conjunctural nature of European unemployment problems and the recent positive developments of the Nordic and Dutch economies, I do not mean to imply that these northwestern European welfare states do not face challenges. I have discussed at length the loss in policy-making discretion resulting from financial liberalization. In the case of the social democratic welfare states, I would contend that the main additional challenge is to adjust their wage bargaining systems to the new international economic environment. Failure to do so could easily result in wage inflation, which will translate into higher unemployment. This will happen immediately and inevitably in Finland, which is a member of the EMU, and immediately in the other three countries if they maintain a fixed exchange rate, and with a lag if they do not via a chain of devaluation, higher interest rates, lower investment, inflationary pressures, and so on. As I pointed out above, the recent literature on wage bargaining and unemployment identifies the traditional Nordic model of central bank dependence, accommodating monetary policy, and real wage restraint but nominal wage inflation as one policy mix that delivers low levels of unemployment (Iversen 1998; Franzese and Hall 2000). With rising capital mobility, this combination became increasing problematic and had to be backed up with devaluations. However, in open financial markets, the devaluations themselves became increasingly costly as they caused progressively higher interest rate premiums. In the end, open capital markets forced all of the Nordic countries to accept German monetary policy leadership and, therefore, nonaccommodating monetary policy.

According to the recent work on wage bargaining and unemployment cited above, this necessitates a move to sectoral level bargaining, the German model, to produce wage restraint. With the decentralization of collective bargaining, it would appear that Sweden is well positioned to deliver the appropriate mix. Based on observations of recent Nordic bargaining rounds and interviews I conducted with the chief economists of the major Swedish union and employer confederations in June 1999, I think that the magic bullet combination suggested by this literature is too simplistic and that we do not know for sure which configuration is best suited to produce noninflationary wage increases in these present monetary and exchange rate environments as these economies approach full employment.[18] While it would take me too far afield to fully develop my arguments here (see Stephens 2000), suffice it to say that it is my judgment that considerable fine-tuning of the bargaining systems, particularly the introduction of stronger coordinating mechanisms to prevent free-riding by the sheltered sector, may be necessary to adapt them to the EMU environment.

As for the Christian Democratic welfare states, Esping-Andersen (1999; Esping-Andersen et al. 2002) argues compellingly that their problems are rooted in the patterns of labor force participation and demographic change generated by the social policy configuration itself. The low level of women's labor force participation is in large part a product of the policy pattern: strong support for male breadwinner benefits; low levels of public sector employment; low levels of social provisions such as daycare, which allow women to combine family and work; absence of a low-wage private service sector; union opposition to part-time work and extended hours in retail trade; among others. Add to this the emphasis of these welfare states on workforce reduction—moving workers to passive supports such as early pensions and disability pensions—as opposed to Scandinavian-style active labor market policy, and one arrives at quite unfavorable ratios of working to transfer dependent populations. Since many women in these postindustrial societies enter the workforce anyway, the absence of policies enabling the combination of work and family has resulted in extremely low levels of fertility. This threatens to greatly increase the ratio of aged to working age population a generation from now, which will make the dependency ratio yet worse. Thus, the solution for the Christian Democratic welfare states would appear to be to move in a Nordic direction of much stronger support for mothers' employment through policies such as more public daycare and longer parental leave, which facilitate the combination of work and family. This, however, would involve raising the level of taxation, not a popular solution in the present situation.

4

Globalization and Social Policy Developments in Latin America

EVELYNE HUBER

Social policy in Latin America has undergone profound changes in the 1980s and 1990s. The thrust of the changes has pointed in the direction of state retrenchment and market expansion in the financing, delivery, and administration of social services and transfer payments. To the extent that the state has retained responsibilities for social services and transfers, they have become more targeted rather than more universalistic. There is no disagreement about the need for social policy reforms, but wide divergence of opinion about the desirable direction of the reforms exists. Proponents of the market-oriented changes are arguing that they have brought greater efficiency, that is, better social services and transfers, particularly for the truly needy, at an affordable cost. Opponents are arguing that the changes amount to an abdication of state responsibility and of the principles of solidarity and redistribution on which social policy should be based.

Similarly, there is disagreement about the causes of the reforms. One point of view holds that the old model of social policy was inextricably linked to the import substitution industrialization (ISI) model and therefore became unviable along with that model. In this view, liberalization of the Latin American economies required a corresponding adjustment of social policy to reflect market principles. Social policy reform was—or should be—part and parcel of a successful overall reform package designed to integrate Latin American economies into the world economy and create confidence among investors, both domestic and foreign. A different view holds that only certain aspects of the old policy regimes were incompatible with economic liberalization and that there was a variety of possible directions for social policy reform. In this view, the power of the international financial institutions (IFIs) weighed heavily on Latin American countries to adopt market-driven social policy reforms, but given a favorable domestic political power constellation, alternative kinds of reforms were possible.

The purpose of this chapter is to assess the validity of the arguments in the debate about the impact of globalization on social policy reform. An understanding of the forces that promoted given sets of reforms also provides insight into the goals to be achieved through the reforms and will allow us to draw out some implications for the debate about the reforms' outcomes. Both of the above-mentioned views on the causes and direction of the reforms attribute great importance to globalization, vaguely defined as the power of international economic forces. The first view emphasizes market logic and investor confidence, the second financial and political power. Clearly, to assess the relative merits of these points of view, I will begin with an examination of the various components of the concept of globalization. I will then identify the nature of the old models of social protection in Latin America and the causes of their crisis, as well as the determinants of the nature of the reforms, with special attention to the relative weight of the various components of globalization and of domestic determinants.

The specification of the dimensions of globalization provided by Glatzer and Rueschemeyer is comprehensive and analytically useful and will be adopted here. The growth of international markets for goods and services, of international capital markets, of international networks of production in the form of transnational corporations (TNCs) or global commodity chains, and the growing importance of international organizations are the four key components of globalization that need to be examined separately and in conjunction in an effort to assess the impact of globalization on social policy developments in Latin America over the last two decades.

Traditional Models of Social Protection in Latin America

Latin American countries differed and continue to differ widely in their systems of social protection.[1] Only six Latin American countries can claim to have built a system of social protection vaguely resembling a welfare state, covering more than 60 percent of the economically active population with some form of social security as of 1980. These countries are Argentina, Brazil, Chile, Costa Rica, Cuba, and Uruguay; at least three Caribbean countries, the Bahamas, Barbados, and Jamaica, also belong to that category.[2] With the exception of Costa Rica, these are pioneer countries that introduced their first social security schemes in the 1920s and 1930s. A second group of six countries had expanded coverage to between 30 percent and 60 percent of the economically active population by 1980: Colombia, Guatemala, Mexico, Panama, Peru, and Venezuela. All but Guatemala belong to the intermediate group that introduced their social security schemes in the 1940s or early 1950s (Mesa-Lago 1994, 15–19). Bolivia, Ecuador, and Paraguay also belong to the intermediate group, but their coverage had not reached 30 percent by 1980. The remaining countries instituted social security systems even later and their coverage remained below 30 percent of the economically active population, with the lowest being the Dominican Republic (12 percent), El Salvador (12 percent), and Paraguay (14 percent).

The reason coverage remained so low in most countries is that social security was employment based; contributions were mandatory for employees and employers. The self-employed were in some cases included on a voluntary basis, in others on a compulsory basis, but in either case evasion was rampant as the self-employed generally had to pay both the employer and the employee share, which made the contributions prohibitively expensive for most self-employed persons. Moreover, a very large sector of the self-employed worked in the informal sector, beyond the reach of labor and social security legislation.

In general, then, advancement of ISI and the related relative size of the formal sector were strong determinants of the extent of social security coverage. Argentina, Brazil, Chile, and Uruguay were among the most advanced industrial countries as of 1980, with 25–34 percent of total employment in industry.[3] At the other end of the coverage spectrum, Bolivia, Ecuador, the Dominican Republic, and El Salvador had never gone through a strong ISI phase and had less than 20 percent of the employed in industry. However, there were clear exceptions to this rule, such as Costa Rica, Barbados, Jamaica, and the Bahamas, all of which had a comparatively low degree of industrialization but high coverage. Mexico and Venezuela, on the other hand, had a high percentage of employment in industry also, with 29 percent and 28 percent, respectively, but they lagged behind in coverage. These exceptions demonstrate that political power distributions and consequent policy choices were important in shaping systems of social protection.

For the most part, social security coverage included pensions for old age and survivors, and health care. Few countries had family allowances, and even fewer had unemployment insurance; coverage under the latter was limited to privileged sectors of workers. Similarly, social assistance was very poorly developed; the most widely practiced form of social assistance was a very low pension for the indigent. Exceptions to this general pattern were the noncontributory scheme for the rural sector introduced in Brazil in 1971, and the virtually universal coverage of the public health care system in Costa Rica. Jamaica and Barbados also had public health care systems with almost universal coverage.

The most advanced systems of social protection were constructed step by step, beginning with the most powerful pressure groups, such as the military, civil servants, and the judiciary (Malloy 1979; Mesa-Lago 1978). With the progress of ISI, other middle- and working-class groups in crucial sectors and with a high degree of organization were added, such as journalists, bank workers, teachers, railroad and port workers, mining, public services, and finally manufacturing. Typically, many of these newly incorporated groups received their own programs, so that the systems of social protection grew to be very fragmented and quite inegalitarian.[4] Even where the distributive impact of these systems on those covered was neutral or slightly progressive, the highly limited coverage in many cases made the systems regressive for the population as a whole, as tax funds were often used to subsidize parts of social security schemes. The military governments of the 1960s and 1970s effected some unification of social insurance systems, but inequalities and lack of coverage of large sectors of the population (those outside the formal labor market) persisted. For those outside the system there was no effective social safety net, except for very low social assistance pensions in the most advanced countries. In health care, several countries legally extended the right to free treatment in public clinics to indigents, but in practice accessibility of these clinics was woefully inadequate, particularly in rural areas. Arguably the most important part of social policy for those outside the formal labor market was the price controls and subsidies on basic foodstuffs and public transport.

As of 1980, the social security systems in the pioneer countries already faced considerable financial problems (Mesa-Lago 1989). Given the roughly five decades of existence of the pension systems, they had matured and the ratio of active to inactive members was deteriorating rapidly. Generally, even where some part of pension funds was invested, the returns were low; often these funds were used to finance other parts of social policy, such as housing. Evasion of contributions among employers was rampant, as was delayed transfer of contributions from those employers who did make contributions to the social security systems, which in times of high inflation greatly reduced the value of these contributions. Frequently the state failed to meet its obligations to the social security system as well. On the expenditure side, benefits for the privileged systems, particularly under the rules that allowed retirement after a certain number of years of service, weighed heavily, as did rapidly escalating costs for medical technology. Finally, administrative expenditures in many systems were very high, as social security agencies along with other public agencies were sometimes used for patronage employment. The economic crisis of the 1980s then greatly aggravated these problems and forced adjustments.

Changes in Social Protection Policies in the 1980s

The key to understanding the trajectory of social protection policies in the 1980s is the debt crisis. Several countries had already experienced severe debt problems in the 1970s, but when the banks reacted to the threat of a moratorium by Mexico in 1982—which was soon followed by similar announcements by Argentina and Brazil—by withholding any new loans, the crisis became a generalized one. Country after country had to submit to austerity programs imposed by the International Monetary Fund (IMF), which plunged the region into the deepest recession since the 1930s. Latin America became a net capital exporter at an annual rate of roughly 3 percent of GDP from 1983 to 1987 (Dornbusch 1989, 11), or, according to Varas (1995, 279), of 3.5 percent of GDP annually between 1983 and 1990. In addition to austerity programs, the implementation of structural adjustment programs became a condition for receiving loans from international financial institutions (IFIs), most prominently the International Monetary Fund, the World Bank, and the Inter-American Development Bank, and for agreements on rescheduling the debt. Structural adjustment was aimed at a general reduction of state intervention in the economy and included liberalization of trade and capital flows, privatization of state enterprises, relaxation of economic regulations, and incentives for foreign direct investment.[5] The combined austerity and structural adjustment measures led to rapidly rising unemployment, underemployment, and poverty rates.

The austerity packages entailed a rapid and deep cut in social expenditures. Expenditures on health, education, and welfare dropped from an average of 9.1 percent of GDP in 1982 to 8.3 percent in 1990 (table 4.1).[6] Given that GDP per capita decreased in this period, the real value of expenditures per capita decreased significantly, from an average of $533 per capita in 1982 to $485 in 1990 (table 4.2; expressed in 1995 constant dollars adjusted for purchasing power parity [PPP]). In some of the larger countries, these expenditures dropped very steeply (Chile and Mexico), whereas in others it only dropped moderately (Argentina) or even increased (Brazil). A similar picture of heterogeneity prevails among the smaller countries. As table 4.3 demonstrates, many countries made great efforts to protect expenditures on health, education, and welfare and managed to hold constant or even slightly increase their share in total public expenditures. That share increased slightly from an average of 38 percent in 1982 to 40 percent in 1990.

This general decline in social expenditures meant a decline in the real value of pensions as they were left to lag way behind inflation, a decline in the quantity and quality of health care due to staff cuts, declining salaries of health care professionals, cuts in operating budgets of clinics and hospitals, lack of investment in new facilities, and so on, along with similar developments in education. A further crucial impact of the austerity and structural adjustment packages concerned the reduction or elimination of price subsidies and controls on basic necessities, which hit the poorest groups hardest since these groups spend the largest percentage of their income on these necessities. Price increases of 200 or 300 percent on some

Table 4.1 Social Security and Welfare, Health, and Education Expenditure
as % of GDP

	Level				Average annual change (%)		
	1973	1982	1990	1997	1982	1990	1997
Argentina	7.42	5.21	6.13	9.22	−.24	.11	.44
Bahamas	8.41	9.04	7.2**	8.08****	.07	−.20[b]	.22[e]
Barbados	16.43	14.48	17.31***		−.21	.40[c]	
Belize			7.07	10.13		−.20	.43
Bolivia	3.31	4.6*	6.23	11.25	.16[a]	.18[d]	.71
Brazil	7.77	10.15	12.85	13.91	.26	.33	.15
Chile	13.86	21.62	11.70	13.24	.86	−1.24	.22
Colombia			3.65	6.59			.42
Costa Rica	10.67	12.24	15.12	14.43	.17	.35	−.09
Dominican Republic	5.28	4.73	3.31	5.18	−.06	−.17	.26
Ecuador	7.36	9.68	4.57		.25	−.63	
El Salvador	5.15	5.33	2.96	4.36	.02	−.29	.20
Guatemala	3.28	1.61	4.06***	7.39****	−.18	.34[c]	
Mexico	5.78	7.21	5.25	7.09	.15	−.27	.26
Nicaragua							
Panama	12.14	10.97	14.22	15.57	−.12	.46	.19
Paraguay	3.64	5.33	2.67		.18	−.33	
Peru	5.11	3.79			−.14		
St. Vincent			10.29	11.77		.03	.21
Uruguay	13.47	19.31	14.46	22.69	.64	−.60	1.17
Venezuela	7.21	8.74			.16		
Mean	*8.02*	*9.06*	*8.28*	*10.73*	*.11*	*−.10*	*.34*

Note: *value for 1981; ** value for 1991; *** value for 1989; **** value for 1995.
[a] Annual average change for 1973–1981.
[b] Annual average change for 1982–1991.
[c] Annual average change for 1982–1989.
[d] Annual change for 1981–1990.
[e] Annual average change for 1991–1995.

items, decreed overnight, were not unusual, and were at the root of what came to be called "IMF-riots" (see, for example, Walton 1989).

The structural adjustment packages had a profound impact on the reach of social protection policies via the decline of employment in the manufacturing and public sectors. Workers in medium and large manufacturing enterprises and public sector employees were traditionally covered by social security schemes, and as they lost their jobs they and their families lost coverage for pensions and health care. Official social policy by and large ignored their plight, as the new guiding principle for social policy was to target the neediest. In the name of efficiency and social justice, and in the context of declining expenditures, nutrition and preventive health campaigns were launched for the very poor. Under guidance from the IFIs, social emergency investment funds were established, mostly based on foreign financing. These funds were to provide loans to the poorest communities for eco-

Table 4.2 Social Security and Welfare, Health, and Education Expenditure per Capita in 1995 PPP Dollars

	Level				Average annual change		
	1973	1982	1990	1997	1973–1982	1982–1990	1990–1997
Argentina	775.01	563.06	552.13	1080.3	−23.55	−1.37	75.45
Bahamas	1195.03	1331.77			15.19		
Barbados	918.74	895.35	1343.1[b]		−2.60	63.96[d]	
Belize		280.81	299.73	437.91		2.36	19.74
Bolivia	76.83	112.79[a]	132.74	246.85	4.50[c]	2.22[e]	16.30
Brazil	398.43	651.97	834.14	934.51	28.17	22.77	14.34
Chile	563.77	960.38	679.87	1099.09	44.07	−35.06	59.89
Colombia			306.75	369.05			8.9
Costa Rica		770.82	949.65	989.46	−2.34	22.35	5.69
Dominican Republic	155.47	179.2	129.07	237.2	2.64	−6.27	15.45
Ecuador	186.37	325.18	148.27		15.42	−22.11	
El Salvador	217.11	180.41	102.66	170.85	−4.08	−9.72	9.74
Guatemala	104.23	57.52	139.03[b]		−5.19	11.64[d]	
Mexico	333.50	591.88	391.48	525.83	28.71	−25.05	19.19
Panama	542.28	605.89	642.45	809.89	7.07	4.57	23.92
Paraguay	109.23	251.77	122.15		15.84	−16.20	
Peru	233.63	200.37			−3.70		
St. Vincent		276.07	436.2	534.37		20.02	14.02
Uruguay	778.69	1330.63	1042.34	1906.39	61.33	−36.04	123.44
Venezuela	534.53	564.06			3.28		
Mean	445.18	533.15	485.4	718.59	10.87	−.12	31.24

Note:

[a] Value for 1981.

[b] Value for 1989.

[c] Average annual change for 1973–1981.

[d] Average annual change for 1982–1989.

[e] Average annual change for 1981–1990.

nomic and social infrastructure, social services, and sometimes production ventures. The targeted health and nutrition campaigns, particularly where they were targeted at the poorest urban communities with relatively good accessibility, were often very useful. The demand-driven social funds, however, were obviously unlikely to reach the poorest sectors since those were the least capable of formulating project proposals. Moreover, the targeted health and nutrition campaigns and the social funds opened space for discretion by public officials and thus were vulnerable to abuse for political patronage purposes.

The overall results of the economic crisis and the changes in economic and social policy were rising rates of poverty and inequality. Poverty increased in virtually every country, from 35 percent of all Latin American households in 1980 to 39 percent in 1990 (CEPAL 1995, 146). During the same period, inequality in the distribution of household income increased (CEPAL 1994, 33–45). The exceptions to the general trajectory of social expenditures and social policies in this period are

Table 4.3　Social Security and Welfare, Health, and Education Spending as % of Total Public Expenditure

	Level				Average Annual Change (%)		
	1973	1982	1990	1997	1973–1982	1982–1990	1990–1997
Argentina	44.29	38	58.03	60.41	−.7	2.50	.34
Bahamas	44.55	42.34			−.25		
Barbados	46.72	47.42	52.18[b]		.08	.68[d]	
Belize		28.30	25.07	34.57		−.40	1.36
Bolivia	35	32.55[a]	38.04	51	−.31[c]	.61[e]	1.85
Brazil	50.75	47.77	35.12	56.77	−.33	−1.24	3.09
Chile	39.85	63.39	57.42	62.46	2.62	−.75	.72
Colombia			31.56	41.01			1.35
Costa Rica	54.97	66.56	59.04	63.86	1.29	−.94	.69
Dominican Republic	30.05	35.03	28.44	31.1	.55	−.82	.38
Ecuador	33.57	35.16	31.51		.18	−.46	
El Salvador	41.69	27.76	27.19	35.35	−1.55	−.07	1.17
Guatemala	34.44	12.95	34.61[b]		−2.39	3.09[d]	
Mexico	45.36	24.91	29.42	43.61	−2.27	.56	2.03
Panama	45.22	32.45	60.04	57.59	−1.42	3.45	−.35
Paraguay	34.40	45.34	28.40		1.22	−2.12	
Peru	28.7	21.53			−.8		
St. Vincent		30.15	30.22	27.72		.01	−.36
Uruguay	59.48	65.22	62.03	74.58	.64	−.4	1.79
Venezuela	34.38	30.15			−.47		
Mean	41.38	38.26	40.49	49.23	−.23	.23	1.08

Note:
[a] Value is for 1981.
[b] Value is for 1989.
[c] Average annual change for 1973–1981.
[d] Average annual change for 1982–1989.
[e] Average annual change for 1981–1990.

equally important. Barbados, Brazil, Costa Rica, and Panama stand out among the countries in the highest category of social spenders in that they increased social expenditures in the 1980s as a percentage of GDP (table 4.1); they all managed to do so even in real terms. In the distribution of household income, only Uruguay and Colombia showed a slight improvement in the 1980s (CEPAL 1994); Costa Rica was not included in the comparative United Nations Economic Commission for Latin America and the Caribbean (CEPAL) study, but Morley (1995, 138) found that inequality rose during the 1980–1982 recession and then declined. Costa Rica and Uruguay, then, were different from the other Latin American countries in spending efforts and outcomes, and as we shall see below, they were also different in some aspects of their traditional systems of social protection and in their approach to social policy reform.

Changes in Social Protection Policies in the 1990s

Most Latin American economies resumed growth in the 1990s, but they remained highly vulnerable to decisions of external economic actors and increasingly of the largest of the domestic private investors. Capital flows returned to Latin America, but mostly in the form of short-term funds and portfolio investment, particularly in the first half of the 1990s. Debt-equity swaps and privatization of state enterprises frequently led to direct foreign investment. Large inflows of short-term capital led to overvalued exchange rates and import booms and left countries highly vulnerable to fluctuations in investor confidence. Where such confidence suddenly declined, massive outflows of capital and pressures for devaluation were the result, such as in Mexico in 1994 or Brazil in 1998–1999. Governments' reactions to these pressures in the form of devaluation, massive increases in interest rates, and austerity then caused renewed recessions.

Overall, employment expanded considerably as well, but not fast enough to absorb the growing labor force. Particularly from 1994 on, solid GDP growth rates have been combined with persistent or even rising unemployment levels, and in the countries that suffered recessions in the mid-1990s unemployment rose particularly sharply (CEPAL 1997). Argentina before 1995 is a dramatic example of an economy with positive growth and at the same time significantly increasing urban unemployment, rising from 6 percent in 1990 to 13 percent in 1994 (CEPAL 1996, 25). With the beginning of the economic crisis in 2000–2001, urban unemployment then rose to 16 percent (CEPAL 2002). Moreover, employment expanded mostly in low productivity sectors, in small enterprises and informal activities, which reduced its contribution to poverty reduction.

With economic growth, social expenditures rose in real terms significantly above the level of the early 1980s (table 4.2), and they also rose as a percentage of GDP and of total public expenditures (tables 4.1 and 4.3). Clearly the highest spenders, with 14–23 percent of GDP were, in descending order, Uruguay, Panama, Costa Rica, and Brazil, followed by Chile with 13 percent. The increase in real expenditures meant some recovery of benefits in cash transfer programs, and some improvement in social services, though it clearly has been difficult to make up for the lack of investment in social infrastructure in the 1980s.

Changes in overall social spending in the 1980s and 1990s, then, can be regarded to some extent as conjunctural, but of much greater and more lasting importance were the many structural reforms of the social policy schemes that were undertaken in the late 1980s and the 1990s.[7] These reforms pointed in two opposite directions: individualization, privatization, and targeting of social policy on the one hand, exemplified by the Chilean model, and unification, maintenance of state responsibility, and universalization on the other hand, exemplified by the Costa Rican approach. Most of the other countries that adopted significant reforms fell in between these two extremes, with Mexico and Bolivia closer to the Chilean pole, Peru, Colombia, and Argentina somewhere in the middle, and Uruguay and—to a lesser extent—Brazil closer to the Costa Rican pole.

Chile was a pioneer in adopting social security reform in two ways: It was the first country to do so, in the very early 1980s, and its reform amounted to the most radical privatization of social security.[8] The reform of the pension system created compulsory individual capitalized accounts administered by private, for-profit companies called Pension Fund Administrators (AFPs). Only the individual worker made contributions to this fund; employers made no contributions. People who had made contributions to the old system had the choice of remaining with the old or joining the new system; there was no possibility to switch back to the old system, and all new entrants to the labor force had to join the new system. In practice, the large majority of people switched to the new system, enticed by initially lower contribution rates, the promise of recognition bonds for their previous contributions to be paid at retirement, and a massive advertising campaign promising higher benefits. By 1990, 90 percent of the insured were registered in the new private scheme; those remaining in the old system were mainly people close to retirement. However, coverage remained restricted; in 1990, 79 percent of the labor force were registered, but only 56 percent made contributions; the corresponding figures for 1993 were 90 percent and 53 percent. If the contributors to the public system and the armed forces system were included, contributors in 1993 reached 61 percent (Mesa-Lago and Arenas de Mesa 1998, 61).

The total value of an individual's pension fund in the new system is determined by total contributions plus investment returns on the contributions minus administrative charges. At the point of retirement the individual has the option of transferring the accumulated fund to an insurance company to buy a life annuity, or to receive a variable pension directly from the AFP. The state assumed the responsibility of paying benefits in the old system, honoring the previous contributions of those who switched to the new system, providing a minimum pension for those with twenty years of contributions whose accumulated funds in the new system would not reach a certain limit, and guaranteeing the life annuity in case of bankruptcy of an insurance firm. There are no solid figures for the combined financial burden of the deficits in the old system and the subsidies to the new system. One estimate sets the costs for this reform at some 4–5 percent of GDP in the 1980s and early 1990s (Diamond and Valdés-Prieto 1994, 279–80); other estimates are roughly comparable (Mesa-Lago and Arenas de Mesa 1998, 74). The deficit in the public system will last for another thirty years, and many people in the private system underreport earnings and make contributions only sufficient to entitle them to a state-subsidized minimum pension.

The presumed advantages of the new pension system were a stronger relationship between contributions and benefits, higher pensions because of investment of the funds, lower administrative costs, and a boost to capital markets. It is highly questionable, though, whether any of them have been realized. The relationship between contributions and benefits is not the same for everybody; it varies by income levels because the element of fixed commissions has a highly regressive impact, and of course investment performance can be highly variable over time. In the early 1990s, average pensions in the new system were higher than in the old, but this was mainly due to the exceptionally high returns from the mid-1980s on, returns that were not sustained in the mid-1990s and are most unlikely to prevail for any length of time again. Administrative costs in the new system are extremely high because of the huge outlays for advertising and for sales personnel; as of the mid–1990s, the administration of the Chilean system was the most expensive in Latin America (IDB 1996). Administrative costs, of course, are passed on to the contributors. In March 1999, CB Capitales, a brokerage firm in Chile, released figures on the returns on contributions after fees and commissions were taken into account and a compounded weighted average had been calculated to take account of capital accumulation over time. These figures showed an average annual return of 5.1 percent from 1982 to 1998, much lower than the 11 percent claimed by the supervisory agency of the AFPs (www.cb.cl, April 1, 1999). Mesa-Lago and Arenas de Mesa (1998, 69) come to the same conclusion as CB Capitales, that the interest paid on bank deposits was higher than the net returns on pension funds during the first fourteen years of existence of the AFPs. Finally, the impact of the pension reform on the domestic capital market is highly disputed; some argue that the reform stimulated an important diversification of financial instruments and created investor confidence (Grosse 2002); others counter that the growth of investment opportunities in the 1980s was primarily due to the privatization of state-owned companies and that the pension funds have had little effect on the national savings rate (Uthoff 1995).

In health care, the public system was decentralized and a new private system of insurance and delivery was created. All members of the new pension system have the option of having their compulsory health contribution of 7 percent of gross income go to a private health insurance company (ISAPRE) instead of the National Health Fund (FONASA). Many ISAPREs charge additional premiums, depending on the level of insurance selected, and they either have their own health facilities or contract with private providers. The National Health Fund also offers a free choice plan, with private providers, but subscribers have to pay the fees for co-payments set by the providers, regardless of their income. Treatment in public primary health care centers is free for those covered by FONASA; hospitals charge a co–payment depending on income. Treatment for the poor is free in the public system. In 1990, about 70 percent of the population was covered by public insurance, and 15 percent by ISAPREs, mostly concentrated in the high-income groups; the remainder was not covered by either system but in practice would rely on the public system (Aedo and Larrañaga 1994, 19–27). Per capita outlays in the public system were a mere 22 percent of those in the private system, with the result that a two-class system of health care exists in Chile, where those relying on the public system receive generally inadequate treatment in dilapidated facilities and by severely underpaid personnel (ibid., 19–27). Increases in spending in the 1990s have improved salaries somewhat but have been insufficient to make up for the accumulated neglect of more than a decade.

In addition to the means-tested social assistance pension, the Pinochet government supported a number of other targeted programs, most prominently the emergency employment program and nutrition and health care programs for pregnant women and children at risk of malnutrition. Eligibility for many of these programs was determined by individual classification of households according to their income levels and possessions, a process that was deliberately stigmatizing and divisive, aimed at undercutting solidarity among the poor (Posner 1997). Meanwhile, universalistic benefits such as family allowances were greatly reduced; by 1989 the value of family allowances was barely 30 percent of what it had been in 1970 (Raczynski 1997). Spending on these targeted programs was much too low to make a dent into poverty, but it did help to prevent a deterioration of internationally observed indicators such as infant mortality.

In stark contrast to Chile, Costa Rica eschewed individualization and privatization in social protection policies in the 1980s and 1990s and instead strengthened the universalistic features of its pension and health care systems and attempted to put them on a more solid financial basis. From the beginning, Costa Rica's pension system had been built in a more unified manner than those of other Latin American countries, with all private sector employees belonging to the Costa Rican Social Insurance Fund (CCSS) and only public sector employees having separate funds with special privileges. In 1991 and 1992 the minimum ages for retirement were raised and all new civil servants were required to join the CCSS under standardized conditions. Both employers and employees make mandatory contributions to the CCSS, and the government provides additional funds.

The health care system in Costa Rica is overwhelmingly public and coverage is near universal. In 1973 all hospitals were transferred to the CCSS, and by 1980, 95 percent of physicians had salaried positions in the social security system. Many of them had some sort of private practice on the side, but only 14 percent of consultations were private (Casas and Vargas 1980, 268). Since the 1980s, efforts have been made to integrate the CCSS and the Ministry of Health into a unified national health system, with the former being mainly responsible for curative care and the latter for preventive care through programs specifically aimed at rural and urban poor communities. Total population coverage for health care through the contributory insurance program and the noncontributory program for the indigent reached 85 percent of the population by 1989, in part because the contribution rates for the voluntary sickness insurance of the self-employed were kept very low (Mesa-Lago 1994, 96–97). Clearly, subsidizing the health care system imposed considerable expenditures on the state budget, and during the economic crisis of the early 1980s the state built up a large debt to the system.

In part, the very success of universalizing access to health care created severe problems for the system. As demand increased and public expenditures declined and then recovered slowly, waiting lists for special services grew, consultations grew shorter, and pharmacological supplies dwindled. One of the results was a growth of unauthorized private consultations, with doctors using the public facilities to treat patients who could afford to bypass the lines for a fee (Trejos et al. 1994). Various attempts were made to improve management and supervision and thus service delivery, such as contracting with doctors on the basis of a flat fee per registered patient, or with enterprises to hire physicians, or with cooperatives or self-managed organizations to provide integrated health care programs, or with private pharmacies to deliver drugs, generally with positive results in terms of client satisfaction and costs (Mesa-Lago 1994, 99–100). Still, the overarching goal remained the provision of universally accessible, good quality health care, and contributions from employers, employees, and the government were increased for that purpose.

Costa Rica also has targeted programs such as pensions for the indigent, a school lunch program, nutritional care for children at risk, and housing subsidies, but, except for the housing subsidy, they predate the 1980s and have always been seen as complementary to the universalistic programs, rather than as substitutes. They are on a permanent financial basis in the form of a payroll tax and a share of the general sales tax, but of course this basis is vulnerable to economic cycles. The school lunch program originally was a universalistic one but later became geographically focused on poor communities. Eligibility for the pensions for indigents is determined by an evaluation by social workers, with considerable latitude for judgment and corresponding problems in the efficiency of targeting (Trejos et al. 1994).

Several other countries introduced pension reforms in the 1990s; the Mexican, Bolivian, and Salvadoran reforms are similar to the Chilean one, whereas Peru and Colombia established systems where the private and the public scheme are competitive, and Argentina and Uruguay introduced mixed systems.[9] In Mexico, the old public pension system for private sector employees, some public sector employees, and the self-employed was closed down, and all the insured were transferred to individual, private, capitalized accounts, but employer contributions were not eliminated. In Peru and Colombia, old and new employees have a choice between the reformed public system and a system with fully capitalized individual accounts. Once Peruvians have joined the new private system, they cannot switch back to the old public one, in contrast to Colombia where this remains possible. In Argentina, all employer contributions continue to go to the public system and employees can choose whether they want to make their contributions to the public or a new private system. The public as well as the private system provide a flat-rate basic benefit plus additional benefits related to length of time and amount of contributions, and in the private system benefits are related to investment performance of the funds minus fees and commissions. The basic pension benefit is set in relationship to average compulsory pension contributions, which results in some form of indexation. In Uruguay, all employer contributions and all employee contributions on wages up to eight hundred dollars per month continue to go to the public system; those under forty at the time of the reform and all new entrants who earn more than eight hundred dollars per month have to make contributions to a new private system; those over forty in that income category could choose the public or the private system. According to estimates at the time, less than 10 percent of the population would be forced to participate in the new system (Madrid 1997). All pensioners will receive a basic pension from the public system and in addition a public or private supplement related to contributions. Due to a constitutional amendment accepted by a referendum in 1989, the real value of public pensions is protected by indexation to the average wage (Filgueira and Filgueira 1997). The Brazilian public pension system was improved by guaranteed minimum benefit levels and an elevation of benefit levels of rural workers to those of urban workers, but the reform attempts to curb expensive privileges in special systems have repeatedly failed, with disastrous consequences for other parts of the unified social protection budget, such as health care (Weyland 1996; Draibe 1997).

In general, health care reforms have been slower and less comprehensive than pension reforms. In most countries, attempts were made to emphasize preventive over curative medicine, to bring rapidly rising costs under control, and to experiment with a variety of public/private combinations in service delivery. In Argentina, health insurance was and has remained largely in the hands of the *obras sociales*, that is, compulsory social insurance funds administered by unions. The uninsured poor have a right to free health care. The rules governing *obras sociales* were changed to foster competition for members among them and to encourage mergers. However, public hospitals have been transferred to the provinces, or closed, or turned into self-administered and self-financing hospitals, with clearly negative consequences for access of the poor (Lo Vuolo 1997). In Uruguay, mandatory health insurance for workers through mutual aid societies, heavily subsidized by the state, complements the public system, providing effective access to health care for virtually the entire population. The deterioration of services resulting from the rapid growth of enrollment in the mutual aid societies and from declining public health expenditures in the early 1980s caused the emergence of private emergency mobile units (Filgueira and Filgueira 1997). To counter the deterioration, public health expenditures have increased markedly since 1985. Brazil legislated a very ambitious health care reform that was aimed at providing universal access and integrating preventive and curative care, but an acute lack of funds, noncooperation on the part of many state and municipal authorities, and strong opposition from private health care providers and drug companies prevented the system from functioning as intended (Weyland 1996, 157–82).

The trend in other areas of social policy led away from universalistic and toward targeted policies. The most widely used forms of these policies were funds to provide no- or low-cost loans to poor communities or individuals for infrastructure or small businesses, and special services, mostly concerning nutrition and health, targeted at poor communities or households (see, for example, Graham 1994). Despite the rhetoric about the ability of these targeted policies to reach the poorest of the poor, it is obvious that the demand-driven social investment funds were most unlikely to do so, as they presupposed a capacity to formulate viable proposals. However, these funds were extremely popular with governments for understandable reasons. First of all, they received strong financial backing from the IFIs; second, they could help to placate the most mobilized and vocal among the poor; third, they entailed much discretion and thus could be used for partisan political purposes and clientelistic practices. The most notorious of these targeted programs, if only because it was by far the largest and best financed, was the National Solidarity Program (PRONASOL), run out of the office of the Mexican president Salinas (1988–1994) (see, for example, Cornelius, Craig, and Fox 1994).

Economic growth and increased social spending in the early 1990s caused a decrease in poverty rates in several countries, but CEPAL (1995, 19) concluded that "for the region as a whole, then, the very moderate progress made in alleviating poverty was insufficient to restore the situation achieved at the end of the 1970s." In addition, because of population growth the absolute numbers of poor people continued to grow. Then, the deep recessions in Mexico and Argentina in 1995 and in Brazil in 1999, the slowdown of growth in other countries after the mid-1990s, and finally the Argentine economic crisis beginning in 2000 caused stagnation or increases in un- and underemployment and thus were setbacks in the fight against poverty.[10] CEPAL (2002) figures show an average for nineteen Latin American countries of 48 percent of the population below the poverty line in 1990 declining to 44 percent in 1999. Moreover, even during periods of growth, extremely little progress was made in reducing the stark income inequalities that characterized the region historically and were aggravated in the 1980s when only the income of the top 10 percent held steady or increased (CEPAL 1995, 27). In virtually all countries inequality held steady or even increased, the only exceptions being the urban areas of Uruguay, Mexico, Bolivia, and Honduras. Uruguay consolidated its position as the Latin American country with the most equal income distribution, in part due to the public sector transfers in the pension system (CEPAL 1998).

The Impact of Globalization on Social Protection Policies

The driving forces behind the cutbacks in social expenditures and the social policy reforms were clearly the debt crisis and the economic policies adopted to deal with the crisis. The debt crisis itself can be seen in part as a consequence of globalization, namely the growth of international capital markets in the 1970s, which made cheap money available to Latin American governments and firms, then transmitted an increase in interest rates in the early 1980s, and finally drove governments to insolvency when all new flows stopped in 1983. Of course, Latin American governments were not simply passive actors, but they eagerly participated in borrowing heavily to deal with the balance of payments problems stemming from the exhaustion of the ISI model. Many of them also pursued imprudent macroeconomic policies, letting the exchange rate appreciate, running budget deficits, and so on. Nevertheless, the growth of international capital markets and the search for customers on the part of large international banks were crucial enabling conditions for the growing indebtedness of Latin American countries. The spread of higher interest rates through these markets, followed by the banks' decision to halt new loans, were crucial precipitating factors for the crisis.

The economic policies adopted to deal with the debt crisis were, at least initially, largely externally imposed, in part with the support of domestic technocrats, and then they created internal beneficiaries that became increasingly strong support groups. Again, this external imposition is obviously a consequence of globalization, namely the growing influence of IFIs. The IFIs assumed a pivotal role not only because of the resources under their control but also because they could give or withhold the stamp of approval for governments' economic policies, which was crucial for banks' and creditor governments' willingness to restructure the debt. The IFIs, bolstered by the balance of power in the international economy, acted on the premise that the costs of adjustment would be borne by the Latin American countries, not by banks from OECD countries. The support from domestic technocrats can also be seen from a globalization perspective, as the result of educational circuits that have increasingly brought Latin American economists to American universities where they absorb a neoliberal view of the world, and as the result of career circuits that rotate these economists between IFI employment and national governments.[11]

The economic reforms, that is, austerity and structural adjustment policies, had, then, both direct and indirect effects on social protection policies. The most direct effects came from the austerity packages in the form of massive expenditure cuts that affected the value of transfer benefits as well as the quality of social services. As part of these expenditure cuts, subsidies for basic foodstuffs and energy were eliminated, which affected the poor very negatively. In addition, large devaluations of the currency caused imports to become much more expensive, which particularly adversely affected the medical system. The structural adjustment policies had for the most part indirect effects that were mediated through the decline in formal sector employment. Rationalization in the public sector and privatization of state-owned enterprises caused the loss of thousands of jobs. Trade liberalization, particularly where it was done very rapidly and indiscriminately, drove many domestic manufacturing enterprises to bankruptcy and destroyed jobs. The employees who lost their jobs in these sectors also lost social security coverage, and the social security schemes in turn lost large numbers of contributors. The combination of loss of contributors, high inflation, and reductions in government contributions greatly aggravated the budget problems in the existing social security systems. Moreover, employer contributions to social security had reached comparatively very high levels which, in the context of heavily protected economies, had simply been passed on to the consumer. In the new context of trade liberalization and competition from imports this was no longer possible, and those employers who were able to adjust to the new environment began to pressure governments for a reduction of payroll taxes. In short, the structural adjustment reforms promoted globalization in the form of increased integration into world markets for goods, and this transition had a clearly depressing effect on the effectiveness of the traditional employment-based social security schemes.

The drive to achieve greater integration into world markets by attracting large transnational corporations or becoming part of buyer-driven global commodity chains (Gereffi 1995) was a further motivation for governments to keep wages and employer contributions to social security schemes low.[12] Strict limits on wage increases, of course, were integral parts of IMF-imposed austerity programs. Real industrial wages fell significantly in 1980–1986 in Mexico and Peru and somewhat less in Costa Rica and Chile; in Argentina and Uruguay they fell and then recovered to slightly above the 1980 level, and only in Brazil did they increase markedly (Roxborough 1989, 92). In the period 1989–1996, then, average remunerations declined in Brazil, improved slightly in Argentina and Mexico, and increased markedly in Chile (Edwards and Lustig 1997, 3). On the whole, then, wage earners had barely made any net gains in a decade and a half. Wages in export processing zones, the parts of production most directly integrated into global commodity chains, were notoriously low. Enterprises in these zones for the most part avoided unionization and had not only low wages but also bad working conditions.

By the late 1980s, the IFIs, particularly the World Bank and the Inter-American Development Bank (IDB) no longer insisted on structural adjustment of the economy only but became increasingly concerned with social policy reform itself. The favorite terminology became "adjustment with a human face." There were three obvious reasons for IFI involvement in social policy reform. First, social safety nets were considered essential to protect the process of economic adjustment from disruptions through social protest. Second, given the size of social security schemes in the more advanced countries, they had an obvious potential to endanger fiscal discipline and budgetary stability. Third, the experience of the early 1990s, where economic recovery and renewed growth did little to alleviate the problems of poverty and inequality in most Latin American countries, jeopardized the claims of neoliberals. It was no longer credible that these problems would take care of themselves if only governments would create the right economic environment for private investors to do their jobs and create wealth and economic growth.

A number of additional factors contributed to a reorientation in the debate about social policy, from seeing it as a trade-off or diversion from growth-oriented policies to recognizing its potential contribution to economic growth.[13] First, the World Bank's interpretation of the East Asian success cases from an essentially neoliberal perspective had come in for heavy criticism, including from Japan. One area where this view could easily be amended without accepting the overall importance of state intervention in the East Asian model was by putting heavy emphasis on investment in human capital. Thus, the World Bank and along with it the IDB began to promote investment in education as an important component of a long-term growth strategy. Improving education in the Latin American context, then, immediately came to include the issues of health care and nutrition since it is well established that malnourished and sick children are unable to learn properly. Of course, the IFIs remained extremely concerned about resource constraints and about keeping the role of the state as restricted as possible, and their views concerning the amount of resources to be devoted to social policies and the models of social insurance and service delivery continued to differ radically from those of left-wing parties.

The following statements are indicative of the IFIs' general stance regarding social policy. Birdsall and Jaspersen (1997, 126) state that "the challenge in Latin America, then, is to find ways to reduce inequality, not by transfers, but by eliminating consumption subsidies for the rich and increasing the productivity of the poor. Investment in education is a key to sustained growth, not only because it contributes directly through productivity effects, but because it also reduces income inequality."[14] The essence of the model of social policy advocated by the IFIs, aside from investment in education, consisted in a combination of privatization or the introduction of private sector activities in competition with public sector activities in pensions, health care, and other areas; of decentralization of responsibility for service delivery; and of targeting of benefits to the poorest groups. In practice, the IFIs consistently advocated and financed the use of social emergency funds for targeted programs, and they insisted on state retrenchment in social security schemes. The IFIs, then, clearly set the agenda for social policy reform, but like in the case of economic policy reform, they were not capable of enforcing full compliance.

It is worth noting here what the IFIs did not emphasize. They did not search for ways to finance universalistic or near universalistic public schemes. The argument that universalistic schemes such as basic citizenship pensions waste resources on middle- and upper-income groups loses considerable validity if there is an effective tax system through which such unneeded benefits can be reclaimed. Tax reform was certainly put on the agenda of structural reforms, but it was not linked to the fiscal health of social security schemes. The fiscal health of social security schemes was to be improved through cuts in benefits, such as reduction of the value of cash transfers, of salaries of health care providers and investment in health care facilities, and an increase in copayments, not a greater infusion of general tax revenue. Moreover, the tax reforms slashed maximum tax rates for individuals and corporations and instead put great emphasis on value-added taxes, with at least potentially rather regressive consequences.

As discussed above, the one country that implemented all these reforms to a greater extent and earlier than anybody else is Chile, and therefore Chile has become the reference case paraded as a model not only in IFI publications but also in international publications like the *Economist.* Yet, despite the devastating impact of the debt crisis on all countries in the region, despite the formidable ideological backing of the IFI's models of social policy reform in international forums and in the leading media outlets, and despite the use of conditionality in structural adjustment loans to get countries to accept that model, the significant differences outlined above in approaches to structural adjustment in the 1980s and to social policy reforms in the 1990s demonstrate that domestic political power constellations had an important mediating effect on those pressures emanating from globalization. To a large extent, neoliberal structural adjustment of economic policy and reforms of social protection policies ran in tandem. Where economic liberalization was embraced rapidly and fully, social protection policies also underwent privatization and state retrenchment and a reorientation toward targeted benefits. In contrast, where economic liberalization was introduced gradually and selectively and the state retained an important regulatory role in the economy, reforms of social protection policies were aimed more at improving the financial health and the reach of public schemes and to supplement rather than replace those with targeted programs. However, the reforms of social protection policies at times generated even stronger organized opposition than economic reforms per se, so that governments in many countries made concessions that deviated from the neoliberal model of social policy.

The Mediating Impact of Domestic Institutions and Actors

The main factors accounting for the differences between countries in economic reforms and in reforms of social protection policies were the balance of power between supporters and opponents of neoliberal reforms, and the degree of power concentration through political institutions.[15] The power distribution between supporters and opponents in turn was heavily influenced by the severity of the crisis. Supporters of both types of reforms, aside from the technocrats in the inner circle of the executive, were mostly the internationalized sector of the bourgeoisie and highly qualified professionals in the private sector. Some members of the internationalized sector of the bourgeoisie, at first mainly based in finance and export production, managed to take advantage of privatizations and to acquire control over large new conglomerates, which made them crucial economic and political actors. Opponents of the economic reforms were the domestically oriented bourgeoisie, and opponents of economic as well as social policy reforms were blue- and white-collar unions, the petty bourgeoisie, and social movements. In the case of social security reform, beneficiaries of existing privileged schemes such as professionals, public employees, and the military, often mobilized in opposition as well. Typically, opposition parties resisted reform attempts for either ideological or partisan political reasons. Clearly, then, the political orientation of the government, the strength of unions and social movements, and the power of opposition parties—at the time of the attempts to reform social protection policies—were important for the outcome of these attempts.

Argentina and Uruguay were traditionally well-organized societies, and in Brazil a large number of social movements emerged during the transition. In Argentina and Uruguay, unions and pensioners, along with opposition parties, mobilized against proposals for radical privatizing reforms and cuts in benefits. The result in Argentina was that the president, Carlos Menem, had to make participation in the reformed scheme voluntary and co-opt major unions by allowing them to administer private pension funds and by promising continued support for their *obras sociales* (Kay 1998). The result in Uruguay was that the new scheme provided only supplements to upper-income earners, and benefits in the public system were protected through an indexing mechanism established by a referendum (Hernández 2002). In Brazil, mobilization by popular forces and competition among parties resulted in legislation of universalistic social policy schemes with improved benefits, which, however, could not be financed without a curtailment of excessive benefits in privileged public service systems. Such curtailments, in turn, were obstructed by opposition from civil servants and their political allies.[16] Costa Rica has developed a comparatively strong civil society also, particularly considering its relatively lower level of economic development, with a significant cooperative movement in the important coffee export sector, and a strong party with social democratic aspirations. This party presided over the worst of the economic crisis and introduced decidedly heterodox economic policies accompanied by a social compensation plan; neoliberal reforms of social protection policies did not even get on the political agenda.

Generally, severe economic crises weakened the unions, made the mass public more willing to accept radical reforms (Weyland 1998, 2002), and increased the leverage of the IFIs, thus tilting the balance toward the supporters of radical neoliberal reforms. These factors clearly contributed to the adoption of radical economic reform policies in Argentina and Peru. Costa Rica escaped this fate in part because, despite the severity of the debt burden, the IFIs were more tolerant of its heterodox approach than they were toward other small countries. The Costa Rican government was granted this room to maneuver in large part because of the strategic location of Costa Rica in the Reagan administration's war on Nicaragua, making it the recipient of very large amounts of U.S. aid. However, the explanatory power of the depth of the crisis and the IFIs' leverage is limited. As just noted, initial plans for radical neoliberal social policy reform in Argentina had to be modified in response to opposition from pensioners and unions. Moreover, Brazil suffered an acute crisis with runaway inflation in 1990 as well, yet resisted radical economic reform and continued to pursue a more statist and universalistic orientation in social policy reform. Thus, we need to understand how the structure of political institutions mediated the effects of the power balance between supporters and opponents of neoliberal reforms.

Power concentration in the executive is an essential factor for overcoming resistance against economic reforms (Haggard and Kaufman 1995). Though it is by no means true that only authoritarian regimes can implement serious economic reforms, nor that they are necessarily better at managing reforms (see ibid.), there is no doubt that the extreme power concentration in the hands of Pinochet goes a long way in accounting for the speed and depth of economic and social policy reforms. The literature on welfare states in advanced industrial democracies has shown that power dispersion through constitutional features like presidentialism, federalism, strong bicameralism, and referenda retards expansion of comprehensive and generous social protection policies, but that it also retards retrenchment of welfare state programs (Huber, Ragin, and Stephens 1993; Huber and Stephens 2001a). Retrenchment of transfers and services is unpopular and politically costly everywhere, all the more so when the affected constituency is larger, with the result that democratically accountable governments are reluctant to undertake such retrenchment (Pierson 1996) and that opponents of retrenchment mobilize to use veto points to block it. The only two cases among advanced industrial societies where radical retrenchment was imposed are Britain and New Zealand, both countries without any power-dispersing constitutional features and with an electoral system that makes it possible to win a majority of seats in the legislature without a majority of the popular vote. In Latin America, the most radical economic and social policy reforms outside of Chile were imposed by overpowering executives (with at times questionable democratic methods), Carlos Menem in Argentina, Alberto Fujimori in Peru, and Carlos Salinas in Mexico. Where politics were more open and competitive or constitutional power more dispersed, such as in Uruguay, Costa Rica, and Brazil, economic reforms were more gradual and moderate, and social policy reforms were aimed at strengthening universalistic basic transfers and services.[17]

In addition to constitutional provisions, the structure of the party system is an important determinant of concentration or dispersion of political power. Where parties are factionalized or there are several parties competing for power, as in Uruguay and Brazil, it becomes difficult to form solid reform coalitions.[18] In contrast, where parties are disciplined and one party or a small coalition manages to win a majority in the legislature, it is easier for the executive to obtain support for sweeping reforms. In the case of Argentina, the Peronists controlled the senate and had almost a majority in the Chamber of Deputies when the pension reform was introduced, making it possible for Menem to push the reform through, albeit after a number of concessions to the unions, the traditional power base of the Peronists (Kay 1998; Madrid 2003). In Mexico, the historically hegemonic (though eroding) position of the Partido Revolucionario Institucional (PRI) and its control over a large sector of the labor movement made it possible for Salinas and Zedillo to neutralize effective opposition against their economic and social policy reforms.

Policy legacies are an additional factor that influenced social policy reforms. The existence of a comparatively unified social security system, such as in Costa Rica, facilitated further unification and consolidation, whereas the existence of a variety of privileged systems, such as in Brazil or Peru, made unification and consolidation more difficult. The impact of policy legacies becomes even more pronounced in cross-regional comparisons, where these legacies differ widely. As Cook's chapter demonstrates, the legacy of universalistic systems of social protection in the former Soviet Union has profoundly shaped people's expectations, and despite a desperate shortage of funds, these systems have not been abolished.

Comparison to Western Europe

The impact of globalization on social protection policies in Latin America was undoubtedly much stronger than it was in western Europe. Two sets of reasons account for this difference. I shall present these reasons very briefly and then provide an elaboration; in this more extensive discussion, I shall also use comparisons to the Latin American past to underline the impact of globalization. First, the various aspects of globalization changed the economies of Latin American countries to a greater extent than the economies of western European countries. The growth of international capital markets facilitated overborrowing in the 1970s, ending in the debt crisis of the 1980s and contributing to the volatility of capital flows to

Latin America in the 1990s. Trade liberalization had a dramatic effect on the domestic manufacturing sectors that had been very heavily protected before and were rather suddenly exposed to competition from imports. Many enterprises were simply unable to adapt and went bankrupt. The IFIs, with the support of the large international banks and the U.S. Treasury, came to play a crucial role in imposing austerity and structural adjustment policies, which in turn maintained the vulnerability of Latin American economies to external developments.

Second, the state itself, democratic institutions, and domestic forces supporting the goal of universalistic and solidaristic social protection policies were much weaker than in western Europe. Parties as institutions were much weaker in most countries, and parties of the democratic left were in a particularly weak position. Unions had been greatly weakened by repression under the military regimes, and the economic crisis continued to weaken them after the transitions to formal democratic regimes. In some cases, such as Mexico and Argentina, unions were for historical reasons closely linked to the parties undertaking the neoliberal reforms and thus could be co-opted. Weak legislatures in what O'Donnell (1994) has so aptly called "delegative democracies" were incapable of preventing overbearing executives from imposing radical reform policies. Finally, the state itself, particularly its extractive capacity, was greatly weakened by the economic crisis and the state retrenchment prescribed by the IFIs, which left it in a precarious position to reform the social protection policies in a universalistic and generous direction, supported by the necessary tax revenue.

The recycling of petrodollars in the 1970s led to a rapid accumulation of foreign debt on the part of Latin American countries. Most of this debt was contracted from foreign banks at variable interest rates. In the early 1980s the restrictive monetary policy in the United States led to an increase in international interest rates; the London Interbank Offered Rate, the base interest rate for most Latin American loans, rose from an average of 8 percent in 1970–1979 to 14.4 percent in 1980 and 16.5 percent in 1981 (Dornbusch 1989, 9). This obviously meant a greatly increased debt service burden, and this at a time when commodity prices on world markets fell and economic growth in the industrial countries declined, which meant a decline in export earnings for Latin America. Accordingly, debt service payments of Latin American debtor countries rose from an average of 25 percent of exports of goods and services in 1980 to 40 percent in 1982 (ibid.). When the banks reacted with a stop of all new loans and only rescheduled old ones under the umbrella of IMF austerity programs, Latin America as a whole became a net capital exporter.

Capital flight in the period 1976–1982 had been massive from some Latin American countries and clearly contributed to the build-up of foreign debt, as foreign loans provided a large part of the dollars that were taken out of these countries. Dornbusch (1989, 8) cites estimates of capital flight in 1976–1982 of $25.3 billion from Mexico, $22.4 billion from Argentina, $20.7 billion from Venezuela, and $5.8 billion from Brazil, and he points out that the accumulated stock of Argentina's foreign debt in 1982 was $44 billion. Now, both capital flight and debt problems have a long history in Latin America, and one might be tempted to argue that globalization has not changed much. However, two factors distinguish the 1980s from the 1930s, the last very serious and generalized debt crisis (Drake 1994, xvii). First, the magnitude of the debt in the 1980s was much larger in both absolute and relative terms than in the 1930s. Second, in the 1930s the debt was owed to a large number of small investors who had bought Latin American bonds and had no leverage over Latin American governments to prevent them from rather universally defaulting. In contrast, in the 1980s the debt was owed to a moderate number of large bank conglomerates whose potential insolvency in the case of a Latin American default was such a threat to the financial stability of advanced industrial countries that the banks were able to enlist the support of those governments and the IFIs in order to keep the debtor nations from defaulting. Of course, the very existence of the IFIs has to be added as a major difference between the 1930s and the 1980s. They became the premier instrument through which Latin American countries were forced to gear their economic policies toward continued debt service.

The increased debt service burden in the early 1980s also aggravated government deficits, which then became a primary target of the IMF-imposed austerity policies. The deep recessions induced by the austerity policies in turn further depressed revenues and stimulated continued expenditure cuts. In 1983 the government deficit in Argentina reached 14 percent of GDP, in Brazil 5 percent, in Chile 4 percent (despite years of austerity in the 1970s already), in Costa Rica 4 percent (it had been 5 percent in 1981), in Mexico 8 percent (down from 12 percent in 1982), in Peru 7 percent, and in Uruguay 4 percent. Total government expenditures as a percentage of GDP declined between 1983 and 1989 from 20 to 10 percent in Argentina, 35 to 26 percent in Chile, 26 to 23 percent in Mexico, and 19 to 13 percent in Peru; the decline in Uruguay and Costa Rica was smaller, from 20 to 18 percent and from 20 to 19 percent, respectively (IDB 1991, 284–85). Taking the highest figure in the years 1981–1983 and comparing it to 1989, current revenues as a percentage of GDP fell in Argentina from 11.5 to 6 percent, in Chile from 37 to 31 percent, and in Peru from 14 to 6 percent. The declines in Costa Rica and Uruguay were more moderate again, from 17 to 15 percent in both cases; in Mexico it held steady at 18 percent (ibid.).[19]

In the 1990s, as discussed above, capital flows to Latin America resumed, but initially mostly in the form of short-term, highly liquid capital. This, of course, left Latin American countries highly vulnerable to loss of confidence by investors, financial panic behavior, and contagion from economic crises in other areas. The first drastic example of this phenomenon was the Mexican crisis of late 1994, early 1995, where speculation about an impending devaluation caused a massive exodus of capital, which in turn greatly aggravated the pressure on the currency and resulted in a massive devaluation, very high interest rates, stringent austerity policies, and a severe recession—and all of this despite a very large financial rescue package from the United States. Through what became known as the "tequila effect," other Latin American countries also lost large amounts of short-term capital and were forced to adopt austerity policies in the wake of the Mexican crisis. The Brazilian crisis of late 1998, early 1999 is another example of a contagion effect, this time across continents. At least according to one convincing account by a highly regarded economist,[20] the catalyst of the crisis in Brazil was the financial crisis in Russia, which motivated large international banks and fund managers to reduce their exposure in emerging markets and thus to withdraw money from Brazil.

Clearly, there are no parallels to these phenomena of debt build-up, capital flight, and subsequent austerity policies in western Europe. Even if government deficits of 4, 5, or even 8 percent of GDP did occur, they could be handled more easily in a context where total revenues on average surpassed 40 percent of GDP. Nowhere were total public expenditures cut in half, as in Argentina, nor reduced by almost a third, as in Chile and Peru. Moreover, European governments were in a position to design their own austerity policies, rather than being subject to a "one method fits all" therapy from IFIs.

Similarly, there are no parallels to the Latin American experience with trade liberalization in western Europe. European integration brought a gradual lowering of internal tariffs and then of nontariff barriers. Tariff reductions like those in Latin America, where average tariff levels were slashed by the reform from 45 percent in the mid to late 1980s to 13 percent in 1995, and average maximum tariffs from 84 to 41 percent (Baumann 2002) were simply unheard of. In this same short period, the proportion of imports affected by nontariff barriers was reduced from 34 to 11 percent (ibid.). Many European countries, particularly the smaller ones, have had highly open economies since World War II, and the degree of openness has not changed dramatically anywhere. This is not true, of course, for two other advanced industrial democracies, Australia and New Zealand, and it is telling that these two countries also undertook a major restructuring of their social protection policies in the wake of opening their economies.

The western European experience demonstrates that high trade openness is compatible with a generous welfare state, based in part on employer contributions to social security schemes. The social wage is like money wages; whether they can be afforded or not depends on how competitive an economy is in high productivity world markets. Thus, industrial upgrading to these types of production is essential not only for wage levels in Latin America, but also for social protection policies. The path of labor-intensive, cheap manufacturing to successful competition in world markets of goods and services is not an appropriate one for Latin America to begin with. Latin America simply cannot compete with countries like China in these markets. The fastest growing new Latin American export activities in the past ten to fifteen years have been raw material–based, be they nontraditional agricultural products, fish, or timber-based products. Only Argentina, Brazil, and Mexico made some inroads into exports of durable goods and technology-intensive products. Mexico was by far the most successful in terms of the contribution of these products to total exports, which rose from 27 percent in 1990 to 58 percent in 1997, followed by Brazil with 24 percent and Argentina with 16 percent in 1997 (Baumann 2002). All manufacturing, including *maquilas* (assembly of imported components for re-export), increased in Mexico from 39 percent of total exports in 1990 to 83 percent in 1998; the average for eight other major Latin American countries is 31 percent in 1990 and 36 percent in 1998 (Stallings and Peres 2000, 158).

Finally, west European countries, of course, are forced to maintain the confidence of international financial markets as well. However, typically this manifests itself in the constraint of having to offer higher interest rates if a particular country's fiscal policy is regarded with suspicion. Massive outflows of capital and speculative runs on the currency, followed by massive devaluations and domestic austerity measures, as happened in Mexico and Brazil, are not part of the west European economic scenario. The west European currency crisis of 1992—when an attempt to peg the currencies failed and country after country had to float its currency—did result in devaluations, but not of the magnitude typical for Latin America.

Turning now to differences in the internal power constellations that mediate the pressures from globalization, the most obvious is the difference in the strength of supporters of generous and universalistic social protection policies. Both the quantitative and the comparative historical literature on advanced welfare states have demonstrated that the crucial forces behind generous welfare states are social democratic or Christian Democratic parties, and the difference between them lies in the emphasis on universalism, redistribution, and public social service expansion, all of which are particular postulates of social democratic parties (Stephens 1979; Korpi 1989; Esping-Andersen 1990; Huber, Ragin, and Stephens 1993; Hicks and Misra 1993; Huber and Stephens 2001a). With some important exceptions, parties as institutions are rather weak in Latin America (Mainwaring and Scully 1995), and parties of the democratic left are among the weakest. Only in Costa Rica and Chile can one speak clearly of effective participation of democratic left parties in national governmental power in the 1980s and 1990s, and in Chile this participation took the form of a junior partnership in the coalition led by the Christian Democrats. One might want to include two other historically prominent parties in the democratic left in this period—the Colorado Party in Uruguay and the Democratic Action Party in Venezuela—but the former has been very highly factionalized and the latter has been on a very steep decline. The Apra Party in Peru under Garcia, in power from 1985 to 1990, identified itself in theory with the democratic left, but in practice it remained deeply populist in its policies as well as its organization. None of the governing parties in Colombia and Argentina can be grouped with the democratic left, nor, of course, can the Institutional Revolutionary Party in Mexico—three other countries in which parties play reasonably institutionalized roles. It is telling that in Uruguay, Venezuela, Argentina, and Mexico formidable electoral challenges from democratic left alliances have emerged. Finally, only in Chile has a Christian Democratic party exercised governmental power while the issue of social policy reform has been on the agenda.

The second pillar of generous welfare states is a strong labor movement. Where labor movements are politically united they provide essential support for social democratic parties; where they are politically split, one part does just that and the others push politically close religious parties toward more pro-labor, pro-welfare state positions. In the social democratic welfare states of northern Europe, union density as of 1980 was on average 71 percent of the labor force; in the northern Continental Christian Democratic welfare states it was on average 47 percent (Huber and Stephens 2001a). Estimates for Latin America vary widely, and averages across several countries are rather meaningless given the poor quality of the data and the wide intercountry variation. McGuire (1996) lists estimates for the 1980s for Argentina ranging from 17 to 36 percent of the economically active population, for Brazil from 12.5 to 37 percent, for Chile from 8 to 13 percent, for Mexico from 9 to 35 percent, Peru 3 to 16 percent, and Uruguay 17 to 21 percent.[21] Even if we accept estimates tending toward the upper limit, they remain far below the degree of organization achieved in western Europe. If we had figures for contract coverage in Latin America, the differences would be even more pronounced. The practice of extending agreements to all workers in a given sector, either by law or by precedent, means that contracts cover on average 84 percent of wage and salary earners in the social democratic welfare states of northern Europe and 78 percent in the northern Continental Christian Democratic welfare states (Huber and Stephens 2001a). This practice is virtually nonexistent in Latin America and therefore contract coverage by and large reflects union density. One notable exception is Argentina where, according to ILO figures, union density in 1995 was 39 percent of wage and salary earners, but contract coverage extended to 73 percent of employees (ILO 1998).

One might assume that the comparatively low union density in the 1980s was conjunctural, caused by physical and legal repression under the military regimes and aggravated by the economic crisis, and that union density would have risen as economic growth resumed in the 1990s under formally democratic regimes. The first part of the assumption is clearly correct (Drake 1996), but the second part is not. Many of the jobs in the 1990s have been created in low-productivity activities, and those are notoriously difficult to organize. Even where there is a considerable expansion of manufacturing, as in Chile, much of the production is done by subcontracting to small enterprises that do not have labor contracts (Díaz 1993, 13). Moreover, governments engaged in structural adjustment and reforms of social protection policies are concerned about potential union resistance and thus have done little or nothing to help organized labor regain strength by liberalizing restrictive labor legislation.

There are additional reasons for labor's political weakness. First, most labor movements in Latin America have several confederations affiliated with different political tendencies, which weaken unions' political influence as they can be played against one another. In addition, unions waste resources in competing with one another for members. Second, where unions have historically been closely identified with a political party, such as in Argentina with the Peronists and in Mexico with the PRI, the parties have by and large controlled the unions. Union leaders were dependent on party approval both for benefits like political appointments and for gaining concessions for their members. Since labor legislation and state intervention in industrial relations have been absolutely crucial for the very existence and functioning of unions, the parties controlled the levers of power and thus were able for the most part to demand compliance from the unions with government policies. Of course there were limits to this subordination of unions, limits set by the danger of defections and the formation of independent unions. Nevertheless, the relationship between these parties and "their" unions was much less equal than the relationship between social democratic parties and "their" unions in western Europe. In western Europe, the union confederations close to social democratic parties have their own experts who formulate not only strategies for wage negotiations but also demands for economic policies, which then become the basis for negotiations with the parties to arrive at a program that both the party and the unions can support.

O'Donnell (1994, 1999) has drawn our attention to important dimensions of institutional weakness in Latin America with his concepts of delegative democracy and lack of horizontal accountability. Delegative democracy captures the behavior of overbearing executives who regard themselves as the repository of the national will and regard the legislature as an obstacle to the effective and efficient pursuit of national goals. Horizontal accountability refers to accountability of the executive to other branches of government and in general to supervision of governmental agencies, accountability and supervision that could ensure compliance with the rule of law. The relevance of these weaknesses for reforms of social protection policies is that popular resistance to privatization, individualization, and deterioration of public services has to be channeled through legislatures to result in effective counterproposals, and legislatures have to be able to influence policy formation and implementation. In delegative democracies, the clearest examples of which among the cases discussed here are Peru under Fujimori and Argentina under Menem,[22] the channels for effective alternative proposals through the legislature are by and large blocked. In Peru there was little open debate in the society or the legislature of any alternatives, and in Argentina the executive attempted to ram the legislation through the legislature without any changes at all. However, since the Peronists did not have a majority in the Chamber of Deputies, Menem had to make some concessions and rely on Peronist leaders to use questionable tactics to push the bill through with the narrowest of margins (Kay 1998; Madrid 2003).[23]

Finally, the effective pursuit of comprehensive, universalistic, and redistributive social policy designs presupposes a high degree of regulatory and extractive capacity of the state, a capacity that is present in extremely few Latin American countries. Even effective neoliberal reforms, such as privatization of pension systems, require substantial regulatory capacity to prevent excessive risk-taking and profit-making on the part of private managers that could leave large numbers of even middle- and high-income earners without protection for old age. The combined ideological and fiscal attacks on the state in the 1980s, though, have left many state agencies debilitated and drained of highly qualified and committed personnel. There is little disagreement that in the early 1980s most state agencies in Latin America employed excessive amounts of people whose productivity was low and whose dismissals were beneficial for budgets without hurting the capacity of these agencies. However, one can certainly argue that the steep decline in salaries of civil servants, the lack of investment in technology for state agencies, the restriction of the functions of such agencies, and the ideological attacks on state agencies as necessarily promoting rent-seeking behavior damaged state capacity.

The most obvious—and for social policy arguably the most damaging—aspect of state weakness is the comparatively very low extractive capacity of the Latin American state. In 1989, current revenue as a percent of GDP among Latin American countries ranged from a low of 6.5 percent in Peru and 7 percent in Bolivia to a high of 30 percent in Chile. In that same year, revenue in the larger of the English-speaking Caribbean nations ranged from 26 to 31 percent of GDP (IDB 1996, 370), thus refuting the argument that the level of economic development of the Latin American nations is the decisive obstacle to raising state revenue. Looking at the tax burden alone, in the northern European countries with social democratic welfare states, total taxes in 1980 ranged from 36 to 56 percent of GDP, and in the Continental countries with Christian Democratic welfare states from 33 to 53 percent (Huber and Stephens 2001a). In the period 1991–1995, when most of Latin America experienced growth, the average tax burden was 14 percent of GDP, an average that was pushed up by the inclusion of the English-speaking Caribbean. The average tax burden for the fast-growing East Asian newly industrialized countries in this period was 17 percent. Among the Spanish-speaking countries in Latin America and the Caribbean, only Nicaragua and Brazil narrowly surpassed 17 percent; the Dominican Republic, Uruguay, Honduras, Costa Rica, Venezuela, and Chile were between 14 and 17 percent, and all other countries below 14 percent of GDP (IDB 1996, 128).[24] The stronger extractive capacity of the state in Spain and Portugal was one crucial factor that enabled governments in these countries to expand the welfare state while opening their economies (see Glatzer, chap. 5, this volume).

Virtually every country instituted some type of tax reform in the 1990s, but with very limited success in raising revenue. First, the reform had to make up for the revenue lost from trade liberalization. In 1980 taxes on foreign trade made up 30 percent of total tax revenue; by 1995 this contribution had fallen to 17 percent (IDB 1997, 44). Second, the reforms slashed marginal rates on individuals and corporations (see ibid.) on the grounds that they promoted evasion and that the loss of revenue could be compensated by closing tax concessions. Third, enforcement of tax collection, both of direct and indirect taxes, has remained highly deficient. The main obstacles to success have been of a political nature. The beneficiaries of the neoliberal reforms, the large economic conglomerates and the top 5–10 percent of income earners, oppose increases in their tax contributions commensurate with their relative ability to pay, and they have the resources to make their opposition effective.

This now brings us back to the initial discussion of the motivations behind and the results of social policy reforms. As the showcase of neoliberal reforms, Chile deserves a closer look. Certainly, the emphasis on targeted programs was designed to mask the overall cutbacks in social expenditures. The pension reform and the decentralization of the public health system were motivated in part by the desire to remove the state as a target for collective action, in line with Pinochet's other policies aimed at atomizing and demobilizing Chilean society (Garretón 1986, 98–103). The pension and health care reforms also meant that in practice efforts at redistribution through these schemes were abandoned, as the value of public pensions and facilities and salaries in the public health service were eroded. The democratic governments in Chile so far have not changed this structure but simply increased expenditures to improve public pension benefits and the quality of public health care. In theory, there certainly is room for a more activist and redistributive role of the state even within this new policy framework, to use general tax revenue to improve minimum and social assistance pensions and to invest in public health facilities. In practice, however, this room to maneuver is limited by the realities of the political power distribution. Shortly after the transition, the Chilean government reached an agreement with business on tax increases for a limited period of time in order to increase social expenditures. However, at the end of this period the agreement could not be renewed since business was not willing to make any more concessions. Employers have come to regard the fact that they do not have to pay any contributions for employees' pension and health insurance as an entitlement, and they resist permanent increases in other taxes that could compensate for this loss of revenue from payroll taxes. Similarly, high-income earners have become used to the idea that they are providing for their own health insurance and retirement and none of their contributions to these schemes are used for redistributive purposes as they would be in any universalistic system of social insurance. Again, they are hardly inclined to accept progressive income tax increases to fund public benefits and services that they and their families do not utilize. This is the logic underlying the well-known phenomenon of much more limited political support for targeted than for universalistic social policy schemes (see, for example, Cook and Barrett 1992, 62).

Let me end with a final summary reflection on globalization. Globalization can be held in part and indirectly responsible for the difficulties of financing social protection policies that would be effective in reducing poverty and inequality in Latin America. The growth of international financial markets was the central antecedent of the debt crisis, in which the IFIs, another component of globalization, attempted to impose neoliberal economic adjustment policies and a set of neoliberal reforms of social protection policies. Where they were adopted, the combination of these reforms then created new sets of powerful economic actors and beneficiaries of the reforms: employers who did not have to make contributions for employee benefits any longer and high-income earners who could afford to purchase superior services and insurance on the market, all of whom became major political obstacles to universalistic and redistributive alternatives. As in other parts of the world, however, pressures emanating from globalization were filtered through domestic institutions and power constellations,[25] which is why globalization can only be held responsible in part. There were and are alternatives, as demonstrated by Costa Rica and Uruguay, but their pursuit requires the formation of strong political coalitions and of democratic institutions that are capable of enforcing accountability. To put the same conclusion in more theoretical terms, following Rueschemeyer, Stephens, and Stephens (1992), power constellations in the international system are only one of three clusters of power that shape political outcomes; power constellations within society and the state arena are the other two.

5

Revisiting "Embedded Liberalism"
Globalization and the Welfare State in Spain and Portugal

MIGUEL GLATZER

Globalization is often seen as severely constraining national policy options in a wide variety of policy areas. Indeed, the even stronger view—that globalization will lead inexorably to downward pressure in social and labor market policy—is still widely asserted. By focusing on the case of Spain and Portugal, where openness and welfare state development occur contemporaneously, this chapter takes issue with that "strong view" of the negative effects of globalization on social and labor market policy. The chapter will show that globalization can place downward pressure at particular moments and in particular circumstances; but overall developments in Spain and Portugal come closer to the view that economic openness tends to be associated with measures of social protection. This linkage is mediated by persistent political responses over a long period of time.

The first section of this chapter briefly reviews the two competing theoretical perspectives: that globalization presents a threat to the welfare state, and, alternatively, that integration into world markets has often facilitated or at least been strongly associated with welfare state development. The chapter then moves to a more explicit analysis of the Spanish and Portuguese cases, focusing on the turn toward openness and the development of social and labor market policies as well as collective bargaining, which frequently provides an arena for social policy negotiation in which welfare provisions can be developed in return for competitive wage restraint. The next sections focus on the shift in monetary policy toward a hard currency regime, along with the effects of the Maastricht criteria. At first glance these might appear to be effects of European integration, and the Economic and Monetary Union of Europe (EMU) in particular, rather than the result of globalization. However, one can also see these European developments as particular versions of worldwide phenomena. A concern with reducing inflation and with reducing budget deficits is not restricted to Europe but has become virtually universal. Understanding how social policy expansion can occur in an environment where pressure to reduce budget deficits is high is a critical aspect of welfare state building in the current period.

The Portuguese and Spanish cases arguably represent the most successful cases of welfare state development among the middle-income countries studied in this book. If the recent debate about northwestern European welfare states has revolved around terms such as the growth to limits, stability, adaptability, and in some cases limited retrenchment, the cases of southern Europe, and of Portugal and Spain in particular, present clear evidence of substantial, if still incomplete, welfare state development. In comparison to developments in other middle-income countries, the story in Iberia has been much more positive. At a minimum, the Portuguese and Spanish cases demonstrate that opening up to the international economy after the Golden Age of the welfare state from the 1950s to the 1970s is still compatible with welfare state development. Like the Costa Rican story in Huber's analysis of the Latin American cases, Portugal and Spain show that there is still room for a domestic politics that combines economic openness with a strengthening of social protection. Understanding the factors, economic and political-institutional, which explain how globalization leads to social policy change in the direction of greater universalism rather than toward safety nets and market-dominated systems, is a crucial aspect of this project.

The Spanish and Portuguese transitions from authoritarian rule to democracy commence in 1974 and 1976, respectively. In Portugal, the process was initiated by a left-wing military coup that threw the country into a period of revolutionary turmoil. This coincided with and was further complicated by the abrupt loss of Portugal's African colonies and the return of its colonial expatriates. In contrast to this unusual beginning of a transition to democracy in Portugal, the Spanish transition was characterized by a high degree of gradualism and consensus.

Democratic Portugal was first governed by a weak series of left coalitions, in which the Socialist Party (PS) played a dominant role. From the mid-1980s on, political stability returned under the leadership of the center-right Social Democratic Party (PSD) and later, after 1995, under that of the Socialist Party. In Spain, the transition was led by the center-right Democratic Central Union (UCD). From 1982 until 1996 the Spanish government was dominated by the Spanish Socialist Party (PSOE), which pursued a complex mix of welfare state development and market-oriented economic policies. Its dominance ended with the victory of the center-right Popular Party, which did not, however, radically change course.

Both Portugal and Spain developed close links to the European Community, joining formally in 1985. The move toward the European Union (EU) with a single currency (EMU), which was initiated by the Maastricht Treaty of 1992, led to difficult policy reorientations in order to meet the conditions for joining the new single-currency area.

It is important to note, however, that welfare state development in Portugal and Spain was not instigated by the European Community. Except for some specific provisions of labor market policy, social policy issues were surprisingly absent from the entry negotiations. With the exception of social funds targeted to very particular populations, the European Community did not support Iberian welfare state development financially. Pensions and health care, which constitute the largest elements of welfare expenditure, were domestically financed. Nor did the European Community protect Spain and Portugal against international competition. In fact, membership entailed an opening to precisely such competition.

Globalization and Social and Labor Market Policy: Two Views

In the last few years globalization has often been seen as a serious threat to welfare states, even those of advanced industrial countries. This current pessimistic view of the effects of globalization stands in marked contrast to an earlier literature that emphasized the complementarities, both political and economic, between the welfare state and greater trade openness and economic internationalization (Cameron 1978; Katzenstein 1985). In the newer view, globalization is seen as threatening—through various mechanisms—the sustainability of the generous social provisions that mark the advanced welfare states.

The two views are remarkably asymmetrical. The newer, pessimistic view offers persuasive causal arguments, but it is not supported by strong empirical evidence. The older view has significant empirical support, but the exact mechanisms, the micrologic by which openness leads to welfare state development, remain unclear.

In the negative view, globalization places economic and political pressure on the welfare state. The economic mechanism focuses on the unsustainability of noncompetitive welfare states. In this view, rich countries with noncompetitive welfare states will experience lower rates of investment (as domestic firms decide to invest abroad, and foreign direct investment dries up), and will suffer unsustainable trade deficits as cheaper imports flood the domestic market and noncompetitive exports remain unsold. Along with the restrictive monetary policies that reduce the risk of capital flight and speculative currency attacks, these factors lead to lower rates of economic growth and higher rates of unemployment. In order to attract capital and to ensure that exports remain competitive, countries might engage in "races to the bottom" whereby social provisions and labor market protections, and the taxes used to finance them, are reduced.

The political mechanism argues that globalization weakens the political power of interests traditionally allied with the welfare state, and strengthens interests critical of the welfare state (Wilding 1997). Thus, the increased exit option of domestic investors as well as the need to attract capital from abroad are likely to make the government pay greater heed to business interests calling for lower rates of corporate taxation or social insurance and less intrusive social and labor market regulations. The need to recalibrate social and labor market priorities in order to enhance international competitiveness certainly informs the apparent wave of tripartite bargaining recently sweeping much of Europe (Rhodes 2001).

In contrast to the pessimistic view stands an earlier tradition in political science that links welfare state expansion to openness. In this tradition, for which Ruggie (1982) coined the term "embedded liberalism" (see also Cameron 1978; Katzenstein 1985; and Rodrik 1997), two fundamental claims are advanced. The first claim is empirical: There exists a positive association between openness and expansion of the public economy (and thus the welfare state).

The second claim is theoretical and offers a broad macroexplanation for why openness should lead to greater public expenditure. In the analyses of Ruggie and Katzenstein, the notion of "embedded liberalism" helps to explain the link between external economic openness and domestic social protection. Seen as part of the postwar compromise, embedded liberalism reduces the threat of protectionist forces by cushioning domestic groups from the vagaries brought about by openness. The cushioning effect of the welfare state in turn makes it possible for economic sectors that are under stress to adjust or decline, thus facilitating a process of creative destruction that should, eventually, result in a more efficient allocation of resources. Without the cushioning effect, the argument goes, the churning of the market in which firms, industries, and sectors rise and fall as a result of international economic conditions would be constrained by political limits on openness.

Although this argument makes two strong fundamental claims (the empirical relationship between openness and size of government/welfare state and the macrologic by which the welfare state makes openness politically feasible), the causal mechanism that would underpin this argument remains underdeveloped. Did politicians involved in the postwar construction of the welfare state understand the macro-logic? Were politicians worried that without a welfare state to cushion the negative economic effects of international economic integration openness would be hard to maintain?

In an alternate formulation of the argument, politicians need not be aware of the macro-logic. Rather, they simply react to social demands for greater social protection in the face of greater perceived risk. For Rodrik this is the mechanism at work: "Societies that expose themselves to greater amounts of external risk *demand (and receive)* a larger government role as shelter from the vicissitudes of global markets. In the context of the advanced industrial economies specifically, this translates into more generous social programs" (53; italics added).

Because the empirical relationship between openness and size of government is strong, and because the macro-logic whereby a welfare state is functional for an open economy is persuasive, the lack of a precise causal mechanism between openness and welfare state development is an open problem.

One of the weaknesses in finding a precise causal mechanism linking openness to larger government size or a larger welfare state lies in the fact that the risks created and attributed to openness can also be produced through domestic processes. One might plausibly argue that these risks will be the larger, the greater the degree of openness. But it would be helpful to have measures of risk (or rather its effects) that are independent of openness and terms of trade volatility. The Golden Age of capitalism often provides the empirical basis for much of the work on the link between openness and government size and welfare state. Yet for much of this period, increasing openness was not accompanied by higher levels of unemployment or high levels of income volatility, raising the question of the degree of risk experienced by populations in countries pursuing a strategy of greater openness.

A more fully determined causal link in the openness argument needs to provide space for politics, which is largely absent from the arguments. These require greater attention to the ways in which risk becomes politically potent. Different institutions of interest intermediation will affect the political aggregation and salience of risk. The Chilean case, which has both a high degree of openness and, because of the structure of its exports, experiences a high degree of terms of trade volatility, illustrates in powerful ways the importance of politics. According to its high degree of openness and terms of trade volatility, Chile should have a large government sector or welfare state, yet this is clearly not the case. The explanation must lie in politics—political systems vary in the degree to which they are responsive to concerns about risk. Thus, the outcome in terms of size of government or size of the welfare state will be shaped by existing institutional capacities and the interests and strength of the different social and political actors. Finally, one should not discount the possibility that welfare state development occurs independent of openness. In this view, the welfare state's effects in making openness politically palatable are a fortuitous side effect of other causes of welfare state development. Although the correlation between openness and welfare state development still holds, and although the macro-logic still applies, welfare state development, in this view, did not occur *because* of openness. Correlation does not, after all, imply causation. For the Portuguese and Spanish cases, the logics of industrialism, modernization, party competition, and, interestingly, "Europeanization" constitute possible alternative causes of welfare state development that are independent of openness.

Combining Economic Openness with Welfare State Development

The processes of Spanish and Portuguese democratization were markedly different. The hallmarks of the Spanish route—the frequent use of political and social pacts and consensus—allowed the Spanish transition not only to become a model in the political science literature but also provided a template for democratic transitions in other countries. The Portuguese route, by contrast, stands alone. Democracy by coup d'état led by a left-leaning revolutionary military remains exceedingly rare.

Despite their very different paths, the timing of democratization in the mid to late 1970s in the two countries forced the Spanish and Portuguese economies to confront similar economic problems. Although both countries shifted their economic strategies toward much greater openness and competition, they differed in the degree of autarchy they inherited from their long-lasting authoritarian pasts. Spain, a much larger economy, had remained significantly more closed than Portugal. Portugal's commitment to an economic development policy based on trade with its colonies did not prevent the development of a parallel policy of European integration. Portugal benefited belatedly from the Marshall Plan and became a founding member of the European Free Trade Association (EFTA). In 1960 Portugal was admitted to the International Bank for Reconstruction and Development (IBRD) and the International Monetary Fund (IMF), and in 1962 it joined the General Agreement on Tariffs and Trade (GATT). Nonetheless, in the democratic period both countries committed themselves firmly to a strategy of integration into the wider European and global markets. The longer experience with openness prevented Portugal from undergoing some of the shocks that the move toward openness brought to Spain. In particular, Portugal did not suffer as much from the Spanish problem of large smokestack industries that had thrived under autarchy and import substitution industrialization but which were rendered uncompetitive by openness.

The opening of the economy, both to domestic competition and to integration in world markets, required many reforms. Trade barriers were lowered and capital controls lifted. Monetary policy during the first years of the transition originally focused on periodic devaluations as a means of maintaining competitiveness, particularly so in Portugal. However, in the mid-1980s both countries shifted monetary policy away from devaluation and toward the maintenance of a hard peseta and hard escudo, principally as a means of combating inflation but also as a way to provide a more stable climate for long-term investment. The democratic period in Spain and Portugal thus witnessed not only the dismantling of what Dehesa (1994) calls "assisted capitalism" (a system based on government favoritism, with extensive use of government licensing), but also the transition to greater openness to the world economy in both capital movements and trade.

Maravall (1993) has argued that Spain and Portugal are successful cases of a triple transition—to democracy, to structural economic reform, and to a welfare state. This "social-democratic approach" allowed Spain and Portugal to build a welfare state involving universal health care coverage, major expansion of public education, and virtually universal pension coverage during a period of major economic restructuring despite a sometimes unfavorable international economic climate. It is true that the southern European welfare states remain small by northern European standards. Average pension levels and the quality of social services remain low. Nonetheless, the increase in the share of GDP devoted to social protection has been very large in both these countries during the democratic period.

Tax revenue in Spain rose from 25 percent of GDP in 1976 to 36.7 percent in 1988 (Maravall 1993). Spanish expenditure on pensions, unemployment benefits, health, and education rose from 9.9 percent of GDP in 1975 to 17.8 percent in 1989. In Portugal, tax revenue (direct and indirect taxes plus social security contributions) rose from 21.5 percent of GDP in 1972 to 34 percent in 1994 (Mozzicafreddo 1997). Social security transfers (comprising expenditure on pensions, unemployment benefits, disability benefits, and child benefits) rose from 7.6 percent of GDP in 1977 to 15.1 percent in 1986 to 20.6 percent in 1993. Expenditure on education and health rose from 3.8 percent in 1973 (the last year of the dictatorship) to 9.1 percent in 1991.

If Portugal and Spain from the mid-1970s on firmly committed themselves to economic globalization through liberalizing trade, foreign direct investment, and capital flows, this process was clearly compatible with major expansion of the welfare state. Globalization prevented neither large increases in social expenditure nor rises in taxation to fund this expenditure. These figures provide no support for the most negative of the globalization theses—that globalization constrains the welfare state and its development. Downward spirals in social provision, social dumping, and an inability to tax are simply not present in the Portuguese and Spanish cases. The aggregate data thus seem to support the contention of the earlier tradition in political science that linked welfare state expansion to openness.

Development of the Welfare State: Labor Market Policy and Collective Bargaining

Portugal and Spain are frequently categorized as similar in the comparative politics and comparative industrial relations literature. Among the poorer members of the European Union, they both experienced long periods of authoritarian rule from the 1930s to the mid to late 1970s. The long dictatorships, which were hostile to independent labor and the development of expensive social policies, nonetheless enacted a substantial and often rigid labor market policy, much of it inherited by the democratic regimes. The combination of long authoritarian rule along with the release of pent-up social demands in the wake of democratization led to a distinctive constellation of social and labor market policies.

Labor market policies are marked by high degrees of formal rigidity that protect workers and employees. Restrictions on firing as well as compensatory costs for employment termination routinely place Portugal and Spain at the top of European rankings of labor market rigidity. Franco's regime, through the Ordenanzas Laborales, for example, produced a legacy of greater labor market regulations than Salazar's regime. The labor ordinances were a highly detailed system of work rules and classifications which, although outdated, limited firms' internal flexibility in the deployment of labor. Portugal's protective labor market regulations, already substantial as measured in dismissals' compensation in the authoritarian regime, increased dramatically during the transition to democracy when dismissals, except for disciplinary reasons, were virtually prohibited. The difficult path to reforming these labor market policies in an equitable manner has been a hallmark of labor politics in both Spain and Portugal since the mid-1980s.

Collective bargaining and tripartite agreements among government, labor, and business have played a central role in the restructuring of labor markets. Collective bargaining patterns in Spain and Portugal share several prominent features that are largely determined by the form of union organization. The two countries have neither a highly centralized bargaining structure as found in the Nordic countries nor a fully decentralized system as in the United States. They combine relatively low union density with parallel unions of rival political orientation. In the assessment of factors contributing to labor peace and wage moderation advanced by Calmfors and Driffil (1988), Portugal and Spain fall in the worst position, which makes wage moderation through national pacts or competition in the labor market less likely. The existence of rival union confederations—the socialist/social democratic União Geral de Trabalhadores (UGT) and the Communist Confederação Geral dos Trabalhadores Portugueses (CGTP-IN) in Portugal and the socialist UGT and Communist Comisiones Obreras (CCOO) in Spain—complicates wage negotiations. This is particularly the case in Spain, where the threat that the CCOO would win an increasing share of union elections made UGT deference to the socialist government's economic policies an increasingly untenable strategy.

In Portugal this form of union competition is somewhat reduced for two reasons. First, the UGT and CGTP represent more distinctive groups of workers than their Spanish counterparts. The Portuguese UGT disproportionately represents white-collar workers, with the bank workers' union being among the strongest UGT unions, while CGTP typically represents blue-collar workers. This differentiation, which is less pronounced in the Spanish case, is more conducive to coexistence and cooperation.

The second reason lies in the long-standing obstructionist stance of CGTP-IN in the process of national social bargaining. The CGTP has frequently boycotted national social bargaining, and when it does participate in the talks it rarely signs the final agreement. The differentiation of worker bases, along with the CGTP's obstructionist stance in social bargaining and its fixed anti-EU and anti-EMU positions have reduced its potential to poach workers from the UGT, thus limiting the costs of UGT bargains with employers and the government.

In the mid-1980s Portuguese labor market policy was still characterized by legislation enacted during the revolutionary period of 1975. The law's restrictions on firing were particularly numerous. Individual firing involved a long and onerous process and was justifiable only under very limited circumstances. Collective firing was also a long process and required administrative approval, which was often denied. The relative ease with which employers could use temporary (or fixed-term) contracts, liberalized in 1976, combined with continued rigidity in other types of contracts, explains the high proportion of the workforce employed under fixed-term contracts.

This rigidity was seen by internal critics and outside advisers such as the OECD as leading to suboptimal outcomes. In this view, labor market rigidity increased the unemployment rate, led to wage arrears, and blocked the entry of youth into the labor market. The PSD government program of 1989-1991, like many others before it, called for substantial liberalization of the labor market. Unlike other governments, however, the impetus propelling labor market reforms was greater. Two new factors accounted for the greater emphasis placed on these reforms. The first was European integration. Membership in the European Community had been achieved in 1985 and brought with it the desire to amend Portuguese law and institutions so that they approached the norms and common practices of the more developed European countries. However, while integration through the *acquis communautaire* as well as the need to implement directives brought about instances of reform that were demanded by the EC, most changes in labor market and social policy were propelled by domestic politics.

Overall, "Europe" played a curious role in these politics. On the one hand, a major goal of the reformers in this period was to reshape Portuguese law and institutions in such a way as to emulate what were perceived to be practices and norms common to Europe's member countries. On the other hand, calling a reform "Europeanizing" was a useful means of increasing the reform proposal's credibility. Intellectual arguments were certainly provided in defense of labor market liberalization; however, the government defended the reforms by arguing that they would bring Portugal into conformity with the common practice of the majority the European community's members.

Table 5.1 Labor Market Segmentation, Spain and Portugal,
ca. 1985–1995, % of Working Age Population

	Spain	Portugal
Working age population not in the labor force	40	25
Unemployed	13	4
Employed under temporary contracts	15	19
Employed with Full Contracts	32	52

The Spanish labor market is characterized by a profound segmentation, which has been likened to the traditional Spanish four-cornered hat (Perez-Diaz and Rodriguez 1995). There are four distinctive groups of people with relatively low mobility among them: (1) those who do not participate in the labor force because of traditional gender and household norms or because they have been discouraged from seeking employment; (2) the unemployed, of whom about half are long-term unemployed; (3) people who work under precarious temporary employment contracts with little social protection; and (4) those who enjoy full employment contracts and who benefit from the full array of social and labor market protection.

This segmentation (see table 5.1 for rough quantitative estimates) presents obvious problems for a social democratic policy aiming at equity and fairness in the labor market. Equity-enhancing labor market reform runs into the problem of divergent interests between insiders and outsiders. Enhancing the chances of discouraged work seekers, the unemployed and those working under short-term and precarious contracts—the outsiders—will encounter the opposition of the insiders, who are in full employment, are receiving the associated social benefits, and are protected by unions. The Portuguese labor market faces a less severe segmentation between insiders and outsiders. Labor force participation is much higher than in Spain, and unemployment is significantly lower. The conflict between insiders and outsiders is thus reduced to the division between those with temporary employment contracts and those with full contracts and social protection.

The OECD *Jobs Study* of 1994 and its reception in Portugal and Spain illustrate similar tendencies. The OECD's recommendations had a decidedly neoliberal tilt, although they also contained proposals for a significant government role in particular areas. Both countries were very selective in their implementation of these recommendations, following, for instance, advice to pursue a more active labor market policy, but resisting many other proposals. The study highlights the fact that in both countries policy stances are deeply grounded in domestic politics. Though receptive to international advice, both countries proved to be "policy makers" rather than "policy takers," much like their more advanced European counterparts.

Development of the Welfare State: Changes in Social Policy

Since the mid-1970s, both Portugal and Spain have engaged in a massive expansion of income transfer programs, moving toward virtually universal coverage. Although minimum pension levels remain low by European standards, they nonetheless increased substantially during this period. Supporting this increase in expenditures, both countries raised tax revenue considerably.

Funding the new and improved welfare provisions was nevertheless not without complications. That these were, over a long period of time, persistently tackled, indicates how strong was the political support for welfare state building. Funded by payroll taxation in a pay-as-you-go system, both countries' pension systems have run substantial deficits requiring the infusion of general government revenue. Particularly in the Portuguese case, these deficits are the result of the large noncontributory scheme that provides benefits to people who, because of the incomplete coverage of the system under authoritarian rule, had never contributed to the system. The universalization of pension benefits has meant that the ratio of contributors to pensioners has approached critical levels and produced a difficult pension politics. Pension levels in the noncontributory scheme remain low, but increasing their value requires additional tax revenue. Increasing the payroll tax, however, elicits resistance from employers and often complicates the process of social bargaining and social pacts. As a result, proposals to adopt a greater role for a private, fully funded tier in the pension system gained prominence.

In 1986 a rationalization of the Portuguese financing system for social security and unemployment benefits was undertaken. In early 1985, unemployment benefits had been integrated into the social security system, but the financing system for these two programs remained separate and bureaucratically and administratively onerous. The creation of the comprehensive social tax (*taxa social unica*) resulted in a system financed jointly by employers and employees who paid contributions amounting to 24 and 11 percent of wages, respectively. The comprehensive social tax reduced this contribution by 1 percent (23.5 for employers and 10.5 for workers). Also in 1986 the social security system was reformed to improve the social protection afforded agricultural workers by merging their scheme into the two principal social security schemes (for the employed and for the self-employed/independent workers) that cover workers in the private sector. The growth in Portugal's social security system was very substantial during the long period of preparation for EMU. In 1985, three years before the abandonment of the crawling peg regime, there were 1,941,000 beneficiaries of the social security system. In 1994, well after Maastricht and amid preparations for EMU, the number had increased to 2,350,000, an increase of 21 percent. Total expenditure had risen by 8.3 percent in real terms. The ratio of contributors to pensioners fell during this same period from 2:1 to 1:7.

Further reforms of the social security system in 1993 attempted to rectify the growing problem of the system's financial imbalances, in which contributions failed to accompany the growth in expenditures. The reform focused on the scheme that covered self-employed workers because the imbalance between contributions and expenditures was greatest there. However, multiple changes were made in the pension system. The retirement age for women was gradually increased over a six-year period to sixty-five so that it would be the same for both men and women. In addition, the eligibility criteria for early retirement were tightened and the starting age for early retirement was raised to sixty. The minimum number of years of contribution necessary to receive a pension was raised from ten to fifteen. The basis for the value of the pension was changed from the highest-paid five years of the last ten to the best-paid ten years of the last fifteen. These values were to be inflation-adjusted so as to eliminate the negative effect of inflation in the pension-determining formulas. To facilitate job mobility across economic sectors, and between the private sector and government service in particular, a unified pension system was created in 1992. This allowed the final pension determination to take into account the combined value of contributions made to the principal social security scheme (covering the private sector) and to the government service scheme.

The changes to the social security system were motivated by a large number of factors, many of them common to the changes underlying reform of the social security systems in other European countries. Policy makers were very aware of changes in the demographic, economic, and sociologic environment surrounding the social security system. Increased life expectancy, lower birth rates, changing family structure, higher unemployment, and lower rates of economic growth were universally acknowledged factors to which social security systems had to adapt. These environmental changes informed the debates on how to balance the need for greater equity and more comprehensive coverage in the system with the obligation to move away from ever greater financial imbalance.

The need for financial balance, however, was only one of many sources of pressure influencing social security reform. Certainly, rectifying the financial imbalance of the system gained importance. The need to protect the hard escudo policy from speculative attacks, along with the general anti-inflationary stance in which the hard escudo policy was embedded, later reinforced by the Maastricht and Stability Pact criteria, all highlighted the problem of growing deficits in the social security system. However, other sources of reform included the desire to rationalize the complicated social security system, facilitate intersectoral mobility, provide greater gender equality, expand coverage, and combat poverty by raising minimum pension levels. Because EMU represents the culmination of an anti-inflationary exchange-rate policy adopted as early as 1988, EMU per se has not brought major changes to the social security system. Rather, EMU should be viewed as consolidating and, through the Maastricht and Stability Pact criteria, reinforcing a preexisting trend that emphasized the need to reduce the financial imbalance of the social security system. Second, this could be done by increasing taxes, and indeed the capacity for government growth in both Portugal and Spain has been substantial. Some of the negative purported effects of EMU thus disappear when the government revenue constraint is relaxed. Where taxes can be raised, EMU is compatible with expansion of the welfare state.

The Shift in Monetary Policy and Continued Welfare State Growth

Monetary policy mediates in complex ways between economic openness and welfare state building. "Printing money" is one way of funding increased public expenditures. The subsequent increased inflation creates, however, not only internal economic and social problems but also problems in balancing external accounts and keeping stable exchange rates. Devaluing the country's currency may give otherwise unprofitable enterprises an extended lease on life, which may be appealing in the transition from autarchy to openness, but it also deflects capital streams from more productive uses. Furthermore, the inevitable inflationary pressures associated with continued devaluation make it very difficult to achieve wage moderation in return for increased social protection. Both Portugal and Spain moved from frequent devaluations to hard currency policies. Aside from internal considerations, this was encouraged and later made obligatory by the process of European integration. Throughout both phases, however, the development of social welfare policies continued.

From 1977 to 1990 Portuguese monetary policy was characterized by a crawling peg regime, in which the escudo was devalued at a predetermined and publicly known rate on a monthly basis. By the end of the 1980s Portugal's economic stabilization and the increased importance given to the fight against inflation suggested a new monetary policy. A policy that relied on devaluation was seen as costly for the long-term health of the economy because it failed to effectively combat inflation, reduced the real value of wages, and provided an artificial crutch that ensured the competitiveness of Portuguese firms without forcing them to rationalize. The move from crawling peg, where devaluation was a principal policy tool, to a hard escudo, where devaluation was to be used only rarely, to membership in EMU, where devaluation relative to Portugal's European trading partners became an impossibility, represented a fundamental change in direction of economic policy. It was a long process, implemented gradually.

The gradual abandonment of the crawling peg regime started in 1988. In October 1990 the government decided to accompany the European Monetary System

(EMS)[1] through "shadowing" without actually participating in it. Less than two years later, on April 6, 1992, Portugal formally entered EMS. The goals were clear. First, participation in EMS would wean Portuguese exporters from a reliance on devaluation and force them to find other sources for their competitiveness, thus leading to a modernization of Portuguese firms. Second, it would contribute to an inflation-fighting strategy and lead to a lowering of interest rates. And third, it would lead to budgetary discipline.

The government expected that the new exchange-rate regime would "force both union and employers' habits of thought and strategy to adapt to economic and financial expectations characteristic of more prosperous and stable economies" (Cavaco Silva 1995, 108). It faced strong protests from important segments of Portuguese industry. In what amounted to the reverse of the Standort Deutschland Debate (which focused on whether Germany's generous social and labor protections could be maintained), Portuguese society embarked on a debate about the future of Portuguese economic identity. Urged by the government to modernize, many firms felt that they would not be able to do so in time. Fears were commonly expressed that the Portuguese market would be swallowed by more competitive firms from abroad. Many in this national debate worried that Portuguese firms, not used to diversified quality production, faced with a low-skill workforce, poor access to technology, and lacking brand management and marketing skills, would quickly find their products rendered uncompetitive in European markets once the crutch of devaluation was removed.

The evolution of Portuguese monetary policy shared many features with Spanish monetary policy. Although the PSOE had embarked on a strong peseta policy somewhat earlier than the Portuguese adoption of a strong escudo, the trajectory is quite similar from 1986 on. The main differences concern the overvaluation of the peseta, which many analysts see as greater than the overvaluation of the escudo. In part because of this overvaluation, the peseta came under stronger speculative attack than the escudo. The Spanish government was thus forced to undertake downward adjustments of the peseta that were both more frequent and deeper than the largely preemptive downward adjustments undertaken in Portugal. Nonetheless, the downward adjustments were generally viewed as salutary for they provided a measure of welcome relief to domestic producers that had been under considerable duress.

Thus, in both Spain and Portugal the painful adjustment to a new monetary policy predicated on sound money preceded EMU. As foreseen by the governments implementing the policy, the abandonment of a crawling peg regime had major implications for both employers and workers. It forced exporters, as well as those firms subject to competition from abroad, to find sources of competitiveness that lay outside the easy crutch of currency devaluation, and thus set in motion a wave of restructuring. For unions, the implications of the policy shift went further. The reduction in inflation also heralded significant changes in wage bargaining. Control of wage costs became particularly important under a strong currency regime, where wage inflation could not be counterbalanced by currency devaluation. The transition to a low inflation/strong currency regime was difficult in both Spain and Portugal.

Social pacts and heightened responsibilities for the social partners were mechanisms used in both countries to smooth the transition from a high to low inflation environment, but in both countries unions increasingly felt deceived by both government and employers. This led to the 1989 general strike in Spain, in which the UGT broke its allegiance to the PSOE, in turn sparking a rise in compensatory social spending. In Portugal, social pacts in the latter half of the PSD's tenure became increasingly fragile and hard to come by and were marred by high levels of mutual suspicion. In part, this was the result of the shift in the way wage agreements were calculated relative to inflation. Past practice, a legacy from the high inflation days following the revolution, involved setting nominal wage gains that would make up for past inflation. Although it failed to protect the value of real wages, which fell considerably between 1976 and 1983, this mechanism tended to perpetuate high rates of inflation. In an attempt to cut inflation, the system of wage determination was changed to reflect anticipated, rather than past, inflation. A provision in the bargaining agreements allowed wages to be pushed up should actual inflation exceed expected inflation by a certain amount. This provision was rarely acted upon, which led unions to criticize the government for reneging on agreements, and made the conclusion of social pacts difficult.

The Portuguese and Spanish cases thus lend only partial support to the prediction that southern European countries, in adjusting not only to globalization but also to the loss of national policy instruments that accompanied EMU, will develop social pacts. Noting the signing of social pacts in a number of countries where national-level social bargaining had been traditionally weak, Martin Rhodes has made the argument that a "competitive corporatism" might be emerging in southern Europe. Although recent pacts, explicitly linked to the macroeconomic criteria embedded in Maastricht and the Stability Pact, have been concluded in both Portugal and Spain, this follows a period of several years in which social pacts seemed to be in eclipse. National level social pacts are not yet a permanent or even dominant element of social and labor market policy making in these countries. Although there are significant forces within and outside the government that wish to give renewed emphasis to social pacts, the pacts themselves have been too infrequent and too frequently broken to be viewed as fully institutionalized forms of policy making. Whether social pacts under EMU will truly take root remains an open question.

Meeting the Maastricht Criteria: Budgetary Consolidation and Consequences for Social Policy

The conventional wisdom posited that Portugal and Spain would have great difficulty in meeting the Maastricht criteria for entering into the Economic and Monetary Union of Europe (EMU), which stipulated upper limits on inflation, budget deficits, and total public debt as a proportion of GNP. Indeed, the doubts about southern Europe's capacity to lower inflation, debts, and budget deficits were so strong that serious debate emerged in northern Europe about the desirability of variable geometry and a two-speed Europe. The southern European countries resisted these proposals but the skepticism about their ability to meet the criteria ran so deep that they were nonetheless given the unfortunate collective label of "Club Med." Portugal, Spain, and Italy, though not Greece, committed themselves to meeting the criteria and to proving the naysayers wrong, and in so doing surprised themselves. This section asks how the two Iberian countries met the criteria; focuses on the budget deficit; and analyzes how the Maastricht criteria, through the budgetary consolidation it demanded, affected social spending.

Portugal was able to meet the Maastricht budget deficit criteria through a combination of judicious policy actions and a fortuitous economic environment that provided high rates of growth, and which consequently lessened the pain of the necessary budgetary consolidation. The strategy relied on (1) lowering interest payments on government debt, (2) reducing the size of the debt, and (3) consolidating the budget through substantial increases in revenue while avoiding stringent cuts in expenditure.

The first goal was made possible by curbing inflation brought about by the strong escudo policy and the commitment to EMU. Lower rates of inflation, along with financial liberalization, resulted in a gradual lowering of interest and bond rates and allowed the debt to be rescheduled at cheaper rates. The second goal was accomplished by earmarking a high percentage of revenues from privatization to debt reduction. Privatization in 1996 alone was to provide revenues equivalent to 2.3 percent of GDP. Over three-quarters of the revenue so raised was to be used for debt reduction.

To reduce the budget deficit, budgetary consolidation relied principally on revenue increases rather than expenditure cuts. Thus, current government receipts increased from 38 percent of GDP in 1994 to 39.3 percent in 1995 and to 40.2 percent in 1996. Substantial increases in current revenues were not matched by cuts in current expenditure. Indeed, during this period of budgetary consolidation, total expenditure exhibited slight growth rather than decline. Expenditures increased from 40.3 percent of GDP in 1994 to 40.7 percent in 1995, and to 40.9 percent in 1996.

The lowering of public expenditure, particularly if it affects the welfare state, is often viewed as one of the ways in which EMU, with its strict budget deficit criteria, can threaten the European social model. However, the Portuguese experience shows that the argument needs to be refined. In these countries consolidation of the budget relied not on cuts in current expenditure but rather in significant increases in government receipts. Models that predict that EMU's budget deficit criteria will lower public expenditure rely on assumptions about tax resistance. To be more credible, these models need to explain under what conditions governments that are forced to undertake budgetary consolidation do so through expenditure cuts rather than revenue increases.

Should the Portuguese road to budgetary consolidation—which relied overwhelmingly on revenue increases—be viewed as anomalous? Traditional conceptions of Portuguese and Spanish political economy suggest that the answer should be yes. In this traditional view, it is argued that relying on revenue increases should be easier for Portugal (and Spain) than for other more developed countries for three reasons. First, these countries are still emerging from a low taxation regime, and thus face more room for tax increases than high taxation regimes. Second, the period of democracy is characterized by a long secular trend of revenue increases, suggesting that this policy tool was frequently relied upon. And third, the desire to build a welfare state—still not fully realized in these countries—meant that budgetary cutbacks, particularly in the social sector, would conflict with the goal of social policy expansion. In these countries, welfare state politics was still much more about development than stability or retrenchment.

The above arguments are misplaced, however. The size of the Portuguese and Spanish public sector is no longer dramatically smaller than the European average. Although it is true that democracy has brought about a long-term secular trend of tax increases, these have been neither steady nor uncontested. Indeed, both countries have relied on difficult cuts in public expenditure on several occasions in the last quarter-century of democratic rule. Austerity budgets imposed by the IMF, or designed to avoid IMF involvement, were passed in both Portugal and Spain. Furthermore, the PSD program had as a major plank the control of government expenditure in Portugal. Finally, welfare state politics are by no means about welfare state development universally. The desire to construct a comprehensive welfare state is frequently opposed by long-standing arguments that, given low productivity rates, low cost competition is central to the economy. Under these conditions, the financing of the welfare state becomes a highly contested issue. Traditional explanations are thus not wholly satisfactory in explaining why Portugal opted for revenue increases rather than expenditure cuts in consolidating its budget.

Like the Portuguese case, the Spanish route to budgetary consolidation involved reductions in both the debt and the deficit, made possible by declines in interest rates and increased revenues from privatization and a surge in economic activity. In contrast to Portugal, however, Spain relied more heavily on expenditure controls. There were certainly disputes on the question of competencies and revenue-sharing between the central government and that of the autonomous regions, but these had more to do with questions of Spain's evolution toward a federal structure than with deep disagreement over the total level of taxation and expenditure.

Although both Portugal and Spain met the criteria for entry into EMU, more recently their paths have diverged. Portugal now runs a substantial budget deficit that is much higher than Spain's and is now in technical violation of the Growth and Stability Pact. The origins of this divergence are twofold. Over the last three years, economic growth, which boosts revenues, has been high in Spain. Equally important, however, has been the lack of success in controlling increases in public expenditure in Portugal. This has occurred in a number of areas, although health care service is the most notorious.

EMU has not reduced welfare expenditure in Portugal and Spain. Budget deficit reduction did not rely on cuts in the welfare state. Furthermore, EMU has not eradicated cost pressures within the welfare state.

Two Radically Different Unemployment Outcomes

If Portugal and Spain followed a roughly similar "social democratic" strategy of social policy development and structural economic reform, the most salient difference in the two countries' economic performance is undoubtedly their experience with unemployment. For the last fifteen years Spain has had the highest rate of unemployment in the EU (hovering around 20 percent, with lower and upper bounds of 16 and 24 percent) while Portugal has often had the lowest unemployment rate, frequently between 5 and 8 percent.

This result is puzzling for many reasons. First, as shown above, both countries shift their policies firmly toward economic openness and integration. It is true that there are differences in the timing of these reforms (particularly their implementation during periods of recession and growth), and that Portugal had a more open economy than Spain during much of the dictatorship period, but nonetheless both experienced very significant increases in trade, foreign direct investment, and international capital flows. Many of the reforms lowering trade barriers and controls over foreign investments are similar.

Second, unlike Spain, Portugal suffered a massive 15 percent increase in the size of its civilian labor force in the short period between 1974 and 1976. While part of this increase was due to the end of outward labor migration to France and Germany (an experience shared with Spain), the vast bulk of this increase came from the return of Portuguese migrants in Africa and military demobilization. Portugal, a country of nine million, absorbed 600,000 expatriates from the African wars and decolonization in 1974–1976. In addition, military employment during those two years shrank from 300,000 to 100,000. Not surprisingly, this increase in the labor force caused Portuguese unemployment to rise rapidly. However, it quickly stabilized in 1979 and eventually declined, in contrast to Spain, where unemployment continued to grow.

Third, trade unions and the radical left were dramatically stronger during the transition to democracy in Portugal than in the Spanish case, and labor unrest was very high. Not only was the CGTP union closely allied with the Portuguese Communist Party, a much stronger political force than the Spanish Communists, but the Portuguese unions did not fear a potentially disastrous right-wing takeover. In the early years of the democratic transition in Portugal wage increases were enormous. In the first six months after the revolution nominal wages increased by 25 percent, and by as much as 100 percent in the textile industry. Yet it was Spain that experienced the greater and more lasting wage shock.

Fourth, Portugal and Spain are regularly classified as having among the most similar and most rigid labor markets in the OECD (Blanchard and Jimeno 1995). Indeed, most studies of the Spanish labor market agree that the institutional configuration regulating the labor market contributed heavily to the high rate of unemployment. Firing costs were high in both countries. Restrictions on individual dismissals and legal penalties for wrongful dismissal were high, and employers, particularly in Spain, were often ruled against in court. Collective layoffs required government approval for most of this period.

As indicated earlier, in both countries collective bargaining fell in the worst position of the Calmfors-Driffil model. Spain and Portugal have neither a highly centralized bargaining structure nor a fully decentralized system and are thus expected to have problems achieving wage moderation. Despite a history of bargaining at the national level and the existence of company agreements, the intermediate level of industry agreements remained the most important. In Spain, though not in Portugal, regional agreements were an additional important source of intermediate-level bargaining. Both Portuguese and Spanish law exacerbated the consequences of industry (and regional level) bargaining by automatically extending the results to companies that did not participate in the bargaining.

The extensive use of fixed-term contracts has reinforced insider-outsider problems that plague both countries' labor markets. Perez-Diaz and Rodriguez (1995), for example, argue persuasively that the divisions among the core employed who benefit from formal labor market protections, the peripherally employed (those on fixed-term contracts or in the informal economy), and the unemployed as well as those no longer in the labor market are particularly salient in the Spanish case. The strong division between the core employed and those workers who do not benefit from social and labor market protections applies equally strongly to the Portuguese case.

Given the underlying similarity in the formal labor market institutions, the difference in unemployment rates remains puzzling. For Blanchard and Jimeno (1996), for example, high unemployment in Spain and low unemployment in Portugal "may be the biggest empirical challenge facing theories of structural unemployment" (218).

Despite similar institutional configurations in labor market regulation, however, Portugal and Spain underwent radically different experiences in their reaction to greater openness. In Bermeo's felicitous formulation, Portugal's reaction to the economic crisis of the 1970s was "labor-protective," while Spain was "labor-compensating" (Bermeo 1994, 198). Portugal's reaction was labor-protective in the sense that unemployment did not rise significantly. Bermeo argues that this was in part the result of a different political strategy whereby bankrupt firms in the private sector were taken over or supported financially by the state. In addition, the number of jobs in the traditional state sector increased substantially, compensating for job losses in the private sector, the return of emigrants and expatriates, and the flow of workers out of agriculture.

The Spanish case was "labor-compensating" because unemployment was allowed to rise, but unemployment insurance and relatively generous assistance schemes were introduced early on. The state thus compensated those who lost their jobs in the process of economic adjustment. Spain experienced an extremely painful *reconversión industrial,* a process whereby thousands of jobs were lost in large smokestack industries that, in large measure because of globalization, were no longer profitable (Smith 1998).

Indeed, it is perhaps symptomatic of the two strategies that the principal labor market issues to have dominated politics during most of the economic adjustment process in the two countries were different. In Spain, the principal issue was that of the *reconversión industrial.* In Portugal, by contrast, the issue was that of wage arrears, whereby bankrupt firms would continue to operate but not pay their workers.

A critical element in making Portugal's "labor saving" strategy possible lies in its wage flexibility. Unlike Spain, which in the words of a Spanish labor market economist "experienced not so much an oil shock as a wage shock," Portugal experienced an extraordinarily high degree of wage flexibility. Real wages in Portugal fell below their 1973 level only two years after the revolution, and took six years to recover.

Portugal's wage flexibility stemmed in part from lax compliance with its labor market regulations. The comparative indices which rank Portugal high in terms of the rigidity of its labor market regulations thus overstate the true level of regulation in the economy (based on interviews with labor ministry officials, Central Bank economists, and union leaders). Surveys show that many Portuguese employers do not perceive labor market regulations as particularly rigid. This is largely related to the high number of small firms in Portugal. Public sector employees and workers in large firms tend to benefit from the strict labor market regulations. However, the numerous employees of small firms, as well as the self-employed, often do not.

Revisiting Globalization and the Welfare State

Spain and Portugal clearly demonstrate that it is possible to open the economy to international trade and capital flows and at the same time build a comprehensive welfare state. This was not a fortuitous by-product of favorable economic conditions and strong economic growth, but required multiple political decisions. Central among these was a readiness—on the part of political elites, major interest groups, as well as the voting public—to raise taxes in order to finance greater social protection. But building these two welfare states also involved, as we have seen, the creation of new institutions and continuous policy innovation to deal with challenging external and internal environments.

The two countries add impressive case evidence to the cross-national statistical findings supporting the view that social welfare policies are linked to economic openness. However, the actual causal processes are still far from clear. Several features of the Spanish and Portuguese story cast doubt on any simple claim that economic openness causes welfare state development.

First, politicians erecting the welfare state defended their project not in terms of openness but in terms of modernization and Europeanization. As later in east-central Europe, "Europe" served as a model for the return to "normality" after the years of authoritarian rule and economic autarchy. In this regard, developing a welfare state was much more than a means to secure openness; it was a primary goal across the vast majority of the political spectrum. Left, center-left, and center-right parties shared a consensus on the desirability of developing the welfare state.

Second, and very importantly, although welfare state development is correlated with increasing international economic integration over the whole of this period, there are many distinct events in which openness constrained welfare state development. Indeed, the two IMF agreements Portugal entered into because of balance of payments crises called for austerity, budget-tightening, and a freer labor market. Spain famously avoided an IMF agreement when Felipe Gonzalez argued that Spain would undertake the necessary measures to reduce the inflation differential with Europe, cut the current account deficit, and prepare Spain for European integration on its own, without recourse to the IMF. Nonetheless, the government's program of devaluation, financial liberalization, budget cuts, industrial restructuring, and social security reform bore great resemblance to the proposals of the IMF team that had visited Spain in 1981 (Bermeo 1994). Budget cuts from 1981 to 1982 covered most categories of public spending, including health, education, social security, and labor. As part of the struggle against the deficit, pension reform passed by the socialist government in 1985 curtailed benefits. Key features of the reform were increases in the number of years of work needed to qualify for a pension as well as reduced payments through revision of the pension formula. In labor market reform, the government's principal achievement was to increase flexibility by liberalizing the use of temporary contracts. Reducing restrictions on firing was one of the government's goals in labor market reform, but it proved very costly politically. By easing employers' ability to hire under temporary contracts, the government circumvented the more intractable problem of restrictions on firing, which applied to permanent contracts.

Under "crisis" conditions in which IMF agreements are either adhered to or imminent, openness of the economy can lead to cuts in social protection. As sketched out above, the solutions to the crisis involve stabilization and structural reform, which in turn consist of budgetary cuts affecting the welfare state as well as important welfare state reforms that limit worker protections and reduce social transfers.

However, one can also identify specific causal mechanisms whereby economic openness leads to welfare state measures. The very process of market-oriented reform can be facilitated in certain areas by selective use, and expansion, of the welfare state. Thus, the painful process of industrial reconversion whereby Spain closed many of the large smokestack industries that had been rendered uncompetitive was facilitated by the use of generous unemployment compensation schemes as well as early retirement to those affected (Smith 1998). In analyzing the process of structural adjustment, Bermeo (1994) writes that "the PSOE offered specific compensation to the groups most likely to be adversely affected by the reforms" (113).

Openness, then, can be tied to changes in the welfare state through a variety of conflicting mechanisms. Although the empirical correlation between openness and welfare state policies holds, the specific mechanisms often seem to go the other way. That is, even though the welfare state expands very significantly during this period in both Spain and Portugal, the most visible political links between openness and welfare state reform are those that link pressures stemming from openness to the need for market-oriented reform, including reform of the welfare state. Politicians explain the need to cut the welfare state by referring to the need for adjustment imposed by balance of payments deficits, rising debts, and pressure on the currency. By contrast, welfare state expansion occurs largely without reference to the increasing openness of the economy.

Nonetheless, the timing of demands from below can on occasion be traced to changes in the international economic environment. Portugal's explosion in social demands occurred in the period 1974–1976 immediately following the collapse of the dictatorship. These demands reflected more than the exalted revolutionary rhetoric of Portugal during those years. As many analysts have shown, much of the collective action from below (street demonstrations, factories being taken over by workers, farm land by landless agricultural laborers, houses by people who had none) was neither instigated nor controlled by politicians. Indeed, "revolutionary" governments tried to limit and dampen these movements fearing loss of control. Although this explosion of demands has generally been traced to the lifting of the dictatorship, which allowed pent-up demands to be expressed, these were years of economic crisis in Portugal, due both to the oil shock and to Portugal's loss of its colonies. Thus, the demands from below for social protection that are so visible in this period can be linked to the increased experience of external risk. It is therefore possible to view the Portuguese experience in 1974–1976 as supportive of Rodrik's (1997, 1999) posited causal mechanism in which openness and external risk translate into welfare state expansion through demands from below.

The Portuguese and Spanish stories do not cast doubt on the macro-logic by which the welfare state makes openness politically palatable and cushions its negative effects. Indeed, in many ways it reinforces the literature by providing examples of late welfare state development where the relationship still holds. However, the relative rarity of the Portuguese and Spanish cases among middle-income countries gives one pause. In many Latin American countries, for example, a similar turn away from autarchy and toward openness did not result in similar levels of welfare state development. Does this mean that embedded liberalism is a peculiarly European story, not found in countries pursuing the "Washington consensus" involving a more neoliberal embrace of the market with only residual social policies and safety nets? In these countries, openness has brought with it a host of severe problems, ranging from the 1980s debt crisis to recurrent attacks on the currency. The lost decade's low rates of growth may have prevented social policy expansion by themselves. It would not be surprising to find that the argument that openness leads to welfare state development holds only when openness leads to growth.

However, even where growth has occurred, its potentially positive effects on welfare state development have been stymied by balance of payments crises and currency attacks. The de facto resolution of these crises has frequently required IMF conditionality involving at least two policies that delay welfare state development. The first are interest rate hikes designed to stabilize the exchange rate by luring capital back; this has the effect of dampening growth. The second are policies designed to reduce recurring budget deficits, often viewed as one of the principal causes of the crises. Budget deficit reduction typically involves cutting back on pension programs and other income transfer schemes and often involves other welfare state departments such as health and education as well.

Whether globalization will eventually lead to welfare state development in Latin America remains an open question. The optimistic view is that the problems faced in Latin America since the turn toward openness, although very severe, will, in the long run, be transient ones. Once they are resolved, there is no reason these middle-income countries cannot choose to follow the Spanish and Portuguese route and develop their systems of social protection. The pessimistic view argues that "embedded liberalism" was a historically and geographically circumscribed phenomenon. Found primarily in western Europe and triumphant during most of the postwar period, it is now being undone by "subversive liberalism."

There is no doubt, however, that Spain and Portugal demonstrate that welfare state development is compatible with economic openness, provided that the domestic political constellations are favorable. Both countries persistently pursued often difficult policies that established, maintained, and adjusted social protection under changing circumstances.

6

Globalization and the Future of Welfare States in the Post-Communist East-Central European Countries

MITCHELL A. ORENSTEIN AND MARTINE R. HAAS

How has globalization influenced welfare state development in the post-Communist states? Since 1989 the leading east-central European accession states, Poland, Hungary, and the Czech Republic, have experienced radically different welfare state developments from their neighbors in the former Soviet Union. The first part of this chapter analyzes the "Europe effect" that we find to be the source of this differentiation and argues that globalization has not had a uniform impact on post-Communist welfare states. Rather, the effect of globalization differs greatly, depending on a country's position in the international economy and geopolitical relations. We demonstrate that countries closer to the European Union have used welfare state programs to compensate citizens for the traumas of system transition and economic openness, while former Soviet states have allowed their welfare state to collapse to a far greater extent.

After showing why east-central European welfare states have taken a different path from their neighbors in the former Soviet Union, we explore the roots of differentiation within the east-central European welfare states themselves. Despite participating in a common process of European integration, east-central European welfare states have taken different routes to Europe. These differences can best be explained with reference to the domestic politics of transition and a "global politics of attention" in social policy advice. The transition period offered extraordinary opportunities for small groups of policy makers to initiate policy change (Balcerowicz 1995), and they did so in fairly idiosyncratic ways that reflected the current state of domestic and international welfare state thinking and priorities.

130

This essay contributes to the debate on globalization and welfare states in several ways. First, contrary to those who argue that globalization necessarily forces states to cut commitments to welfare, we find that central and eastern European states maintained a strong welfare state commitment during a period of rapid economic liberalization and globalization. Second, we argue that the effects of globalization on welfare states are mediated by politics in three ways: (1) by a country's geopolitical position, in this case proximity to a regional trading bloc with strong welfare state norms and commitments; (2) by the domestic politics of decision making, in this case taking place in an extraordinary period of systemic transition; and (3) by a global politics of attention, in this case influencing the specific paths countries take on the way to Europe.

For the purposes of this chapter, we adopt a carefully conscribed economic definition of globalization that encompasses five trends, following Glatzer and Rueschemeyer (this volume). Under this definition, globalization consists of:

- Expanding international trade in goods and services
- Expanding international capital flows
- Increasing globalization of production (through transnational corporations and global commodity chains)
- The growing role of international organizations such as the World Trade Organization, the World Bank, and the IMF
- Greater transnational flow of economic ideas

We define welfare states as the collection of state programs, regulations, and actions that are intended to directly fulfill a state's declared commitment to the economic welfare of its citizens.

The Europe Effect

Starting in 1989, the post-Communist countries of east-central Europe, southeastern Europe, and the former Soviet Union were swept by a dramatic systemic transformation that fundamentally altered many of the social and economic conditions upon which their welfare states were built. This upheaval created pressures on post-Communist welfare states that went far beyond those experienced by more stable states under conditions of globalization. Systemic transformation or "transition" involved not only very rapid trade liberalization, but also radical changes in economic structures, political institutions, and state administration. Developments in all of these spheres forced a radical reorientation of welfare state conditions, commitments, and structures—but directions were highly unpredictable at the outset of transition. In contrast to Pierson's (1994, 15) concept of "systemic retrenchment," the post-Communist transition created systemic pressures on welfare states, but not necessarily in the direction of retrenchment. Upheaval made it certain that old structures could not be maintained forever, but uncertain, for instance, whether welfare state spending would rise or fall, whether commitments would be changed or maintained in a new way, or whether the socialist safety net would simply cease to exist. Given similar pressures of globalization and transition, one might have expected the post-Communist welfare states to react in broadly similar ways (Frye 2001). But this was not the case. Instead, a process of rapid differentiation began. East-central European states maintained a high commitment to welfare that actually grew as a percent of GDP, while at the same time falling in absolute levels, in line with declines in GDP. Former Soviet welfare states experienced a dramatic decline in both absolute and relative terms (though less pronounced in the latter). Because this differentiation so neatly correlated with geography, we call it a "Europe effect," underpinned by economic and political trends.

Transition Outcomes

In a comprehensive study of post-Communist welfare state adjustment, the World Bank (2000) found that in the first decade of transition, post-Communist states separated into two categories of adjustment, European and Eurasian. These two categories appeared for the most part to be geographically determined. According to the World Bank, the "European" category included the east-central European countries (Czech Republic, Hungary, Poland, Slovakia), the more successful Balkan and former Yugoslav republics (Slovenia, Croatia, FYR Macedonia, Romania, Bulgaria), and the Baltic states (Estonia, Lithuania, Latvia). The Eurasian category encompassed the former Soviet republics (Belarus, Uzbekistan, Kyrgyz Republic, Kazakhstan, Russia, Turkmenistan, Azerbaijan, Tajikistan, Armenia, Ukraine, Georgia, Moldova), minus the Baltics, plus Albania.

What differences did this study find between the two adjustment regimes? Compared to the Eurasian countries, the European countries restructured their economies more aggressively and effectively after 1989–1991. The European transition countries experienced lesser transitional recessions, and their per capita incomes were higher (see fig. 6.1). The European countries also enjoyed stronger institutional and administrative capacity. By 2000, in the leading European transition countries, growth had resumed and real wages had increased, though unemployment remained a problem (World Bank 2000, 2).

All of these factors pointed in the direction of higher welfare state spending for the European transition countries. Starting from very similar pretransition levels, by 1996 the European transition countries spent an average of 10 percent of GDP on pensions, compared to 5 percent for the Eurasian countries (see fig. 6.2). Since pensions are usually the largest portion of cash social benefits in the post-

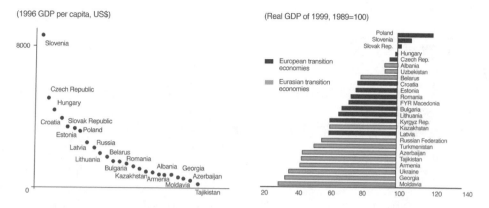

Fig. 6.1. Transition economies fall into two broad groups in terms of economic performance. Data from World Bank 2000, 2.

Communist countries, this gives a good sense of the direction and magnitude of changes in welfare state spending. Unemployment benefits and minimum wages were also substantially higher in the European countries (ibid., 3). The World Bank data concludes that overall economic, social, and administrative performance since 1989 is a good indicator of total social spending in the late 1990s, and performance correlates strongly with geography.

Despite starting with very similar welfare state structures and spending levels, European and Eurasian countries diverged dramatically during the first decade of transition. During the first ten years, welfare state spending increased on average in the European countries, while it stagnated or fell in the Eurasian countries. But why has geography had such a significant effect? What is it about the geographical position of east-central European countries in particular that helped them navigate the post-Communist transition with far less of an economic collapse and far greater commitment to welfare? We propose that the answer is Europe. In short, those countries with good prospects of joining the European Union faced an entirely different set of economic, political, and administrative opportunities and incentives that pulled in the direction of higher economic growth, increasing these states' commitment to, and ability to support, welfare state spending. Our hypothesis here is consistent with the findings of Frye (2003), who concludes that EU integration correlates with higher spending on health and education in transition countries. Like Kopstein and Reilly (2000, 28), we suggest that the EU provided "the crucial external push that has altered domestic interests in favor of accomplishing some of the key tasks of postcommunism."

Integration, however, is a relational process and east-central European countries also were pushed toward Europe by internal factors. Their prospects of joining Europe depended not only on the European Union recognizing east-central Eu-

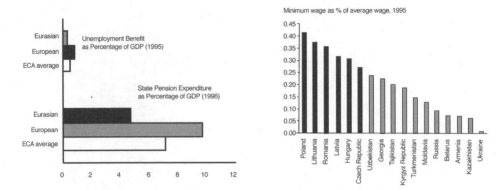

Fig. 6.2. Social protection systems also differ. Data from World Bank 2000, 3.

ropean countries as potential members, but also on their similarity to current EU members in culture, organization, and history and their expressed desire to become more "European," adhering to European norms of political and economic organization. Such internal factors also differentiated east-central European countries from their neighbors to the south and east.

The Regional Politics of the European Union

The radical disjuncture between the European and Eurasian experience suggests that the international position of the east-central European countries was the most significant determinant of their post-Communist welfare effort. We believe that this is because of a pervasive "Europe effect" that can be seen in the domains of economics, politics, and state administration. This section will show why European ties and influence in all three domains may have supported continued commitment to high levels of welfare state spending in the accession countries. We focus on the three largest countries in the first wave of EU membership negotiations, Poland, the Czech Republic, and Hungary. However, the argument applies equally to the smaller first-wave countries, Estonia, Latvia, Lithuania, Slovakia, and Slovenia, and to a somewhat lesser degree to the second-wave countries, Romania, Bulgaria, and Croatia, that is, to most of the World Bank's "European" group, but particularly the leading countries among them.

In the economic sphere, the east-central European countries quickly carved out a privileged place in European trade and investment networks. In the first years of transition, they underwent a massive trade reorientation. Partly this was natural, due to shared borders and previous periods of industrial cooperation. To a degree it was facilitated by state treaties called "association agreements" with the EU, which reduced tariffs on trade with a goal of eventual elimination. Expectations of future EU membership also enhanced inward foreign investment, after a lag period during the chaotic, early years of reform. Soon, east-central Europe was perceived as an attractive, relatively low-cost manufacturing base within Europe. Over time, several leading east-central European countries, particularly Hungary and the Czech Republic, began to show evidence of increasing involvement in European intra-industry trade networks and higher-value-added production. Distinctive among the post-Communist countries, east-central Europe quickly and successfully integrated into the global economy (Kierzkowski 2000; Fidrmuc 2000; Eichengreen and Kohl 1998). In this, east-central Europe differed sharply from some of its neighbors to the south and east (compare Cook, this volume).

Like the rest of the post-Communist world, east-central Europe experienced a severe trade shock in the early 1990s as a result of the collapse of Soviet bloc trade that contributed to a reduction in GDP. Brenton and Gros (1997) estimate that trade collapsed to 87 percent of the pretransition level in Hungary, and to a lesser extent in Poland. Remarkably, east-central European countries quickly reoriented their trade toward the West. Between 1988 and 1996, the three largest east-central European countries, Poland, Hungary and the Czech Republic, doubled the share of their exports going to the EU from the 30–37 percent range to 59–67 percent by 1996 (Kierzkowski 2000, 15). Germany quickly became the largest trading partner for all of east-central Europe. In 1996, Germany took 29 percent of Hungary's exports, 35 percent of Poland's, and 36 percent of the Czech Republic's (ibid., 18).

In addition to successful redirection of trade toward the West, quality of trade also began to improve in east-central Europe. Whereas early in the transition questions were raised about the ability of these economies to integrate into global production networks, between 1990 and 1996 intra-industry trade with the EU increased from 43 to 62 percent in the Czech Republic and from 47 to 57 percent in Hungary. Slovenia's share of intra-industry trade also reached 60 percent in 1996. At that point, the leading east-central European transition economies matched the EU intra-industry trade levels of Sweden, Spain, and Italy. Poland was somewhat of a laggard, with intra-industry trade increasing from 36 to 41 percent in 1996 (Fidrmuc 2000, 87). However, Poland and Romania, whose economies have been fed more by low-cost production, are expected to swiftly move up the production chain in the coming years. Brenton and Gros (1997) conclude that "the more advanced countries in Central and Eastern Europe are indistinguishable from Western market economies." These economies have successfully carved out a niche in EU trade and moreover appear not to be replacing southern European trade, but rather inducing increased specialization in the EU (Fidrmuc 2000, 91). In line with the "compensation hypothesis" of welfare state development, we suggest that successful trade integration in east-central Europe will support and enable continued high levels of social spending, as in other European countries.

Foreign direct investment lagged trade growth during the first decade of transition, but again the most successful east-central European countries, particularly Hungary, have begun to achieve levels of foreign direct investment (FDI) per capita that approach developed-country levels (Kierzkowski 2000, 20). The largest trade partners tend to be the largest investors, with Germany, the United States, and the Netherlands leading the way in FDI (Hunya 2000, 91). Such investment in east-central Europe appears to be fully compatible with high social expenditures since it is premised on European Union membership. Indeed, there is no evidence that among the post-Communist countries, investment seeks the lowest wage, as FDI is far higher in east-central European countries than in the former Soviet republics. Instead, FDI flows to those countries with relatively stable political and social environments. In addition, the promise of joining the European trade zone have helped, as have domestic "European" factors such as good schooling, high skill levels, a history of capitalist industrial organization, and reliable social protection systems, including unemployment and health insurance.

Successful integration into global, but particularly European, trade and production networks appears to be one major factor enabling maintenance of relatively high levels of welfare state spending in east-central Europe. However, there are other aspects of the Europe effect. In the political sphere, the drive to rejoin Europe has reinforced institutions of parliamentary democracy, enabling interest groups to lobby more effectively for a continuation of high levels of welfare provision. Garrett and Nickerson (this volume) argue that democracy mediates the relation between globalization and state spending. European Union membership prospects may also constrain political parties' views of the range of possible policy options. For instance, anticipating EU membership, political parties on the right and left in central and Eastern Europe have felt compelled to commit to European norms and levels of social expenditure (Cook, Orenstein, and Rueschemeyer 1999). The advent of membership negotiations in the mid-1990s reminded east-central European officials that Europe feared mass immigration from the East. East-central European countries that aspired to EU membership would have to maintain social provisions on a European level, to avoid "social dumping." Starting in the mid-1990s, the EU began to work with east-central European ministries to provide experience and expertise on European social welfare, through twinning projects with west European ministries and other projects. Thus, economic, political, and administrative developments related to the project of rejoining Europe all tended to push in the direction of increased social spending and continued commitment to social welfare in east-central Europe.

We believe that this Europe effect explains the significance of a regional variable, measured often as the distance from Brussels in many studies of differences among the post-Communist states (for example, Cameron 2001; Kopstein and Reilly 2000, 10). Distance from Brussels really is significant, not for purely geographic reasons, but because it is a proxy for the cultural, political, and economic commitment to east-central European accession that has placed these countries in a privileged position in the global economy (see also Kapstein and Milanovic 2003, 52).

In short, while the countries of the former Soviet Union provide evidence for the "efficiency" hypothesis that globalization forces countries to scale back welfare state spending, the experience of east-central Europe argues for the opposite "compensation" hypothesis, that greater economic integration provides both the economic basis and need for high welfare state spending (Cameron 1978; Glatzer and Rueschemeyer, introduction; Frye 2003). We suggest that the east-central European experience shows that geopolitics matters. The place of states in the international economy and geopolitical relations has a fundamental impact on the way they will react to similar pressures of economic globalization. In the case of east-central Europe, proximity to and promises of eventual membership in a free trade zone that symbolizes and embodies norms of welfare state provision, parliamentary democracy, and trade openness together facilitated the adoption of like policies in the accession states.

Welfare State Choices within East-Central Europe

So far, we have discussed general trends in welfare state spending across the post-Communist region and argued that EU accession countries have been distinguished from their Eurasian counterparts by higher spending levels overall. At the level of individual country adjustment, however, the picture becomes much more complex, and the variation among the individual states within east-central Europe is quite stark. Below, we describe this variation and also point to some trends toward increasing similarities, focusing particularly on the cases of Hungary, Poland, and the Czech Republic. We then address the causes of these differences and similarities, and explain them through an analysis of decision making in transition. We argue that the large number of programmatic problems for welfare states generated by the post-Communist transition overtaxed the policy capacity of these governments and forced them to seek out new policy ideas and solutions in a relatively unsystematic fashion. New ideas and solutions came from domestic and foreign sources. The foreign sources included international organizations, bilateral aid agencies, and their consultants. However, international organizations paid little attention to social policy in the first years of transition, instead focusing on macroeconomics and privatization (Kapstein and Milanovic 2003, 47). We argue that this relative neglect left domestic policy elites reasonably free to set transition social policy. They did so in an idiosyncratic manner that reflected momentary alignments of intellectual and political resources and historical conditions in a particular country. Thus, policy differed widely from country to country. However, starting in the mid-1990s, a more coherent and forceful international social policy agenda began to appear for the post-Communist states, crafted by a World Bank that was increasingly cognizant of east-central European countries' EU aspirations. Although east-central European welfare states still display unique features, reflecting prior institutional paths, and the particularities of transition decision making, which has long-term path dependencies of its own, this international agenda has had a growing impact. Overall, we stress the power of policy ideas, those of the international community and domestic elites, in reshaping post-Communist welfare states.

Major Policy Developments

A general picture of how social policy evolved in Hungary, Poland, and the Czech Republic after 1989 is shown in table 6.1. These countries followed broadly similar patterns of social policy transformation in a time sequence that generally concurred with that mapped out for them by the World Bank and leading economists of transition. In the first years of the transformation, the emphasis was largely on setting up unemployment systems, since unemployment was widely expected to be the most serious and potentially destabilizing social issue of transition (Blanchard et al. 1991). Later, post-Communist welfare states began to focus on transforming their systems of social assistance, then health and pension systems.

Developments in unemployment insurance were broadly similar in the three countries. After the initiation of unemployment insurance in 1988-1990, benefits were scaled back as unemployment rates rose. Initially, benefits were provided for twelve or even eighteen months at fairly generous levels, but were later cut to six months and reduced in size (Godfrey and Richards 1997, various chapters). Poland, for instance, began to offer a flat-rate unemployment benefit of 36 percent of average wage starting in 1992. Eligibility rules were also restricted. Minimum wage regulations were introduced or reintroduced in all countries at the start of transition, but provided only a low level of protection for low-income workers (Standing and Vaughan-Whitehead 1995).

Social assistance policies in east-central Europe differed substantially when these countries started the transformation, and these differences persisted during the first several years. A major World Bank study by Braithwaite, Grootaert, and Milanovic (1999) showed that in 1993, social assistance systems in the region divided into three groups: concentrated, dispersed, and irrelevant. In concentrated systems (Poland and Estonia), only a small percentage of households received assistance, but this assistance was relatively important for them. In dispersed systems (Hungary and Russia), a high percentage of households received assistance, but this assistance was often only a small proportion of household budgets. In irrelevant systems (Bulgaria), social assistance was unimportant to households and only a

Table 6.1 Welfare State Transformation at a Glance in East-Central Europe

Policy Area	Hungary	Czech Republic	Poland
Labor Market Policies			
Unemployment insurance founded	1988	1990	1989
Restricted/reduced	Reduced in 1993	Reduced in 1991, 1992	Reduced in 1992
New minimum wage legislation	1989	1991	1990
Level (1990–1993)	50–60% of avg. wage	40–50% of avg. wage	30–40% of avg. wage
Social Assistance			
Minimum living standard established	n/a	1991	n/a
Social assistance system targeted	1995	1996	
Health and Pensions			
Health fund payroll tax	1992	1993	1999
Private health insurance funds	1993	1993	n/a
Total health expenditures (% GDP)	1989 (5.7%) 1994 (10.8%) 1998 (8.0%)	1994 (7.8%) 1998 (7.2%)	1989 (3.0%) 1994 (4.5%)
Retirement age increased	1996 to 62 for men and women	1996 from 60/55 to 62/57–61 by 2007	constant at 65/60
Voluntary private pension funds	1993	1994	1999
Mandatory private pension funds	1998	n/a	1999
State pension spending (% GDP)	1989 (9.0%) 1994 (10.8%)	1989 (8.3%) 1994 (8.4%) 1998 (9.1%)	1989 (6.7%) 1994 (15.8%)
Summary Indicators			
Payroll tax levels	1995 (60%) 1999 (53.8%)	1996 (49.4%) 1999 (47.5%)	1996 (48%)
Total social expenditures (% GDP)	1995 (28.6%)	1994 (21.3%)	1995 (26.7%)

small percentage received benefits in any case (Milanovic 1999, 136).

Among the east-central European countries, Hungary was exceptional in the coverage and generosity of its family benefit system, which was one of the most developed in Europe (UNICEF 1994), while Poland had a less extensive, more targeted system that provided a higher average benefit for a much smaller number of recipient households. The Czech Republic was not included in the study, but probably fell closer to the Hungarian model.

Starting in 1995, however, all three countries began to target their social assistance systems, in line with neoliberal thinking and advice primarily from the World Bank (compare World Bank 1995d; Barr 1994, 192). In fact the Braithwaite, Grootaert, and Milanovic study (1999) was part of this effort to make the east-central European welfare states more focused on providing benefits for the poor. The shift was most dramatic in Hungary in 1995, when a socialist government initiated severe cuts in family benefits under the so-called Bokros package of reforms, to respond to a serious fiscal and balance of payments crisis. The Bokros reforms touched off vigorous public protest and a stormy period of reform that ended in 1996 with finance minister Lajos Bokros's resignation from office. Targeting also proved controversial in the Czech Republic, where it was initiated by a right-wing government. Therefore, in social assistance, major structural variation among the three countries in the initial period of reform gave way to increasing structural similarity after 1995, under the influence of the World Bank.

Health and pension systems also saw major variations initially, followed by convergence in the late 1990s. Both Hungary and the Czech Republic established independent health insurance funds early in the transition, funded by special, earmarked health insurance payroll taxes. Poland did not do so until much later, due to concerns about the expense. This difference was important, as Ringold (1999, 34) shows that countries that established such a payroll tax spent significantly more on health than countries that did not. The Czech Republic and Hungary developed systems of private health insurance funds in 1993, while Poland established regional funds in 1998–1999, as part of its later health reform.

In pensions, Hungary and the Czech Republic founded voluntary pension funds with significant tax or budgetary advantages in 1993 and 1994, well before Poland, which took this step with its major pension reform in 1999. Poland, meanwhile, spent far more on public pensions during the first years of transition than either Hungary or the Czech Republic. In 1994, Poland spent 15.8 percent of its GDP on pensions that were more generous than the central European norm. This is largely because pension levels were higher. Poland's average replacement rate (the percent replacement of previous income) was 74.8 percent, compared to 46.8 percent in the Czech Republic or 56.9 percent in Hungary in 1994.

Poland's more rapid increase in pension expenditure has concerned policy makers and analysts alike. Several authors (Cain and Surdej 1999; Kapstein and

Milanovic 2000) have tried to explain why Poland's pension system expanded so rapidly, causing serious fiscal strain and placing downward pressure on other social spending. It was not until 1999 that Poland finally dealt with its problems by passing a comprehensive pension reform that would reduce spending as a percentage of GDP over the long term. The Czech Republic had been more successful in containing pension spending early in the transition. In 1996, both Hungary and the Czech Republic gradually started to increase the statutory pension age in an effort to control spending. And in 1998 and 1999, respectively, Hungary and Poland conducted major reforms of their pension systems, partially replacing their pay-as-you-go public systems with mandatory, private, defined-contribution funds (Müller 1999; Orenstein 2000). Differences in the methods and timing of change, however, had major impacts on pension spending, creating significant long-term path dependencies for reform.

To summarize, in unemployment benefits, Hungary and the Czech Republic were more generous at first, but quickly scaled back. Poland offered less generous benefits from the beginning. In health insurance, Poland did not create an earmarked health insurance tax until after a decade of transition, constraining health spending relative to its neighbors. However, Poland spent more on pensions than either Hungary or the Czech Republic as a percent of GDP. In part because of higher spending, Hungary and Poland conducted major structural reforms of their pension systems in the late 1990s, while the Czech Republic did not. And in social assistance, after wide early variation in policies, all three countries began to target assistance and to reduce universality starting in 1995–1996. While clear trends are visible, so are major differences among the three countries. These differences are important to analyze, not only because they had a major impact on welfare during the transition, but also because they marked paths of welfare state development for the future.

Explaining Trends and Differences

To what extent are trends and differences in east-central European welfare state transformation explained by globalization? We argued in the previous section that the east-central European countries' relatively successful integration into the international economy—reflected in rapidly expanding international trade, particularly with Europe, higher FDI, and integration into European production networks—was associated with a general upward trend in social spending during the transition, and the continued commitment of these states to social protection. However, we have also seen that the extent and paths of this adjustment have varied from country to country.

These differences among country adjustment paths cannot be explained by any consistent theory about exposure to trade or trade openness. For one, the impact of trade is not precise enough to account for numerous policy differences among these three countries. Openness to trade also does not explain differences in spending levels among these three countries. Hungary and the Czech Republic are the most advanced and successfully integrated, as well as the smallest, most open economies in this set. Poland stands out by being four times larger in population, therefore less exposed to trade than its smaller neighbors, and poorer and less advanced economically. By any version of the compensation thesis (compare Cameron 1978), which posits that smaller, more open economies spend more on welfare states, Hungary and the Czech Republic would be expected to spend more during the transition. Also, if welfare states were a luxury that could be afforded by wealthier states, the same result would pertain. However, it was Poland that increased its social spending most rapidly and radically during the transition, as a percent of GDP, mostly through a dramatic increase in pension spending (Hagemejer 1999).

Various political economy explanations for Poland's rapid increase in social spending all come up short (Cain and Surdej 1999; Kapstein and Milanovic 2000). Cain and Surdej use a combination of transition politics and public choice theories to convincingly explain the expansion of pension spending in Poland, but they do not address other cases, where spending was not so extreme. Kapstein and Milanovic argue that political leaders faced a strategic choice during the transition, whether to curry favor with pensioners, and therefore increase pensions and slow privatization, or with workers, and therefore speed privatization and reduce pensions. Poland, they suggest, took the former strategy, while Russia and the Czech Republic took the latter one. However, they have yet to defend this thesis with reference to Polish voting statistics, and it seems implausible that the early Solidarity governments that ruled Poland would have intentionally favored pensioners over workers. Also, our previous work suggests that east-central European leaders were guided more broadly by economic ideas in their choice of transition strategies, whether neoliberal or social democratic, rather than by narrow appeals to age-based constituencies (Orenstein 2001).

Another surprising point about post-Communist social policy is that many developments do not seem to be closely related to party ideology. While previous work (Cook, Orenstein, and Rueschemeyer 1999) showed that left parties in post-Communist countries advocated broadly social democratic welfare state themes, they were just as likely as right parties to implement austerity measures when fiscal crisis threatened, as in Hungary in 1995. Therefore, cross-national studies show that the partisan hue of government has little relation with overall social spending in the first decade of transition (Lipsmeyer 2000), and in fact, there is some evidence that right governments have spent slightly more. Of course, this ignores variation in long-term structural changes that may differ between right and left, but not show up in yearly spending figures. However, it does suggest that social policy transformation has been largely driven by other factors (such as transition upheaval) that transcend party affiliation.

In what follows, we propose to explain this variation among countries' social transformation paths by the dynamics of transition decision making. During a chaotic transition, small groups of specialists were often granted extraordinary authority by executives and parliaments to set social policy along new lines. At the same time, decision makers drew upon available domestic and international sources of policy advice to formulate responses to the plethora of transition problems they confronted (compare Cohen, March, and Olsen 1972). However, policy thinking and advice received differed in each country, often idiosyncratically, explaining a large part of the seemingly unsystematic differentiation in countries on more or less equivalent paths toward Europe.

The Domestic Politics of Decision Making

At the national level, transition social policy was set by small groups of politically connected social policy experts (Jenkins 1999). These expert groups occupied various spaces in the state apparatus, whether at ministries, social security agencies, or government research institutes. They were often granted a great deal of autonomy in the early transition years, both from civil society and parliamentary pressures, as well as from the executive branch. However, they were all relatively small and lacking in resources compared with their west European counterparts, for instance. Small groups of policy experts flowed in and out of government, based on personal connections with particular political parties and leaders. Once located in the executive branch, these groups were confronted with numerous overwhelming problems that were unlike those faced by their counterparts anywhere in the world, at that moment in time.

In the fluid institutional moment of transition, in the face of many conflicting pressures and relatively few available solutions, the ideas of these people about how to reshape social welfare commitments could be extremely powerful (Balcerowicz 1995; Kolodko 1999). Therefore, it is important to examine the terms of their ideological discourse. Broadly speaking, there were three main trends in post-Communist thinking on social policy that correspond fairly well with Esping-Andersen's (1990) typology of European social welfare state ideas. First, and most prominently, was the liberal or neoliberal strain of thinking that swept east-central Europe after 1989. Liberal ideas about rendering welfare states as means-tested "safety nets" began to be heard in east-central Europe (Deacon 1997; Szacki 1995). However, the influence of liberal ideas in the social policy area was muted by the fact that neoliberal thinkers' emphasis lay elsewhere. Post-Communist economic programs emphasized price and trade liberalization, privatization, and stabilization (Blanchard et al. 1991). Neoliberals often left social policy matters in the early years to experts who came from other ideological camps (Orenstein 2001). The primary one, of course, was the broadly socialist or social democratic camp. East-central European social policy experts generally disagreed with neoliberal principles (Nelson 2001; Müller 1999) and tried instead to steer the transition from paternalist socialism toward a more European concept of socialism. While they tended to stay in the background, one could say that this socialist strain dominated east-central European welfare state thinking during the first five years of transition, and will perhaps remain a dominant trend over the longer term. Finally, and less significantly, conservative social thinking was on the rise in east-central Europe, sponsored primarily by Christian Democratic right parties who wanted to emphasize church and family in state social support (Kulczycki 1995).

Since the political backing (by the Communist Party and trade unions) for socialist welfare states had fallen apart dramatically in 1989, small groups of reformers occupying strategic places in the executive branch could have great influence on the course of social policy early in the transition (Balcerowicz 1995). However, the fluidity of transition politics and the relatively low priority of welfare state reform made the disposition of these power resources somewhat haphazard. When reformers did get into positions of power, they often chose to do things on purely ideological grounds that were not necessarily well supported by careful planning or structural preconditions. This autonomy of small groups of reformers in a fluid political situation, armed with new ideas, challenged by a host of problems, and not so constrained by past legacies, gave the early years of post-Communist social policy reform a chaotic character. It meant that countries faced with identical problems would choose to address them in very different ways, depending on the specific policy discourse and opportunities of small expert groups.

The Global Politics of Attention

International organizations, economists, and consultants provided another major source of policy ideas after 1989. However, the international policy community was not primarily focused on social policy in the early transition years (Deacon 1997; Ringold 1999; Kapstein and Milanovic 2000). The transition years can be divided into two periods of international attention to social policy transformation: a first period from 1989 to 1995, in which international attention to this issue domain was low, and a second period, starting in 1995, when social policy moved to the top of the international agenda (Sachs 1995; World Bank 1996c). At that time, a variety of international organizations began to implement and further develop a social policy agenda that pushed east-central European countries more consistently toward a single model of welfare state reform. This influence often came through the international organizations' vastly superior capacity for policy development and argumentation, as well as their control over critical financial resources.

During the early years of transition, international actors paid little attention to social policy in the post-Communist states. Setting up unemployment systems was the only area of priority concern (Blanchard et al. 1991), but otherwise neoliberal policy makers focused on the stabilization, liberalization, and privatization policies that were at the heart of their strategy. All this began to change in the middle of the 1990s for a number of reasons. First was the "return of the left" that demonstrated frustration with neoliberal reform agendas, and popular willingness to support parties, even discredited former Communist ones, that promoted a more social vision of economic change (Sachs 1995; Cook and Orenstein 1999). Second was a widespread recognition that poverty had increased dramatically in central and Eastern Europe during the early transition years. Early on, prominent economists disputed this fact (Sachs 1995), arguing that poverty had not been measured properly, and that living standards had not fallen at all. But gradually, as evidence piled up, this position became impossible to maintain, and a widespread consensus developed during the middle of the 1990s that the transition had been accompanied by massive increases in poverty (Milanovic 1998; Gomulka 1998), even in relatively successful east-central European countries. Third, neoliberal economists began to realize that their lack of attention to social policy matters in the early stage of transition had not caused social welfare states in the east to wither away, but rather to grow dramatically in some cases, like Poland. Neoliberal economists began to view this welfare state expansion as a major impediment to growth—and cutting spending a top policy priority (Sachs 1995). Fourth, major international organizations, particularly the World Bank, shifted their global policy priorities toward issues of poverty, which had not been a primary focus before (World Bank 2000). The EU increased its attention to the accession process at the same time, bringing to the table its greater concern with social issues in transition. All of these international trends encouraged greater attention to issues of poverty and social policy reform in central and Eastern Europe. In the mid-1990s, social policy transformation became the subject of major international conferences and debate, and World Bank social sector lending to the post-Communist countries took off in 1996, rising from around five hundred million dollars to two billion dollars in just two years, as shown in figure 6.3 (World Bank 2000).

Increased global attention had a material effect on post-Communist welfare state transformation, for it led to the development of a more consistent global agenda, and placed greater homogenizing pressures on east-central European welfare states. This emerging global social policy for the region (Deacon 1997) emphasized targeting of social assistance, partial privatization of pension systems, and systemic reforms in health and education. While each of the major international organizations had different emphases, and even conflicting programs in some areas, the World Bank tended to dominate the agenda, coordinating with the EU on issues of preparation for accession. Indeed, the World Bank conducted major re-

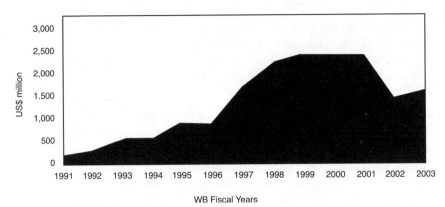

Fig. 6.3. Social protection World Bank Europe/Central Asia lending portfolio

views of east-central European countries' economic policies in preparation for accession that included extensive analysis of social welfare systems and state administration in addition to macroeconomic policy, financial sector regulation, and other economic policy areas that were central to the early transition agenda. As a result, east-central European countries found themselves part of a social policy discourse that primarily included their governments, the EU, and the World Bank, with the latter doing much to set the agenda for these discussions. It is notable that both Hungary and the Czech Republic made efforts to target their more diffuse social assistance systems in 1995–1996, while Hungary and Poland implemented radical pension reforms in 1998–1999. Both of these events, and others, show the strong agenda-setting influence of the World Bank (Müller 1999; Orenstein 2000).

Country Studies

Domestic and international pressures and agendas combined to produce welfare state transformation in east-central Europe after 1989. In the early period, where international attention to social policy matters was low, domestic policy elites had more room to maneuver. Starting in the mid-1990s, though, social policy was increasingly dominated by an international agenda set largely by a World Bank that was cognizant and supportive of east-central European countries' EU membership preparations. In order to illustrate these trends, we use examples of decision making on the transformation of pension systems in the three largest east-central European countries, Hungary, the Czech Republic, and Poland. We show that this decision making was driven by a desperate search for solutions to overwhelming social policy problems, that small elite groups often had considerable leeway in restructuring welfare state policy in the early period of reform and that these early choices had strong path dependencies. These case studies show that east-central European countries have made a range of adjustment choices that reflect distinct paths of decision making in transition, but that there is also increasing evidence of similar overall trends that are driven by the global politics of attention.

Poland

Poland experienced a dramatic pension crisis after 1989, with spending increasing at a much higher rate than in most east-central European countries. Spending on pensions almost doubled from 8.7 percent to 15.8 percent of GDP between 1990 and 1994, creating serious problems for the government budget. To make up a growing social insurance fund deficit, the government had to make substantial subsidies to the two pension funds (employees and farmers), amounting to 3.9 percent of GDP in 1996 (Cain and Surdej 1999, 150).

Pension spending shot up in Poland during the early years of transition mainly because the government took a set of decisions to use the pension system as a buffer for unemployment (ibid. 1999, 167); this was not well thought out. Polish policy makers loosened eligibility requirements for pensions and guaranteed their levels relative to the average wage. As a result, between 1990 and 1994 the "system dependency ratio," which measures the number of workers per pensioner, declined in Poland from 2.49 to 1.75 (ibid. 1999, 150). Meanwhile, the "replacement ratio," which measures the size of the average pension as a percent of the average wage, increased from 57 to 66 percent over the same period (World Bank 2000, 75). Although all the post-Communist east-central European countries faced similar issues of how to deal with rising unemployment and the increasing need for social protection, Poland was the only country to dramatically loosen eligibility requirements in this way while increasing the value of pensions as a proportion of the average wage.

Why did Polish governments react in this way? Cain and Surdej (1999) point to the transitional policies of Solidarity governments between 1989 and 1993. The first Polish reform governments, under finance minister Leszek Balcerowicz and labor minister Jacek Kuron, extended generous early retirement benefits to ease the transition out of the labor force for older workers, and to provide social protection for existing pensioners. These compensation measures were directed toward compensating people for the collapse of the Communist system and the new stresses of market competition, including exposure to foreign trade and investment. Despite the worthy goals of labor minister Kuron, the fiscal laxity of his pension policies is striking, given that this was completely at odds with Solidarity government policy in other areas. At the same time, finance minister Balcerowicz launched a major "shock therapy" restructuring of the Polish economy, which included measures to cut public sector deficits and civil service pay. Why would the same government make decisions to dramatically expand subsidies and guarantees for pensioners?

Such behavior can only be explained with reference to the lack of attention the finance ministry and leading reformers paid to the social sector under neoliberal adjustment plans. Labor minister Kuron provides ample evidence in his 1991 book, *Moja Zupa,* to suggest that he did not understand the Polish social system well when he was appointed labor minister and made a number of decisions, including on pension eligibility, that he later regretted. For instance, one decision extended pension benefits to veterans of the Polish home army and other independent fighting units during the Second World War who resisted the Nazi and Soviet occupations. An important political gesture, this extension of pension benefits, however, raised serious administrative problems since the records, if any, of these groups had mostly disappeared over the years (Kuron 1991). The Ministry of Labor was deluged with requests from pensioners accompanied by little documentation. Pensions were also extended to victims of layoffs, with no provisions for withdrawing them when people found new work. As a result, many middle-aged people claimed benefits and continued to work. Poland's eligibility problem ballooned between 1989 and 1992, when a major spike in the number of people collecting pensions occurred. Later governments restricted eligibility, again suggesting that the increase had been a mistake. When Balcerowicz later wrote that failure to reform the social security system had been the major error of the reform governments, he explained that reformers had simply been unable to deal appropriately with all issues confronting them because of lack of time and problem overload (Balcerowicz 1995).

The Polish case therefore offers clear evidence connecting the expansion of pension spending to the lack of attention to social sector restructuring in early neoliberal programs. Local officials' lack of attention to social sector reform reflected priorities articulated by major Western international organizations and their consultants during the first period of transition. In this sense, local and global officials agreed about the low priority of social policy making in the overall transition program. Therefore, officials like Kuron with little economics, public administration, or social insurance training had great latitude to make policy decisions that did not support or even contradicted major principles of the economic reform that was taking place in the chaotic environment of 1989–1992. Starting in 1995, as international attention was drawn to the problems of social sector reform in east-central Europe, Polish governments began to seriously confront reform of the pension system. The World Bank sent its own experts to help establish a pension reform team within the Polish government. Succeeding governments were successful in implementing major pension reform legislation in 1997 and 1998 that is expected to reduce government spending and replacement rates over the long term (Müller 1999; Orenstein 2000). This reform was conducted with extensive World Bank involvement, financing, and advice, and implemented key elements of a "new pension orthodoxy" (Müller 1999) promoted by the World Bank. Poland, therefore, offers a clear example of unusual deviation during the early adjustment period, taking a path in pension spending far more exaggerated than its neighbors, while later conforming to World Bank policy advice.

Czech Republic

Pension developments unfolded in the Czech Republic in an even more distinctive way. Early Czechoslovak governments paid a relatively high degree of attention to reforming the social system from the early days of transition. This is because early Czechoslovak governments were not completely dominated by neoliberals, but rather by a broad coalition of neoliberals and social democrats (including former Communists on both sides) that implemented a "social-liberal" strategy for transformation (Orenstein 2001). Czechoslovak reformers passed a social reform program, drafted by Social Democrats, at the same time as a radical neoliberal economic reform program in late 1990. The social program included a variety of structural measures designed to maintain the fiscal health of the system during transition. Since international organizations were at the time paying very little attention to social policy reform, Czechoslovak policy makers were left to their own devices. Therefore, as in Poland, small groups of domestic policy makers had extraordinary influence on shaping the future development of the Czech pension system. Under the initiative of a team of experts at the Ministry of Labor, including Igor Tomes, who later became a World Bank consultant, early Czechoslovak governments got rid of many special pension benefits enjoyed by numerous and well-organized groups, like miners. They did this in part through direct negotiation, making a variety of side payments and guarantees to ensure compliance. One was the establishment of a system of private, optional pension funds that would allow for additional funded pensions for different occupational groups. Miners were among the first to found such a fund. The Czech Republic adjusted to the increased burden on its pension system by steadily reducing the proportion of pensions to the average wage, from 64 percent in 1989 to 52 percent in 1992 and 44 percent in 1994. The neoliberal government of Prime Minister Vaclav Klaus also passed legislation gradually increasing the pension age (Müller 1999, 136–37).

The radical differences in the domestic adjustment strategies implemented in the Czech Republic and Poland reflected very different approaches to the problems of transition among small groups of policy makers located mainly in Czech and Polish Ministries of Labor between 1989 and 1992. International influence on these decisions was very limited, as was the influence of top neoliberal policy makers in government at the time. As a low-priority area, social policy reform was delegated in both countries to the Ministry of Labor (and Ministries of Social Affairs or Social Policy), and developments took place that were seemingly out of sight and out of line with neoliberal government economic policies in other areas. For instance, interviews with top policy makers suggest that finance minister Vaclav Klaus seriously opposed the overall social policy of the early Czechoslovak governments and tried to alter it when he became prime minister in 1993 (Orenstein 2001).

However, these initial social policy strategies shaped the paths for future developments. Because the Czech Republic managed to transform its pension system without creating a high degree of debt or fiscal imbalance, it did not come under serious international pressure to adopt a World Bank model of reform after 1995 (Müller 1999). Although Poland and Hungary engaged in almost simultaneous and similar reform efforts in 1997–1998, the Czech Republic has so far been unaffected by this trend, though several domestic analysts have begun to promote a fully funded system based on individual accounts (Jelinek and Schneider 1999).

Hungary

Developments in Hungary took a rather different direction in the first period of transformation. Hungary's pension system was experiencing increasing problems and fiscal imbalance already during the 1980s (Müller 1999), but the first democratic governments were not ready to do much about it. Still, their adjustment strategy differed both from Poland's with its dramatic spending expansion, and from the Czech Republic's, which managed to hold the line by cutting benefit levels. Hungary took a middle path, slightly reducing benefit levels through incomplete indexation, while the pension system dependency ratio increased. In Hungary, the average pension/average wage ratio declined from 65 percent in 1990 to 61 percent in 1994, while the system dependency ratio increased sharply. Increasing reliance on pensions forced the system into a deep deficit, supported out of Hungary's increasing budget deficit, which reached 7 percent of GDP in 1994 (Cook and Orenstein 1999).

In 1995, Hungary adopted a neoliberal reform program under finance minister Lajos Bokros that, among other things, cut family benefits and targeted them. Bokros also initiated a process of pension reform planning that bore fruit in subsequent years, after he was forced from office. In 1996 and 1997, Hungary planned and implemented a major pension reform that was remarkably similar in design to that implemented a year or so later in Poland (Müller 1999; Orenstein 2000). As in Poland, the Hungarian system partially replaced the state-run pay-as-you-go system with a mandatory, private system based on fully funded individual accounts managed by private pension investment funds. There were a few notable differences between the two programs. Hungary diverted a slightly smaller share of payroll tax to the new private system than Poland, and the regulatory structure for the private funds was somewhat different. Most importantly, Poland simultaneously conducted a complete reform of its state system, while Hungary only changed it in parts. But both systems were clearly cut of the same cloth, and both were advised and supported by the social protection division of the World Bank.

Conclusions

East-central European welfare states have generally grown as a percent of GDP since their entry into the global economy. This contrasts sharply with the experience of most former Soviet Union countries, where social spending as a percentage of GDP has stagnated or even declined, and where transitional recessions were both deeper and longer (see figs. 6.1 and 6.2). Broadly speaking, east-central European countries' trend toward higher social spending is underpinned by their privileged position as potential EU members, and the resulting regional politics of EU accession. Prospects of EU membership have helped to foster successful trade integration and foreign direct investment, increasing the ability of east-central European countries to pay for continued welfare state guarantees. At the same time, EU prospects encouraged more representative democracy, greater openness to interest group pressure, and greater political and administrative commitment to social welfare norms than in most former Soviet states. Of course, east-central Europe's better prospects of EU membership were determined not only by external, but also internal factors, particularly their greater similarity and proximity to core EU member states in politics, economics, and culture. However, EU membership was not a natural phenomenon, but a state project that gave overall direction to the east-central European transitions (Orenstein 2001). It was a choice that demanded a great deal of the prospective member countries, including placement of certain parameters on their social policy transformations.

At the individual country level, the picture is far more complex. Social policy was dominated by small, domestic, elite groups located in strategic executive positions during the early transition years. Overwhelmed by numerous problems of transition, the domestic politics of decision making was often driven by a rapid search for solutions that resulted in idiosyncratic policies being adopted. When international organizations, particularly the World Bank and the EU, began to pay greater attention to social policy transformation in east-central Europe, and focus their enormous policy resources in this area, a more consistent policy agenda began to emerge across the region, reflecting the global politics of attention. The resulting social policy transformations bear the marks of both periods, with the effects of early decisions persisting as pressure from a global social policy agenda grows.

At the outset of transition, likely paths of welfare state development were unclear. It was possible that the former socialist welfare states would contract because these relatively weak economies could not sustain generous spending. But it was also plausible that they might grow in order to buffer people from the impact of system transformation. Indeed, analysts frequently predicted intense conflict between populations with high welfare state expectations and states with insufficient means. However, the outcomes of post-Communist welfare state adjustment turned out to be less homogeneous than either of these predictions suggested. Former Soviet welfare states declined along with the collapse of Soviet state structures generally, while east-central European countries found themselves in a corner of this globalizing world that supported continued welfare state commitment and provided the means to finance it through increased trade, investment, and growth. Globalization thus appears to have very different effects on welfare states, depending on their geopolitical position and the interplay between their domestic politics of decision making and the global politics of attention.

7

Globalization and the Politics of Welfare State Reform in Russia

LINDA J. COOK

The present volume has at its core two competing theses about the impacts of globalization on social welfare. The first claims that integration of established welfare states into global economic and policy networks leads to retrenchment. According to this "efficiency thesis," stronger political economies lose control over welfare expenditures to the competitive pressures of international trade and financial flows, weaker ones to IMF conditionalities and creditors' dictates as well. At the same time, international financial institutions (IFIs) promote welfare state restructuring according to a liberal paradigm of minimal public provision, targeting, and privatization that increasingly influences the principles and substance of national welfare policies. The efficiency thesis stresses the growing limits of states' policy autonomy and their weak capacity to resist the downward pressures of globalization on social provision.

The alternative thesis argues that economic openness need not force down social spending, and may in fact lead to compensatory increases in social provision for globalization's losers (Garrett, this volume). More important for the present analysis, it holds that domestic political actors continue to have considerable influence over the size and shape of social provision. The argument is that welfare policies build strong constituencies that make retrenchment politically difficult. The weight of those constituencies in domestic political constellations affects states' responses to globalizing pressures. In northern European and some Latin American cases, as previous chapters have shown, politically dominant defenders of established welfare states have maintained high levels of public provision and

153

universalism despite pressures for retrenchment and restructuring (Stephens, Huber, this volume). In sum, according to this thesis, politics stands as a counterweight to globalization.

Russia presents a very interesting case for this debate. The Russian Federation inherited from the Soviet Union a broad (though low) provision, universalist welfare state. When the Soviet-era economy collapsed, part of the revenue base of that welfare state collapsed with it. The existing levels of subsidies and benefits became unsustainable. In the ensuing decade Russia became progressively integrated into the world economy and concluded multiple conditional agreements with the IMF. Several years of nearly continuous economic contraction ended in the 1998 financial crisis, currency devaluation, and temporary default. Although the economy has revived and resumed growth, it is heavily dependent on international energy markets, and debt remains high. In sum, economic pressures to cut government expenditures have been strong, and real spending on social programs has fallen at least in line with the decline in GDP (OECD 2001). At the same time, the World Bank and other international organizations have strongly promoted restructuring of the old welfare state according to the liberal model.

On the other hand, past commitments and long-established entitlements had created large constituencies for social provision, making retrenchment unpopular and politically difficult even for Russia's powerful and insulated executive. Moreover, despite the weaknesses of Russian democracy and civil society, these constituencies were somewhat empowered by a domestic political constellation in which the Communist-led left dominated the legislature (Duma) in the latter half of the 1990s. Programmatically committed to defense of universalism and established entitlements, the Left opposed the liberal restructuring efforts of the executive and the IFIs, frequently producing stalemate on social policy. Even when liberalizing efforts succeeded, the Russian state often lacked the administrative capacity or political authority to implement them, and they became mired in institutional and attitudinal residues of the old welfare state. In sum, domestic political constellations and interests resisted pressures to scale back the state's obligations. They could not, however, prevent the fall in social expenditures that followed the decline in GDP. After a decade of declining real social spending with little structural reform, the Russian welfare state most resembled an impoverished and ineffective universalism.

Shifts in the legislature and the executive branch in 1999–2000 broke the stalemate, and under Putin the liberal restructuring program has progressed steadily. A key factor here is the change in the composition and political orientation of the legislature. The Communists lost their dominant position in the 1999 elections and have since been weakened by internal divisions and defections. Pro-government parties were strengthened and the legislature began to produce a pro-government majority on most social, as well as other, issues. The liberal model still faces obstacles in Russia: the old welfare system remains institutionally embedded, and the Russian state needs to build stronger administrative and regulatory capacities in the social sector. Still, we can clearly see the key role of domestic politics in shaping the Russian welfare state, in vetoing or enabling the project of liberal restructuring.

The first part of this chapter will review developments in the Russian welfare state over the past decade as well as Russia's integration into the international economy. The second part will present case studies of liberal restructuring efforts in three policy areas, focusing on the roles of IFIs and shifting domestic political constellations. Globalization will, as elsewhere in this volume, be defined as:

(1) expanding international trade in goods and services,
(2) expanding international capital flows,
(3) increasing globalization of production through transnational corporations and global commodity chains,
(4) a growing role of international organizations such as the World Bank and IMF,
(5) a greater transnational flow of ideas.

The conclusion will assess the impact of globalization on Russia's welfare state and draw comparisons with other cases in the study.

The Soviet System of Social Protection

The Soviet-era welfare state was nearly universal, providing a broad range of benefits, though generally at quite low absolute levels, to most of the population. These included consumer and housing subsidies, basic health care, maternity and child benefits, pensions, and education. In 1991, for example, just before the onset of economic reform, the state owned nearly 80 percent of urban housing and paid most of the costs of building and maintenance. Almost 25 percent of the population received pensions, many of them several years below the normal pension age for industrial societies (Goskomstat 1998b, 146). Education was free to the university level, maternity leaves were guaranteed, and child benefits universal. Many benefits were employment-linked or work-based, but with the nearly full-employment economy and high levels of female labor force participation, comparatively few were excluded.

This system's coverage was by no means adequate or equitable. Shortages were endemic, the real value of some benefits eroded over time, and many programs were bureaucratic and rigid in design. Large cities and scientific-military and academic centers had far more and better services than average, while rural areas had the worst. Privileged categories of industrial workers received preferential treatment, and access to benefits was manipulated to differentiate and control workers. Special facilities were available to political and military elites, and separate, categorical benefits (or "privileges") were provided to civil servants, war veterans, and others. In sum, the system combined egalitarian and universalist features with elements of differentiation and privilege more characteristic of the conservative, corporatist welfare state tradition (Deacon 1997). As poverty was not recognized in the Soviet period the system included almost no need-based benefits. It provided no guaranteed income or income floor, nor did it make provisions for unemployment.[1]

This welfare state derived from a combination of socialist ideology, the imperatives of industrial modernization under conditions of state monopoly, and a social contract that helped legitimate Soviet authoritarianism. Beginning in the 1930s the state provided housing, education, and basic health care as part of an effort to build a stable and skilled industrial labor force from a largely rural society. During the 1950s Khrushchev expanded social provision in order to raise living standards and gain greater acceptance from the population. Maternity and child benefits were designed to keep women working in the labor-devouring Soviet economy, and other benefits were added to secure loyalty or reward service. Underlying this process was a basic premise that, rather than prosperity or freedom, the regime owed its people social security. The resulting welfare state, inherited by the Russian Federation when it became independent in 1991, was highly institutionalized, embedded in legislation and popular expectations, and already under economic stress (Cook 1993).

The 1990s: Social Protection under Severe Stress

In 1990 the Russian economy began a period of decline that lasted nearly a decade. Overall GDP fell by some 40 percent, a drop greater than that suffered by most Western economies in the 1930s depression. The economy also underwent a major transformation, encapsulated in the policies of liberalization, privatization, and stabilization that were adopted by the Russian government in late 1991 and pursued, however inconsistently, over the decade. Real public social expenditures fell sharply as a result of the fall in GDP, with expenditures stabilizing around 16–17 percent of the declining GDP in the mid-1990s (see table 7.1). Some consumer subsidies were eliminated as part of the January 1992 price liberalization, a move that increased the costs of food and other necessities by multiples and led to hyperinflation.

In other areas, available funds could not keep up with mandated entitlements. From 1994 social assistance benefits were increasingly in arrears because of both insufficient funds and the collapse of delivery mechanisms (World Bank 1999a).

Table 7.1 Public Social Expenditures as a Percent of GDP

	1994	1995	1996	1997	1998	1999 (estimate)
Total social spending:	17.9	15.1	16.2	17.3	16.4	12.6
Pensions, total	5.9	5.3	5.5	6.5	5.7[a]	5.0
Social insurance	1.2	1.0	0.9	1.1	1.2[b]	0.8
Employment fund	0.4	0.3	0.3	0.3	0.3[b]	0.2
Health, total	4.1	3.4	2.5	3.5	3.1	2.4
Education, total	4.4	3.4	3.7	4.2	3.6	2.7

Sources: OECD 2001, 37.

Note: [a]Goskomstat 1997, 194; 2001, 169; [b]IMF 2001, 22.

Numbers do not add to total spending because of a residual category and other adjustments. Housing subsidies, regarded as producer subsidies, are shown separately.

By 1995 there were constant and months-long delays in payment of child grants, and in many regions these and other benefits were simply no longer provided. Salaries of teachers and medical personnel fell to poverty levels and their work conditions deteriorated, leading to sporadic demonstrations and strikes that temporarily closed schools and clinics in many regions. Because these services were largely funded from local budgets the effects were highly uneven across regions, with those hardest hit by the economic decline suffering most.

Social provision by enterprises was the second major piece of the inherited welfare state. In the Communist period enterprises often directly provided housing, utility networks, health care, child care, and recreational facilities to their employees, and in some company towns to the surrounding community.[2] After privatization and the withdrawal of many government subsidies in the early 1990s, enterprises faced intense financial pressures to cut social expenditures. Moreover, government policy demanded that they shed social assets in order to become competitive. Under these dual pressures managements divested infrastructure to municipalities and privatized or terminated many social services. Estimated at 2–4 percent of GDP in the early 1990s, enterprise social expenditures were cut to less than half that amount by the mid-1990s (World Bank 1996c; OECD 1995). While the specifics varied from case to case, virtually all employers scaled back provision (OECD 1996; Vinogradova 1999).

A third example of fallout from the inherited welfare state in Russia was the substantial portion of social spending that came from four extrabudgetary funds (EBFs), in which money was collected for social, medical, unemployment insurance, and pensions (by far the largest of the four). Employers paid almost the entire contribution to the funds in the form of high payroll taxes, and the collapse of production damaged the fiscal base of these funds. The labor force shrank by 16 percent between 1990 and 1998, real wages declined by 40 percent, and wage arrears mounted. Enterprises began to rely on barter transactions and illegal cash payments to avoid taxation; employment in the informal economy, which could not be taxed, grew rapidly. The IMF estimates that revenues of the funds declined from 11 percent of GDP in 1992 to 8.4 percent in 1998, with many corporate entities behind in payments (IMF 1999, 64). As a result pension arrears mounted from mid-decade, and by its end payments had fallen below the subsistence minimum. The employment fund, which stagnated throughout the period (see table 7.1), did little for the growing ranks of jobless; benefits stood below 20 percent of the subsistence level, blocks to eligibility were high, reductions and delays in payments frequent, active labor market policies unaffordable.

In sum, by the mid-1990s the inherited social welfare system was deteriorating and official benefit programs provided little relief to the substantial numbers of new poor and unemployed in the transition economy. According to official statistics, one-quarter to one-third of the population lived in poverty during the 1990s. Unemployment grew more modestly, rising to a peak of over 13 percent in 1999 (*Russian Economic Trends*, 2002, April 15, 2). Substantial numbers of additional workers stayed at their jobs for the remaining benefits despite sporadic work and pay, constituting the "hidden unemployed" who were not included in the data.

Inequality also grew rapidly, moving Russia from a fairly egalitarian society to one with high levels of income inequality, well exceeding those in the transitional Eastern Europe states (see table 7.2). Inequality has remained high well into the recovery period.

The problems of the Russian welfare state were universally recognized, but opinions diverged as to the solutions. Domestic and international reformers pointed out that social expenditures were relatively well maintained as a percent of GDP, and some argued that spending was sufficient, even excessive, but badly misallocated by the inherited subsidy and entitlement programs (Aslund 2002). These liberal reformers pressed for cuts in the old system that would free funds for more effective poverty relief and other need-based allocations. Opponents of liberalization argued that much of the population was already under financial stress and could not absorb further cuts, and they generally resisted reductions in entitlements or in the state's obligations. We will return to the politics of reform after considering the economic aspects of Russia's globalization.

Table 7.2 Gini Coefficient for Russian Federation, with Comparisons
to Poland and Hungary (Income per Capita)

	1987–1988	*1993–1995*
Russia	24	39
Poland	26	28
Hungary	21	23

Source: World Bank 1999a.

The Impacts of Global Economic Integration and Policy Interventions on Russian Social Policy

To what extent was globalization responsible for deteriorating social provision in Russia during the 1990s? The major decline in Russia's real welfare expenditures was not caused by integration into the international economy, as this is usually conceived in the globalization literature. The biggest factor was the fall in GDP as the Soviet economy and COMECON (Council for Mutual Economic Assistance) trade network collapsed in 1991. Social spending generally fell in line with the GDP decline, which was most severe in 1992–1994; later decline, which paralleled Russia's growing global economic links, was much more gradual and uneven (see table 7.3).

The collapse itself was in large part the unintended result of internal decisions. In the mid-1980s the Gorbachev leadership initiated a series of unsuccessful reforms. These reforms both destabilized the Soviet economy and led to the breakup of the political empire and the collapse of the Soviet-dominated trade block, precipitating Russia's steep economic decline. The Soviet economy was not deeply integrated into global markets, had very little foreign investment, and was a protected system that had exhausted its potential for growth. In an economic sense, the causes of the collapse were largely endogenous.

But the international economy was implicated in at least three respects. First, the Soviet state was deeply invested in political, military, and technological competition with the United States. Rapid change in international technologies—changes that placed Russia behind not only the United States and Europe but developing East Asian states—highlighted the inefficiencies and barriers to innovation in the Soviet economy and shocked the leadership into reforms. Second, the

Table 7.3 Selected Economic Data for the Russian Federation, 1991–2001

	Real GDP (annual % change)	Exports ($USD bn)	Imports ($USD bn)	FDI (net $USD bn)	Portfolio invest (net $US bn)
1991	−5.4	50.9	44.4		
1992	−19.4	53.6	43	0.7	
1993	−10.4	58.3	44.2	1.2	0
1994	−11.6	67.8	48.5	0.64	0
1995	−4.2	82.7	64	2.02	2
1996	−3.4	90.6	72.8	2.48	4
1997	0.9	89	77.4	6.63	46
1998	−4.5	74.8	56.8	2.76	9
1999	5.4	73	42	2.2	−1
2000	9.0	106	45	3	−1
2001	5.0	102	53		

Sources: IMF, *World Economic Outlook 2000*; *World Economic Outlook 2002*; accessed at www.imf.org; *Russian Economic Trends 4* (2002) (table D5); portfolio invest data from Slay 2002, 35.

economies of the largest East European states were more heavily integrated into the global economy than the Soviet states, and Poland's failed integration strategy and deep debt in particular contributed to the crisis and collapse. Third, the sector of the Soviet economy most involved in international trade was energy, and the high oil prices of the 1970s had led to a large expansion of exports and a commensurate increase in hard-currency revenues, some of which were used to fund consumer imports and subsidies. The fall of world energy prices in the 1980s, combined with inefficiencies in the domestic energy sector, contributed to the decline of welfare in the last Soviet period (Aven 1994; Gustafson 1989).

The secondary cause of declining social welfare in Russia was the liberalization-privatization-stabilization model of economic reform that the Yeltsin leadership initiated in early 1992. This model was not directly imposed on Russia by creditors and stabilization agreements in the way that Huber describes for Latin America. When the Russian government began "shock therapy" by slashing consumer subsidies it was not under direct agreement with the IMF, nor did it face a balance of payments crisis. Russian technocrats were not heavily integrated into global educational and career circuits; indeed, Western economists wondered openly whether many of their Russian colleagues really understood how markets worked. But Russia did confront mounting foreign debt, a large budget deficit, and most importantly, sharply contracting production that threatened serious food shortages and other crises in domestic markets, problems that had to be addressed (Aslund 1995).

The Russian leadership turned initially to Western advisers because these advisers were purveyors of Western models that carried prestige and the promise of economic revitalization. Russia's leaders had no more internal solutions; the Soviet economic model, then Gorbachev's efforts to reform it, had failed. By contrast, market models were delivering economic growth in the United States, Europe, and even more dramatically in East Asia. Ideas carried to Moscow by Harvard's Sachs, the IMF's Camdessus, and others had influence in part because of their demonstrated effectiveness. But abstract models cannot be so readily separated from global economic pressures. The G-7 had made it clear that Russia had to adopt an orthodox stabilization program if it wanted debt restructuring (Gould-Davies and Woods 1999). Governmental reformers believed that they needed IMF credits to revive their economy, and the Fund's conditions were well understood. The reality is nicely captured by Greskovits: "It is simplistic to believe that 'somebody' imposed these programs from abroad. It is also simplistic . . . to assert that a government 'freely' elected a certain program that was 'later' approved by the IMF. What we are really facing is a convergence of determinations" (quoted in Greskovits 1998, 60).

Russia's leaders were, at least at the outset, well positioned politically to transform their economic system and impose the necessary social costs. In late 1991

Yeltsin enjoyed a strong popular mandate as the first elected president of the newly independent Russian state. He had tremendous personal authority, and the legislature had granted him broad decree powers. The fledgling Russian democracy had few effective accountability mechanisms. Yeltsin put in place a highly insulated reform team, led by Yegor Gaidar, that mapped out its economic program in consultation with international advisers, much like similar teams in Eastern Europe (Greskovits 1998). Gaidar knew that his policies would be unpopular, and that he had a narrow window to make them a fait accompli. Soon those models were subject to internal political bargaining, conflict, and corruption from which a narrow stratum gained while much of the population lost. Moreover, Russia did conclude formal agreements with IFIs and opened itself to trade and capital markets, thus becoming more vulnerable to pressures from the global economy.

Integrating into the International Economy

From the early 1990s Russia progressively liberalized its trade regime, lowering tariff barriers and export restrictions sufficiently to gain the IMF's second most positive ranking on trade openness (IMF 1999). Foreign trade expanded forcefully, with imports and exports increasing from about 10 percent of GDP at the end of the Soviet period to 30–40 percent in the mid-1990s. Russia has maintained a positive trade balance, with the trade surplus eroding in the mid-1990s and increasing again after 1998. Imports consist mainly of food and machinery; textiles and other consumer goods have also been imported as unregistered "shuttle" trade. Estimated at one-quarter to one-third of total imports in the mid-1990s, the shuttle trade mainly brought in goods from low-wage bordering countries such as China and Turkey, contributing to the recession in the female-dominated textile and related consumer industries and the flow of labor into the informal trading sector (IMF 1999, 101; OECD 1997, 67). Imports from high-wage Western countries also competed effectively on quality grounds with Russian-made products.

Exports are heavily dominated by energy, other raw materials, and semi-finished goods, with primary products comprising more than 75 percent of the total in 1997–1998 and energy the largest part (IMF 1999, 99; OECD 1997, 65). The share of finished and especially high value-added products has dropped, producing a trade composition much more like the Latin American model than the European. Most Russian finished goods are too poor in quality to compete in international markets, though exports have also been restricted by antidumping laws against Russian products in Europe and pressure to limit arms sales, one of the few high-tech areas in which Russia has some advantage. Russia has, according to one commentator, "lost its chance to at least retain the place of the Soviet Union in the international division of labor" (Shishkov 1996), though this was admittedly in the protected COMECON market. More to the point here, heavy reliance on energy and raw materials for export earnings made Russia highly vulnerable to the sharp decline in world demand for these products that began in mid-1997.

Russia's opening to international capital markets had harshly negative effects in the 1990s. Its central feature was large-scale capital flight, estimated by the Russian Central Bank at well over ten billion dollars annually on average for 1994–1998 (IMF 1999, 106). Russia was a net exporter of capital throughout this period, starving most sectors of fixed investment. Foreign direct investment (FDI) remained very low, estimated at one to three billion dollars annually through the mid-1990s, much lower per capita than in the East European transition economies. Foreign direct investment was invested mainly in the food processing and retail trade sectors of a few major cities, with more than half concentrated in Moscow, and in oil extraction (Westin 1999). The major inflows of foreign capital came to Russia in the form of short-term portfolio investment, mainly in government securities (GKOs and Eurobonds) (see table 7.3). Attracted by high interest rates, portfolio investment took off spectacularly in late 1996 and increased to $46 billion in 1997, producing a rapid rise in federal debt and overvaluation of the ruble. Then declining investor confidence in emerging markets, triggered by the Asian financial crisis, led to massive capital outflows that ever-higher interest rates failed to stem. In spring 1998 debt service rose to 40 percent of federal expenditures, and in August the Russian government defaulted and sharply devalued its currency (OECD 2000, 41).

Because the stabilization program imposed costs and failed to bring economic recovery it was challenged from many quarters. After months of conflict Yeltsin used force to dissolve the legislature in fall 1993, partly because of conflicts over the budget deficit and privatization policies. The December 1993 Duma elections produced a nationalist and Communist backlash against policies that, the Left charged, were turning Russia into a "raw material appendage" of the West. Public opinion surveys showed broad distrust of Western advice and its motives. The reformers reacted by buying the support of the country's most powerful economic elites with insider privatization of industry, loans-for-shares programs, access to lucrative export licenses, high interest rates, and tolerance of large-scale capital flight and tax evasion (Shleifer and Treisman 2000). The reform, in other words, was co-opted and corrupted. A narrow stratum of wealthy and politically influential individuals emerged, the primary beneficiaries of the failed policies. Their enrichment is reflected in the increase in inequality (see table 7.2) that further undermined both popular welfare and the credibility of the reform program.

The 1998 financial crisis highlights the negative impacts of global economic integration for the Russian welfare state. Integration made Russia vulnerable to shifts and shocks in the international economy, and access to financial markets enabled it to take on high official debt. When export revenues declined and investors withdrew, the ensuing financial crisis took a heavy toll on welfare. Real budgetary expenditures on social policy declined at every level of government (OECD 2000, 68). Inflation flared briefly, poverty increased markedly, unemployment and pension arrears rose to their highest points in the transition period, and social distress increased measurably for a large part of the population.

The financial crisis initially increased Russia's dependence on IFIs. Russia's debt to multilateral creditors grew from $5.4 billion in 1994 to over $26 billion in 1998 (IMF 1999). The IMF, far and away the largest contributor, lent increasing amounts of money on conditions of fiscal stabilization. It should be said that Russia never met these conditions fully; budget deficits ran well in excess of IMF guidelines, many prices remained subsidized, and progressive demonetization of the economy frustrated monitoring efforts. Tranches were regularly withheld, but in the end usually disbursed. There is evidence that Russia was given special treatment, that the United States pressured the Fund to relax conditionality and dispense money at key points in order to effect political outcomes, in particular to aid the 1996 re-election of Yeltsin, and to try to avert the financial collapse of a nuclear power in 1998 (Gould-Davies and Woods 1999).[3] At the same time, IMF conditions contributed to pressures for price liberalization and budget austerity. In the end, the failed stabilization effort left Russia with billions of dollars of debt to the Fund.

The year 1998 also precipitated a temporary crisis in Russia's long-term foreign-currency debt. After the Soviet collapse, the Russian Federation took on the accumulated debt of the failed state. Restructuring agreements with the London and Paris clubs in 1996–1997 greatly increased the maturity of its foreign debt, so Russia had a modest debt servicing burden and was regularizing relations with external creditors (OECD 2000, 35). With the ruble's devaluation in 1998, though, debt service soared to unmanageable levels, increasing from less than 7 percent of exports on average in the mid-1990s to over 18 percent in 1998, though still only a fraction of the Latin American level (IMF 1999, 2000). In 1999 Russia simply ceased servicing the Soviet debt, which would have required 80 percent of federal tax revenues, and continued to service only the Russian debt.

After the initial shock the 1998 crisis led to recovery. The currency devaluation made most foreign goods prohibitively expensive, leading to a 40–50 percent decline in imports in 1999 and an import-substituting spur to domestic production (IMF 1999, 99). Increased domestic production and demand, combined with high international energy prices, have produced sustained growth. Investment has increased modestly, and capital flight has declined. While external debt servicing peaked in 2003 and will continue at a high level, the government is managing its debt repayment well, has ceased borrowing from the IMF, and is seeking WTO membership. Welfare indicators have improved somewhat, in part because of economic recovery and in part because the Putin government has committed itself to re-funding welfare provision even as it restructures the system. But the economy remains heavily dependent on international energy prices and faces high debt service. In sum, Russia's export structure and debt leave it vulnerable to shocks that could take a heavy toll on welfare

Global Policy Interventions

Interventions by international organizations that advance policy constructs, provide technical assistance, and grant loans to promote substantive social policy change comprise the second dimension of globalization. In Russia and most East European countries social policy was given little priority in the early reform years. Governments concentrated on economic transformation, assuming that resumed growth would alleviate mounting social problems. According to Bob Deacon, "Into the vacuum of national social policy making in the wake of the 1989 events stepped the international organizations . . . an army of human resource specialists descended on the region" (1997, 92). Here, as for Eastern Europe, the World Bank has been the major international architect of social policy reform. The World Bank's approach favors more reliance on markets, privatization, and competition in the social sector, with the state confining its role mainly to providing income-tested, or targeted, benefits to the poor. In Russia its personnel have proposed overall conceptions for restructuring the welfare state according to the liberal paradigm, influenced the terms of policy debate, and helped to develop legislative proposals. The World Bank has sponsored projects in every area of social policy—pensions, employment, health, education, housing, and poverty alleviation—and worked at every level of government, from federal ministries to local pilot projects (World Bank 1999a). The simplest keys to its influence are money, the coherence of its approach, and the sheer scale of its work.[4] As Orenstein and Haas argue for Eastern Europe, the World Bank crafted "a coherent and forceful . . . social policy agenda" for the post-Communist states (Orenstein and Haas, this volume). The World Bank provided hundreds of millions of dollars in social sector loans, with disbursement conditional on progress in specified areas of social policy.

In *Global Social Policy,* Bob Deacon argues that international institutions gain access to polities mainly through counterparts in the governing institutions: where those counterparts have liberal orientations, the World Bank prevails; where ministries retain a socialist orientation and labor movements are stronger, the ILO has played the dominant role (Deacon 1997). Governmental counterparts were surely a key factor in Russia. Social reform agendas were promoted by a synergy of liberal social ministers and World Bank advisers and money. Yeltsin had the constitutional power to appoint those ministers without legislative approval, and Bank advisers saw social ministers' orientations as key to their potential influence. Beyond this, the World Bank could provide funds for cash-strapped ministries and engaged the elite of Russian social scientists with these models through consulting contracts. The soft side of the Bank's influence is perhaps well captured by two quotations that speak to the key issue of means-testing. The first, a remark by a Russian social scientist at a Moscow conference on social policy reform: "The world hasn't made up anything else, so we have to get started with means-testing."[5] The second, by a representative of the World Bank's Moscow office: "We have helped to build into minds the concept of targeting, but not much has been accomplished in terms of real policy" (Alexandrova 2000).

A number of European organizations, mainly OECD (Organisation for Economic Co-operation and Development) and TACIS (Technical Assistance for the Commonwealth of Independent States) have also been active in the social policy sphere in Russia. Though both are based in countries with more solidaristic social policies, they have not articulated a distinctive model for Russia and have generally endorsed liberal positions on such issues as targeting and privatization of social assets such as housing (Deacon 1997; OECD 2000). They also rely on weaker instruments of influence than the World Bank, mainly technical assistance and policy advice. A third group of UN-based agencies, including the ILO, UNICEF, and United Nations Development Program (UNDP), have played an important role as analysts and international publicists of the social costs of reform.

Domestic Political Constellations

Previous chapters in this volume have argued that domestic political constellations play a critical role in mediating globalization's effects on welfare states. Both the balance of power between supporters and opponents of liberal reform, and power concentration through political institutions, matter. In Russia most societal constituents of the welfare state are poorly organized, and labor unions, which have played a central role in resisting reform elsewhere, are extremely weak. Furthermore, Russia's constitutional system privileges executive power, and it is the executive that has pressed for both economic liberalization and welfare state retrenchment. Nevertheless, domestic political constellations presented serious obstacles to reform. The structure of the party and electoral systems for a time maximized the weight of the left in the legislature (Duma), giving it a veto over proposed changes in the legislative base of the welfare state, though its power remained severely constricted in comparative terms.

For much of the 1990s the Russian Duma was dominated by a largely unreformed Communist Party that combined, in the apt phrase of one scholar, "the social values of the left with the state-patriotic political values of the right" (Vujacic 1996, 122). The Communists placed defense of the old welfare state at the center of their platform, calling for an essentially restorationist social policy that would return to citizens rights to jobs, subsidized housing, free education and medical care, and state regulation of prices for necessities ("Za Nashu" 1995). Its main constituency consisted of retired people, the low-skilled, and rural residents, all reform's losers. Pensioners were central, both to the party's voting bloc and to its grassroots organizations. The 1995 legislative election gave the Communists, along with their leftist Agrarian and Popular Power allies, chairmanship of almost half of the Duma's committees, and control over nearly enough votes to pass or block legislation (Cook, Orenstein, and Rueschemeyer 1999; Remington 2001). For the remainder of the decade, as will be illustrated in the case studies below, the legislature functioned as a veto actor against many of the executive branch's reform initiatives.

The Limits to Liberal Restructuring in the 1990s

The Defeat of Targeting

In one of the executive branch's major welfare reform initiatives, in spring 1997, President Yeltsin initiated a broad program to streamline and rationalize social spending. Its central thrust was to eliminate inherited universal subsidies and privileged entitlements and replace them with a system of means-tested benefits that would both save money and target spending on the poor. Proposals were formulated within the executive branch, covering housing subsidies, social insurance, state transfer payments, and other benefits. The World Bank supported this reform effort with an eight-hundred-million-dollar Social Protection Adjustment Loan (SPAL) (World Bank 1997). The government's reform program would have moved Russia toward the model of the "liberal" welfare regime, in which the state provided for the poor and unemployed while the bulk of the population provided for itself through private income and social insurance (Esping-Andersen 1990).

Taken together, the government's program constituted a frontal challenge to the Communists and their leftist Duma allies and threatened to cut the social protections that the latter were committed to defend. Both the content and packaging of the reform—the government's clearly stated intention to remake Russia's welfare state in the liberal image—doomed it politically. The first package of reform legislation comprised a disparate group of draft laws that would have cut subsidies and privileges for the families of veterans and government officials, reduced sick pay and maternity benefits, and replaced the universal system of child allowances. The Duma rejected, by substantial majorities, almost all these measures.[6] After meetings of conciliation commissions throughout the summer and the defeat of a second legislative package in the fall, the government acknowledged its failure in reorienting the social sphere to targeting. In contrast to its East European counterparts, Russia's move toward more targeted social assistance was stymied (Orenstein and Haas, this volume).

Leaving aside for a moment the political obstacles, the move to targeting would have posed serious problems in the Russian context. An OECD study (that nevertheless endorsed targeting) points to the most serious problems: "the creation of the informational and administrative infrastructure necessary for an effective targeting of social benefits will take some time in Russia, especially in view of the prevalence of unrecorded incomes. Conceivable alternatives include the targeting of specific groups or geographic areas—but these can only have limited effect at present because . . . poverty is relatively common in most household types and regions" (OECD 2001, 14). World Bank and Russian reformers seemed to take little account of these problems, or the implicit costs of building the necessary administrative capabilities from the underpaid workers and poorly equipped offices of the social sector. On the other hand, with no reallocation of Soviet-era commitments, unemployment benefits and other transitional aids were starved of funding.

We will next examine reforming efforts in two key areas of Russia's welfare state: pensions and housing. These two case studies will show the influence of international organizations (IOs) on efforts at substantive policy reform. They will also illustrate how domestic constituencies and political constellations limited international influence, and how attitudinal legacies of the old welfare state frustrated liberal initiatives. The Russian state's weak capacity for implementation, innovation, and adaptation of policies further hobbled the reforms promoted by the IOs. Even when these were passed into laws or decrees the Russian state often lacked the administrative, technical, and regulatory capacities to make them work, or the authority to gain compliance with its mandates.

Pension Reform

As in other systems, pensions in Russia constituted one of the largest social expenditures and a key benefit program. Earlier sections of the chapter have shown that, by the mid-1990s, the Russian pension system confronted problems of declining revenues, poverty-level pensions, and payment arrears. Beginning in 1995 the government proposed numerous reform initiatives that were designed to reduce established benefits, restrict eligibility, increase contributions, and transfer more or less of pension provision from the public sphere to individual savings and financial markets. With the aid and advice of the World Bank and other international organizations the government proposed various combinations of these solutions, producing conflicts with the Duma and within the government, but failing to implement any substantial reforms.

Constituencies and the Obstacles to Reform

Initially, reformist officials sought to change the rules of entitlement to pensions in Russia in order to provide immediate fiscal relief to the pension system. They targeted the liberal eligibility rules and special benefits, bonuses, and privileges inherited from the Soviet period, proposing changes that, inter alia, would raise the retirement age, restrict rights to early retirement, cut or eliminate payments to Russia's seven million "working pensioners," eliminate privileged pensions, and so on. In return, they promised timely payment of pensions and an increase in the minimum sufficient to pull the poorest out of poverty. From the rationalizing perspective of Russian reformers and their World Bank advisers these reforms would bring the system closer to fiscal balance and social justice, providing at least short-term relief for the pension system while taking benefits from younger and more able-bodied pensioners and channeling them to the most needy.

Although some were proposed repeatedly, not one of these measures passed into law. As we know from other studies of welfare state retrenchment (Pierson 1994), such immediate and visible benefit cuts are the most difficult politically, and the reformers' broad forays into the entitlements of different subgroups of pensioners spread the damage. In any case the political realities of Russia doomed short-term reform proposals that imposed clear-cut costs on pensioners. The Communist-led left majority that dominated the Duma promised to reject any diminution in pensioners' welfare rights. The lower house also blocked the government's repeated attempts to change the pension contribution formula, refusing to shift even a modest share of the burden from employers to employees. In the words of a knowledgeable World Bank official, "good intentions are stranded at the door of the Duma" (Sederlof 1999).

The proposed reforms also generated opposition from pensioners' and veterans' organizations. Veterans' organizations, particularly the large Union of Veterans, reportedly lobbied the legislature daily on pension and other issues. Its leadership included many former high-ranking military officers whose links with current leaders contributed to their effectiveness (Avtonomov 1999; Kozmina 1998). The few pensioners' organizations generally opposed cuts, and some blamed corruption for the problems. According to a spokesperson for the Pensioners' Party, for example, "We are sure that the declarations concerning absence of money are not true; pensions could be doubled without tension in the budget. . . . Stealing occurs at all stages of collecting pension money" (Petrov 1999). This quote reflects the problems of building consensus in Russian society around the government's pleas for belt-tightening. Pensioners also used the press and courts, producing an outcry over proposed benefit cuts that sometimes led the government to back down. Overall, according to a range of experts, short-term, highly visible pension benefit cuts were simply "politically unacceptable."

The Limits of State Capacity

The government did manage to generate, and pass through the legislature in 1996–1998, some important pieces of pension reform legislation. These avoided the politically unpopular approaches of reducing benefits and restricting eligibility and instead sought to change incentives, shift responsibilities, and expand the possibilities for pension savings in order to increase the inflow of money and lessen the burden on the general fund. Legislation on personal or individual pension accounts was designed to provide incentives for contributions and longer labor force participation, without requiring later retirement. Legislation on individual coefficients was to bring pension levels more in line with past contributions. Legislation on non-state pension funds was to encourage individual savings and occupational pension accounts in a voluntary third tier, moving some pension provision to markets. While the Duma passed all three measures, their intended effects were largely undermined by the limitations of the Russian state's administrative, taxing, and regulatory capacities.

The Russian state could not, in fact, create individual pension accounts because it lacked the capacity to track individual contributions; in the existing system, managements simply contributed (when they did) for the labor collective. In 1995 the Russian government, with World Bank assistance, began to establish a system for individual tracking. It could not bring pension levels in line with past contributions, partly because of resistance from constituencies that would lose from this measure, but mainly because it could not collect sufficient taxes to differentiate pensions. Nor could the state regulate non-state pension funds in Russia's chaotic and corrupt markets. The funds suffered from corruption scandals and some collapsed in the wake of the August 1998 financial crisis, demonstrating clearly the weakness of market solutions to Russia's pension problems in the absence of a stronger regulatory system.

The Legacies of Solidarity and Equality

In spring 1997, as part of the broader reform initiative discussed above, pension reform gained new momentum. It was a major objective of the World Bank's SPAL. Bank documents set out in some detail, as conditions for receipt of tranches, the parameters of the pension program Russia should adopt. The World Bank had two central goals: to provide a minimum pension income that would alleviate poverty; and to move Russia's main system of pension provision away from public financing and solidaristic principles (that is, pay-as-you-go [PAYG], based on transfers from current workers to current pensioners) toward individual, private, funded, or accumulative schemes. Social Protection Adjustment Loan documents recommended gradual introduction of funding, beginning with fictional (or notional) individual accounts and, as obligations to current pensioners lessened, moving to real funding. In the Bank's "optimal structure," the second or main tier would eventually be fully funded, a major departure from the existing system (World Bank 1997).

Deputy minister of labor and social development and former associate at the

Moscow Carnegie Center Mikhail Dmitriev, placed in charge of pension reform, favored a much more radical version of reform. Dmitriev, impressed by the Chilean success with raising pensions through market investment and convinced that the Russian system must be divorced from politics, proposed that Russia transfer most age cohorts to individual financing of pensions through funded schemes within several months. All those participating in funded schemes would lose their right to draw a state pension, while the state would provide only means-tested benefits for the poorest. Dmitriev's studies were financed and published through Carnegie as he cycled into (out of, and then again into) the Russian government, illustrating the networks that developed among Western foundations and the Russian government. In any case, the nearly total rejection of Dmitriev's proposals by the then-reformist Russian government shows the limits of acceptable change, and the intense debate surrounding it gives evidence of the normative as well as institutional legacies of the old system.

Critics of Dmitriev's plan, from among both academic specialists and government, argued that under current conditions it would abandon large numbers of future pensioners to poverty and further exacerbate the deep inequalities and growing stratification in Russian society. Many workers, they argued, could not afford to save for retirement at current wage levels, and would be left without pension security. Women, with lower wages and longer life spans, would see their pensions drop from the present near-equality with men's to less than half. There was at base also a broad normative consensus against abandoning the redistributive and solidaristic elements of Russia's pension system in the face of current realities, voiced by officials from the labor ministry, the Pension Fund, the executive branch, specialists, and advisers. According to one participant, "Everyone criticized Dmitriev—the government, the Ministry of Labor. The main criticism was that the accumulative system doesn't protect the poorest, and that the mentality of the Russian people is accustomed to security. Dmitriev was almost alone in his support for the pure accumulative system" (Bochkareva 1998). In any event, the reform commission was broadened and a compromise draft produced that combined distributive and accumulative principles (PAYG and funded elements), before the August 1998 crisis brought a temporary end to efforts at systemic reform.

The 1998 reform bore the clear stamp of the World Bank's influence. The Bank succeeded in focusing the policy debate on the shift to a funded or accumulative system and provided incentives for Russia's government to conclude a contentious policy debate and approve a reform program. According to the assessment of Hjalte Sederlof, the main World Bank official involved in Russian pension reform efforts, the SPAL succeeded in "bringing about a government decision on pension reform; introducing a second pillar with notional accounts; influencing improved legislation for voluntary pension schemes" (Sederlof 1999). The reform that was finally passed by the Duma in 2002–2003 is based largely on this model.

Housing Reform

A third major area of reform initiatives was the housing sector. Reformers were determined to introduce privatization and full cost recovery into this heavily subsidized sector. In late 1992 the government set out a concept and passed legislation that has remained the basis for housing reform. It proposed to privatize most housing, transfer costs to residents, eliminate subsidies, and provide means-tested benefits to the poor. Enterprises would transfer (divest) their housing to municipalities, which would privatize it to residents for a nominal fee. Housing maintenance and utility charges would then be raised steadily to achieve full cost recovery from residents. Targeted housing allowances would be provided to compensate the poor. Most residences would form self-managing condominiums, while a residual public housing sector was envisaged. The reform is a textbook case of World Bank-supported policy: from the coherence and "fit" of its various provisions, to its insistence on nearly full privatization, to its reliance on means-testing and targeting, to the anticipated residual nature of the public sector.[7]

Constituencies

As the reform began to create costs and benefits, though, constituencies and institutions within Russia reacted, selectively supporting and opposing various elements. The post-1995 Duma majority claimed commitment to housing as a "public good" and opposed increases in rent and utility payments. Since reform legislation was already in place, it took measures that shielded parts of the population from the effects. Housing privileges for veterans, various categories of civil servants, and others, usually provided as an exemption from a percentage of charges, were entrenched in Soviet-era legislation. When housing charges began to rise, these groups lobbied to protect and extend their privileges and the Duma cooperated, passing the Law on Veterans, which increased the share of families receiving housing privileges, and rejecting government proposals that would have reduced privileges for civil servants. It also passed legislation to slow cost recovery and increase the discretion of local authorities in implementing the reform (Kosareva and Struyk 1997). These measures significantly undercut the reformist efforts. The Duma also delayed legislation on condominiums, which had to be in place before municipalities could hand over management of apartment buildings—by far the largest part of Russia's housing stock—to resident-owners. Local governments also reportedly added privileges, illustrating the claims of established patterns of social provision on government authorities.

State Capacities

The state's weak capacities also frustrated housing reform efforts in several ways. First, the federal government was unable, despite legislative requirements, to make municipal governments take over divested enterprise housing, to complete privatization, or to enforce a schedule of rent increases. Municipalities often refused divested housing because the federal government lacked the financial resources to provide the promised transitional aid. When municipal governments did agree, divestiture became part of a complex and murky deal between enterprise and municipality involving taxes and services (Kuraishi 1999). The state also lacked the information and administrative capacity to calculate a reasonable rate structure for rents and utilities in various regions and repeatedly revised its schedule of rent increases, trying with little success to gain regions' compliance. Many municipal governments lacked the capacity to means-test and target housing allowances, and at best their housing allowance programs reached only a tiny fraction of those believed eligible.

In sum, despite the reform, a large part of the Russian population, as well as municipal authorities that directly administer the housing sector, continued to treat housing as an entitlement. About half of eligible Russians declined even the virtually free privatization of their apartments, preferring to rely on a legacy of strong tenancy rights and leaving a large public housing sector. Most who did privatize failed to form condominiums, leaving management and maintenance of their buildings to the state. The population did pay higher rents, rising to about 50 percent of housing costs by 1998 (Belkina 1998). But most who could not pay the newly assessed rents were simply left in their apartments, and eviction, though legal, has been rare. The reform's intended deep structural transformations and reallocations of financial responsibility were blocked by politics together with institutional and attitudinal legacies of the old welfare state. Housing subsides remained substantial, equaling 3.5 to 4.5 percent of GDP during the mid-1990s (OECD 2001). Subsidies cushioned the impact of reform on the population but imposed a heavy burden on municipal governments, crowding out spending in other areas and nevertheless remaining sorely inadequate to maintain the deteriorating housing stock.

A Weak Opposition to Reform

The Left's opposition helped defeat restructuring efforts in the areas of targeting benefits, pensions, and housing, and kept broad entitlements on the books and some subsidies in place, but it could not restore financing. The constitutional system limited it largely to blocking legislative changes in the structure of the welfare state. The president vetoed most measures that would have raised spending levels, while others went out as unfunded federal mandates to regions that lacked the resources to implement them. The government arbitrarily withheld some federal budgetary funds that had been allocated to the social sector. Moreover, the Communists' social policy was backward-looking and included virtually nothing innovative. While the party had a social democratic faction it was, under Zyuganov, dominated by a nationalist and patriotic orientation that isolated it from more moderate socialists, both domestically and internationally, who might have been sources of programmatic innovation on welfare policy. The party's uncritical restorationism served mainly to "freeze up" allocations; the Left failed to generate alternative policies of adjustment or compensation.

The Russian left's power was comparatively brittle in other respects as well. While the Communists were by far the largest and most stable political party, consistently getting about a quarter of the popular vote, they had few ties to labor unions or other traditionally pro-welfare organizations in Russia's weak civil society. The major union in Russia, the Federation of Independent Trade Unions of Russia (FNPR), would not affiliate with the party, and the few new democratic unions were both small and committed to the liberalizing government. In any case, though union density was high, the FNPR was a weak organization characterized by low legitimacy, membership attrition, and poor mobilizing capacity. It engaged in tripartite negotiations but these were largely a sham, with virtually no impact on fiscal or distributive policies (Cook, 1997; Connor, 1996). In other words, the antiretrenchment political constellation in Russia had less depth and breadth, in an organizational sense, than those in the other cases. Moreover, most political parties remain weak and unstable, and the executive has focused great energy on neutralizing potential sources of opposition. In the 1999 election the Communists, though retaining their share of the popular vote, lost their legislative allies and strategic position. Three new parties that have taken a generally pro-government orientation entered the legislature, and liberalization of the welfare state moved forward (Myagkov and Ordeshook 2001).

Politics Matters: Restructuring with a Compliant Legislature

In spring 2000 the new Russian government under newly elected President Valdimir Putin laid out a comprehensive program of welfare state restructuring based on rationalization, privatization, subsidy cuts, and targeting of state assistance to the poor. This program, encapsulated in the Gref Plan for Social and Economic Development of the Russian Federation, essentially revived the program of social sector reform that was initiated during the Yeltsin period. Putin put into place many of the same key governmental policy actors. The policy environment is now quite different from that of the mid-1990s, however. The economy is growing, wages are increasing (though they have not yet recovered to precrisis levels), the government has more money at its disposal and appears more capable and efficient. It has distanced itself from the World Bank after disputes over the appropriateness and effectiveness of past advice, and has limited borrowing (Gimpelson

2002). But the influence of the liberal paradigm remains pervasive, and while the reforms are far from complete, a number of restructuring measures have passed though the legislature.

First, the Putin administration has revived efforts to reduce privileges and benefits for various categories of the nonpoor population. The first of a series of draft laws, cutting privileges for some groups of civil servants, has passed, and several others are pending. The legislation includes compensation in the form of salary increases or monetization of benefits, and such compensation mechanisms have been characteristic of the current reform cycle (Karagodin 2002). The government has also cut, or limited eligibility for, a number of federally mandated social benefits, reallocating funds to those who meet stricter eligibility requirements. The legislature stopped passing unfunded federal mandates, and Putin has announced that some of those passed in the 1990s will simply be dropped. In sum, the process of dismantling the complex system of subsidies, benefits, and privileges for myriad population categories has begun.

The legislature has also passed a major pension reform that individualizes most pension savings and introduces an accumulative, or investment, element into the system. The reform is supposed to increase incentives for pension savings, avoid the anticipated crisis of the pension system as Russian baby boomers retire, and provide investment resources for the domestic economy. The government helped generate legislative and public acceptance by funding the current pension system more fully, raising and indexing pensions. The reform moved through the legislature slowly, with considerable conflict over the risks of investment in Russian markets and amid broad public distrust of most financial institutions. The outcome is a compromise that retains a large role for the state pension fund and introduces the accumulative element gradually, but it limits state guarantees, phases out the solidaristic system, and restricts the possibilities for redistribution.

Housing and communal services, education, and health care reform are also on the agenda. In the housing sector the government is moving cautiously toward full cost-recovery rents, with promised compensation for poorer groups. In education and health care it promises to establish minimum standards, introduce more competitiveness and efficiency into service delivery, and increase reliance on private payment and insurance mechanisms. These reforms are still being developed. The legislature has not opposed them, and cooperation in passing proposed measures is anticipated, though the government expects even this compliant Duma to become more defensive of welfare entitlements as elections near (Karagadin 2002).

Comparisons

The Putin-era reforms might seem to move Russia somewhat in the direction of east-central Europe, where the welfare state is liberalized in the context of increased social spending and the state provides compensation and a decent level of social security (Orenstein and Haas, this volume). Indeed, Putin has used growing state revenues to pay off benefit arrears, increase payment levels, and raise minimum and public sector wages. The government promises increases in real social spending and very modest improvements in welfare state effort (that is, percent of GDP expended). Tax collection has become more effective, though only after the introduction of a flat income tax and regressive social tax. The Putin administration has shown itself to be far more cognizant than its predecessor of the need to build the administrative and institutional capacities for a liberalized system. It has regularized the budget process and made itself more accountable administratively.

But Russia differs from its east-central European counterparts in being both more fragile economically and far less accountable politically. Social policy agenda-setting is still largely dominated by a small group close to the executive, with little input from the social groups affected. As argued above, civil society organization in Russia remains weak. More importantly, the political system provides few mechanisms that would allow society to hold political elites accountable for their promises, or punish them for policy failures. Political parties are unstable, often disappearing from one election to the next. Many lack coherent policies or even clear political orientations, and this has become an increasing problem (Oates 2000). There are no major social democratic parties of the sort that support welfare policies in east-central Europe, nor any democratic left parties whose constituency extends beyond the intelligentsia. Moreover, the legislature exercises little control over the government, and the superpresidency dominates the system.

Liberalization may allow the executive branch to construct policies of compensation while the economy is strong, but it reduces the responsibility of the state for social protection and shifts costs to a population that still has very limited resources. It risks leaving social protection for the bulk of a relatively poor population more exposed to the vagaries of the market.

Conclusion

In terms of globalization's impact on its welfare state, Russia stands between east-central Europe and Latin America. Pressures from the global economy were not the driving force behind welfare state retrenchment in Russia, as they were in Latin America. The collapse of COMECON and of Russia's internal economy were the primary causes of declining welfare. In their aftermath Russian leaders, bereft of internal solutions, were drawn to liberalization mainly because it promised economic revitalization. The international flow of ideas was important here, and its influence was greatly strengthened by the economic resources that IFIs provided when Russia adopted their models. These ideas were also appealing to Russia's politically insulated executive branch because it had the power to impose them on its population, then to distort them in its own interests. An affinity between international technocrats with prepackaged policy blueprints, and politically insulated governments with limited democratic accountability, is evident throughout the Russian reform process. The liberalization-privatization-stabilization program placed additional downward pressures on welfare, and the corruption and cooptation of that program by its elite beneficiaries led to significant increases in inequality.

In the ensuing decade Russia has integrated into the global economy, though not as deeply as many other countries. Its level of trade openness remains modest, multinational corporations are confined to a few sectors (though this includes the key energy sectors), and debt does not approach Latin American levels. The IMF and the Paris and London Clubs have treated Russia rather liberally, indicating that global political considerations may trump global economics. Nevertheless, trade liberalization opened Russia's consumer sector to competition from low-wage neighboring states and higher-quality foreign consumer products, contributing to the depression of domestic production until the 1998 financial crisis, and produced an export structure that is likely inimical to future social provision. Russia produces little of the high value-added exports that have enabled the maintenance of welfare, for example, in northern Europe described by Stephens, nor has it reoriented and diversified its trade structure in the pattern of the east-central European states described by Orenstein and Haas.

In the 1990s the liberalization of capital flows led mainly to massive capital flight and short-term, speculative portfolio investment. Russia's resulting vulnerability to fluctuations in investor confidence contributed to severe economic volatility and financial crisis, default, and devaluation. Overall, the effects of economic globalization on Russia look rather more like those on Latin America. To quote Evelyn Huber, "Massive outflows of capital and speculative runs on the currency, followed by massive devaluations and domestic austerity measures, as happened in Mexico and Brazil, are not part of the west European economic scenario" (Huber, this volume). They are part of the Russian scenario.

Russia has displayed a relatively high level of political-cultural dependency in seeking and accepting policy guidance from international organizations. IFIs have played a significant role in the attempted reform of Russia's inherited universalist welfare state, a role that follows Latin American and East European patterns but has no counterpart in western Europe. The World Bank, the major influence on substantive social policy reform, has promoted a liberal model that has informed both the largely failed restructuring efforts of the Yeltsin period and the somewhat more successful contemporary reforms.

This volume's central contention is that "politics matters"—that domestic political constellations and institutions play a key role in mediating the impacts of globalization on welfare states. This was the case in Russia; IFIs' interventions were largely frustrated by a domestic political constellation that gave the left-dominated Duma a veto over measures to restructure the inherited system of social provision. The Duma mounted an effective defense of universalist principles, as well as entrenched privileges. This was so despite the concentration of power in the executive branch that normally facilitates retrenchment, which highlights the importance of veto points in the institutional system. The progress of social sector reform since 1999 shows that the same institutions, with a different political constellation and more capable leadership at the top, could produce progress on liberalization.

But we must pay attention to the comparative limits of influence of the old welfare state's political defenders in Russia. The Left did keep social security issues on the Russian political agenda. But unlike Stephens's social democratic European governments and some in Latin America, they did not preserve welfare expenditures. Most of their efforts to maintain the real value of benefits were vetoed or canceled out by the continuing economic slide. In the end, the polarization between the executive branch and the legislature produced a policy stalemate. Efforts to deal with the poverty of transition competed with existing entitlements in a context of declining resources. The structures of the old welfare state were preserved, but real social provision deteriorated.

The Russian left is in other respects weaker and more brittle than the social democratic movements that have preserved expenditures and universalism elsewhere. Russian civil society is poorly organized and fragmented. The Communist party lacks the strong base in labor or social movements that underpins the Left in, for example, Costa Rica, and its dogmatism isolates it even from Russia's weak moderate left. Moreover, most other parties and the party system as a whole are unstable. The Communists' strength in the latter 1990s resulted from a particular political conjuncture in which the electoral system and the multiple divisions among their competitors magnified their representation, and they made effective tactical use of their resources for legislative alliance-building. But the universalist welfare state they defended was no longer viable, and they had no alternative.

Finally, my essay argues that the institutional embeddedness of Russia's welfare state, and limits of state capacity for policy innovation and adaptation, contributed to continuity. As both the World Bank and the IMF have belatedly acknowledged, Russia lacked many of the institutions and regulatory structures that are assumed in international policy models for both economic transformation and social policy reform. Even when measures overcame or avoided political obstacles, they were often blocked in the implementation stage by the state's failures, and by institutional and attitudinal holdovers of the old welfare state. The Russian state's capacities to tax, regulate, administer, and gain compliance with its laws and mandates were weak, and we have seen how these weaknesses undermined reform efforts in housing and pensions. A legacy of expectations, entitlements, and orientations toward social provision, not only within the population but in state and local institutions, sustained old practices. How much these legacies will affect the future development of social provision in Russia remains to be seen.

Political constellations have shifted now, and restructuring is proceeding. One hopes for Russia a future that tends toward the east-central European model, with the economy diversifying, democracy deepening, and a restructured welfare state providing adequate social security. But, after several years of economic recovery, poverty and inequality remain high and welfare effort has increased little. There are reasons to fear that Russia will tend toward the Latin American pattern, in which popular political power remains weak and fragmented, the economy is vulnerable to sharp downturns, and the restructured welfare state provides less protection for the population.

8

Globalization and Social Policy in South Korea
The Politics of Social Protection and Structural Adjustment

HO KEUN SONG AND KYUNG ZOON HONG

Until recently, Korean society was unfamiliar with the concept of the welfare state. Welfare was thought of as social benefits that the state benevolently provided to the extremely poor and disabled. For a people accustomed to making a living through their own effort, welfare was never perceived in terms of social rights. Although the state had long been a tax collector, even in social emergencies it rarely provided people with cash assistance. Social benefits given to the extremely poor were rarely enough to live on, as these consisted primarily of small amounts of grains, condiments, garments, and small amounts of cash for heat. Poor elderly people with no family were provided with a small amount of cash benefits under the title of "consolation money."

The absence of public welfare makes the family a central locus of welfare. It is commonly accepted as an individual and social responsibility that children take care of parents who retire or lose their capacity to earn a living. Where public support for housing, education, and health is absent, the family head is responsible for most aspects of the family members' lives. Under these conditions, the self-help ideology became so universal that most people have tended to think of welfare recipients as lazy and immoral.

In the absence of public welfare, the company becomes a main provider not only of employment but also of private welfare. "Company welfare" is prevalent in East Asia, including Japan and, to a lesser extent, Taiwan, in part due to Confucian values that identify firms as family. There are, however, many reasons company welfare is more advanced than public welfare. Economically active people view company welfare as a principal source of support; employees in prosperous and

179

prestigious firms such as the chaebol receive many kinds of benefits, including cheap subsidized loans for housing, payment of school fees, and vacation facilities. Company welfare is quite beneficial to people with good jobs, but it gives rise to increasing inequality relative to people with undesirable jobs and the self-employed. The growth of company welfare was interrupted only in 1997 under the impact of the foreign debt crisis, which severely strained the financial conditions of most private firms.

Thus, family and firm were the two essential pillars of welfare in South Korea. "Universal" social policy was largely neglected during the period of high-speed growth (1961–1987) because governments always placed a political priority on growth. Economic policy took precedence over most other policy areas. Governments stressed the importance of a "growth-first-and-distribution-later" strategy under which most financial and economic resources were saved for economic development. President Park Chung Hee, dictator and creator of the economic miracle, argued that welfare was a poor instrument to combat poverty. He stressed in public speeches that a successful economy was the most efficient road to welfare and that what poor nations needed most were jobs. The logic that employment is the bedrock and guarantor of welfare became the dominant ideology. This persisted until the mid-1980s when social actors started to discuss the importance of social insurance policies in areas such as pensions, health, and unemployment.

However, elements of a social insurance framework had been erected under the authoritarian regime of 1961–1987. For instance, President Park introduced the national pension scheme for military officers, teachers, and bureaucrats soon after the success of the 1961 military coup. Injury insurance for industrial workers was introduced in 1963, although it was restricted to workers in large firms. Health insurance was first enacted in 1976 for employees of large firms and state officials, and was expanded to the entire nation in 1988 just after the demise of the authoritarian regime. The military government provided such benefits only to the military, teachers, and state officials for obvious political reasons—the dictatorship wanted to strengthen the political support and loyalty of persons in public organizations and the security forces. The government restricted coverage of injury and health insurance to employees of large firms for financial reasons: The state wanted to minimize the risk of financial deficits by collecting insurance fees only from the most financially solid sectors.

It is interesting that President Chun Do Whan, who grasped power through another military coup in 1980, set the creation of a "welfare state" as a political goal for the first time in Korean history. He promised improved social policies in order to reduce discontent following the Kwangju massacre and the assassination of President Park. Despite the stated aim, and with the exception of two reforms, little substantive change occurred during the seven years of his government. The two exceptions were regulations on the use of union funds for worker welfare and the establishment of preschool facilities for the children of the working poor. Korea had to wait for the collapse of authoritarianism before "welfare" could go beyond poverty policy and become universal, covering all wage earners.

Nevertheless, the expansion of social insurance to universal programs in the transition to democracy did not alter the structure of the social security system. From 1961 to the present this structure has remained relatively untouched in terms of individual contributions, insurance administration based on sectoral divisions, and government budgetary support. The state undertakes the administrative role in all four social insurance programs, each operated by independent offices. Since the state allocates only a small portion of the annual budget to these programs, the financing of these four insurance programs relies principally upon contributions from employers and employees. For instance, employers and employees each pay 1.92 percent of the monthly wage for health insurance. The pension system is largely pay-as-you-go and its structure remains unchanged even in the reform undertaken by the Kim Dae Jung government. The reforms involved an increase in the contribution rate, expansion of recipients, reduction of pension benefits, and administrative integration of separate programs (the latter temporarily suspended due to various difficulties).

Nonetheless, the Korean case provides strong evidence supporting the argument that globalization and market opening can lead to positive developments in the provision of public welfare, provided that developments in domestic politics support such policy responses. Social security programs covering the four basic types of social insurance were completed in the few years following democratization in 1987. Health insurance was expanded to the entire population in 1988; a pension scheme for all wage earners was introduced in 1988 and expanded to agricultural workers in 1996 and to the self-employed in 1999. Unemployment insurance was introduced in 1996 and became the most useful and effective measure during the foreign debt crisis. Clearly, these are improvements in state welfare that have much to do with democratization, but they came about simultaneously with the opening to world markets both in trade and financial markets.

Most advanced industrialized countries have maintained their welfare regime or at most modified benefits only at the margin, and only a few have undertaken significant retrenchment (Esping-Andersen 1996). It is hard to find a strong negative causality between welfare regimes and lower rates of economic growth, casting doubt on the neoliberal argument that welfare institutions are a direct cause undermining economic performance in Europe (Pfaller and Therborn 1991; Fligstein 1998; Janoski and Hicks 1994; Pierson 1996). These findings suggest that national governments adopt different strategies toward the restructuring of welfare regimes in response to globalization. Several variables mediate the response. The strategy also differs by policy areas. While reliance on market mechanisms has increased in financial markets and in the employment system, institutional protections remain largely unchanged or only slightly modified. At most, the emphasis in public benefits has shifted from unconditional and universal protection toward greater conditionality with the aim of promoting work incentives.

What light does the Korean case shed on the debate surrounding the uncertain causality between globalization and the welfare state? How has the incorporation of Korea into a global economy affected government social policy? Has there been a paradigmatic shift in the social policy regime, either toward welfare state expansion or retrenchment?

Globalization and Social Policy: The Korean Case

As described above, the authoritarian regime prevented the development of a universal social policy. Instead, it introduced selective social insurance programs for social groups that were regarded as important for maintaining political stability. The regime legitimized this underdevelopment by appealing to the high rate of economic growth and the substantial job creation this produced. The democratic transition following the demise of the authoritarian regime in 1987 allowed popular interest in public welfare and social policy to be voiced. As a result the government began to pay more attention to basic needs and social security. The increased demand for social protection was concurrent with the opening of the domestic market to foreign manufacturers and capital.

As in so many of the other countries studied in this volume, democratization and globalization proceeded simultaneously in Korea at the end of the 1980s. Although Korea is typically categorized as a small open economy in terms of trade volume in world markets throughout the period of high-speed growth (see table 8.1), the reality was quite different, for people could neither see nor buy foreign commodities in the domestic consumer market. Furthermore, the share of transnational corporations' production in GDP was relatively small prior to 1987. South Korea was distinguished as one of the middle-income countries foreign investors most avoided. It was an export-led economy with almost complete protection of domestic markets. From 1987 onward, the Korean government rapidly opened domestic markets to foreign investors and manufacturers. Under external pressure, particularly from the United States and Japan, market opening and liberalization proceeded so rapidly that by the early 1990s Korea was fully integrated into the global economy. This major shift from export-dependence to true integration into the global economy characterizes globalization in the Korean case. At the same time, Korea successfully transited to democracy as part of the "third wave of democratization" (Huntington 1991).

In order to examine the relationship between globalization and the development of social policy in Korea it is important to observe developments over the

Table 8.1 Globalization, Social Expenditure, and Taxation

Year	Tradea Bil. $	Tradea (%)	Capital mobility (million $) Outflow	Capital mobility (million $) Inflow	Capital mobility (million $) Total	Social insurance	Welfare service	Social expenditure	Ratio of tax burden
1980	39.7	(63.4)	17	143	160	0.5	–	–	17.8
1981	47.3	(67.7)	28	153	181	0.5	–	–	17.9
1982	46.1	(61.8)	101	189	290	0.5	–	–	18.1
1983	50.6	(61.3)	109	269	378	0.5	–	–	18.4
1984	59.8	(65.6)	50	422	472	0.8	0.1	–	17.3
1985	61.4	(65.1)	113	532	645	0.2	0.1	–	17.1
1986	66.2	(61.1)	183	355	538	0.2	0.1	2.6	16.6
1987	88.3	(64.8)	410	1,063	1,473	0.2	0.1	2.6	16.9
1988	112.5	(61.8)	216	1,284	1,500	0.2	0.1	3.2	17.2
1989	123.8	(55.8)	570	1,090	1,660	0.3	0.1	3.6	17.7
1990	134.8	(53.4)	959	803	1,762	0.8	0.1	3.9	18.6
1991	153.3	(52.0)	1,115	1,396	2,511	0.9	0.1	3.8	17.7
1992	158.4	(50.3)	1,219	895	2,114	1.0	0.1	4.2	18.2
1993	166.0	(48.0)	1,262	1,044	2,306	0.9	0.2	4.4	18.1
1994	198.3	(49.3)	2,300	1,317	3,617	0.9	0.2	4.7	18.7
1995	260.1	(53.2)	3,071	1,941	5,012	0.8	0.2	5.1	19.2
1996	280.1	(53.9)	4,246	3,203	7,449	0.9	0.2	5.3	19.7
1997	280.8	(58.9)	3,229	6,971	10,200	0.9	0.2	6.8	19.6
1998	225.6	(70.2)	3,891	8,852	12,743	1.02	0.2	6.9	19.2
1999	193.4	(64.8)	2,553	15,541	18,094	1.19	0.4	7.2	19.5
2000	332.7	(72.0)	4,855	15,216	20,071	1.60	0.5	10.2	21.8
2001	291.5	(68.2)	5,031	11,291	16,322	2.0	0.7	n/a	22.5
2002	314.6	(66.0)	3,030	9,101	12,131	2.0	0.6	n/a	21.8

Source: National Statistical Office.
Note: ªTrade (%) = (export + import)/GDP.

period of market opening. Table 8.1 displays two sets of statistics: trade as a percentage of GDP and capital flows as proxies for globalization, and social expenditure as a percentage of GDP as a proxy for social policy development. Table 8.2 displays Pearson's correlation coefficients between variables of globalization and social expenditure during these years.

Social expenditure increased gradually over the observed period. With the exception of 1997, there was no dramatic change to this overall trend. Compared to the advanced industrialized countries, social expenditure as a percentage of GDP was quite low. It went beyond 20 percent in most European countries and rose above 10 percent even in some Latin American countries. In 1999, when the Korean government allocated its largest budget for social welfare, it reached a mere 7.2 percent. Throughout the period observed social insurance fluctuated below 1 percent but showed an increasing trend. In contrast, social services seemed to be

Table 8.2 Globalization and Social Expenditure,
Correlation Coefficients between Variables

		CAPMOB	Social	Tax	Trade
Pearson Correlation	CAPMOB	1.000	.923[a]	.777([a])	.913[a]
	Social	.923[a]	1.000	.925[a]	.941[a]
	Tax	.777([a])	.925[a]	1.000	.951[a]
	Trade	.913[a]	.941[a]	.951[a]	1.000

Note: CAPMOB = capital mobility; Social = social expenditure; Tax = ratio of tax burden; Trade = ratio of trade/GDP.

[a]Correlation is significant at the 0.01 level (2-tailed).

almost fixed. Nevertheless, the increasing trend of social expenditure suggests that the Korean government began to pay attention to social policy and to allocate greater budgets for welfare. What, then, are the relationships between social policy and the globalization variables?

The trend in capital flows contains an abrupt increase in 1987, 1991, 1996, and 1998, supporting the rapidity of market opening after 1987. Capital outflow mainly from light industries such as the textile and garment industries is explained by the sudden rise in labor costs following the massive labor disputes of 1987 and the ensuing employers' concessions to workers' demands for higher wages. Capital outflow during the first half of the 1990s was accelerated by the chaebols' investments in low-wage regions. Since 1987 foreign capital has also flowed into Korea more rapidly. Table 8.2 indicates that this capital mobility is positively related to social expenditure (r = .923), supporting the argument that even in Korea, a welfare laggard compared to upper-middle-income countries, economic openness stimulates welfare state expansion.

There is also a statistically meaningful and positive correlation between trade and social expenditure. The increase in trade was especially astonishing in the 1990s. This positive and strong correlation is consistent with Dani Rodrik's argument (1997) that increases in trade generate negative impacts on workers and thus stimulate government efforts to compensate for worker distress. Nonetheless, it is unlikely that trade played a greater role than capital mobility. Trade has long accounted for over half of GDP, fluctuating between 50 and 67 percent of GDP between 1980 and 1997. It is unlikely that increases in trade from an already very high level would have major effects on social policy. It is thus more likely that the opening of the domestic market to multinational corporations and the removal of restrictions on capital mobility have had a greater impact on social policy than fluctuations in trade. Although social expenditure increases over this period, its rate of growth is far lower than the growth of trade and capital mobility.

The financial crisis that occurred in December 1997 and devastated the Korean economic miracle served as a turning point in Korea's social policy regime in various respects. President Kim Dae Jung, elected at the end of 1997, announced a "war on unemployment and economic disaster." Tens of thousands of firms went bankrupt and unemployment soared in the wake of the foreign debt crisis and the IMF's stringent bailout conditions. For the first time in Korea, the Kim government introduced the concept of social safety nets in the hope of securing a minimum standard of living for the unemployed and the poor. As a result the government allocated tremendous amounts of money for social emergency measures during the first two years and made an effort to improve the social policy regime with larger social expenditures. With the change of political leadership in 1998, bureaucrats began to turn their attention to social policy. It was a turning point in Korea's social policy not only because the Kim government allocated substantial financial resources to this area but also because social policy began to be recognized as an independent sphere separate from economic and industrial policy.

The Poverty of Social Policy before the Financial Crisis

The Authoritarian Legacy

Korea is a welfare laggard compared to upper-middle-income countries because of the policy emphasis placed on growth rather than social performance during the authoritarian regime. To promote national competitiveness in world markets the authoritarian government provided tremendous benefits and privileges to the chaebol and large firms. In the absence of benefits provided by the state, private firms undertook the role of welfare provider. Company welfare was well accepted in a society in which the firm was perceived as a second family. No one doubted that the family was responsible for the welfare of all its members, including child-rearing, education, and care for elderly parents. The state concentrated its resources on creating and providing jobs through which people could meet their basic needs and receive fringe and other benefits from employers, which explains why only in 1995 when unemployment insurance was legislated were the four basic social insurance programs complete. When the state implemented the unemployment insurance scheme in 1996, it excluded workers in small firms with thirty employees or fewer, even though these constituted a priority group in terms of need. These workers had to wait for protection until July 1998 when the government decided to expand eligibility in the face of soaring unemployment.

Social policy before the financial crisis of 1997 was implemented through the following provisions: social insurance, tax exemptions for the working poor, the livelihood protection law, price caps on basic goods and public services, and wage policy. Most of these were not universal, covering the whole economically active population, but rather were applied only to legally defined target groups. Social insurance programs illustrate this well. Authoritarian governments legislated industrial accident insurance (1963) and the National Pension for Public Officials and Military Officers (1961) just after the military coup, and national health insurance (1977) for a segment of industrial workers. Only gradually were these programs expanded to cover all wage earners. The National Pension Program, first introduced in 1988, was expanded to workers in small firms with five employees or fewer in 1992, to farmers in 1996, and to the self-employed in the urban sector in 1998. It took almost thirty years for these programs to become universal. There was no urgent need for the state to enrich and broaden social insurance benefits since private firms provided considerable welfare benefits to their employees. Especially in monopoly firms, company welfare was larger than state welfare, which is still true in large firms where company welfare benefits can amount to one-third of the monthly wage. As a result, employees of large firms can start a small business with the severance pay they receive upon retirement. According to a survey (Song 1996), there are over sixty pecuniary and nonpecuniary benefits provided by company welfare programs. As an inducement, the state provided tax deductions for firms to compensate for part of their welfare costs. However, with the severe recession of the early 1990s, welfare often became quite costly for firms to provide. Nonetheless, employers could not avoid union demands that company welfare benefits be raised since they recognized that work stoppages and strikes would inflict greater damage.

Since most wage earners were protected by company welfare, it was sufficient for the state to take care of the working poor, disabled, and the elderly without family (Koh 1998), which is why public assistance and public aid were at the center of Korea's welfare policy. In this regard, the Korean welfare system was highly dependent upon the Livelihood Protection Law that secured a minimum subsistence for the extremely poor. The number of beneficiaries under the law declined steadily from two million in 1990 to one million in 1996, amounting to less than 2 percent of the whole population, while social insurance gradually increased in recipients and coverage (see table 8.3 for the composition and overall trend of social expenditures). Because of the extremely low poverty line defined by the government only a small part of the working poor could receive benefits. For the rest of the working poor public assistance consisted simply of a tax exemption. How helpful the exemption from the income tax was for poor households suffering from irregular employment and low wages is questionable. Thus the Livelihood Protection Law, a Korean version of poverty policy, was no more than an inexpensive and bare-bones welfare program. Although public work programs existed for the working poor, they were not effective in relieving poverty.

Prior to 1996, when unemployment insurance was introduced and administered by the Ministry of Labor, the Ministry of Health and Social Affairs was responsible for most welfare administration. It developed the basic outline of poverty policy, implemented the health insurance and pension schemes, and was in

Table 8.3 Trends in Social Security Expenditures, 1990–1998 (%)

Category	1990	1991	1992	1993	1994	1995	1996	1997	1998
1. Old age cash benefits	14.67	16.35	18.29	20.71	21.11	22.01	19.87	17.51	17.65
2. Disablement cash benefits	1.94	2.45	2.34	2.21	2.12	1.89	1.84	1.57	1.03
3. Occupational injury and disease	4.82	5.85	6.23	5.06	4.82	4.48	4.57	3.96	2.22
4. Sickness benefits	1.88	1.91	1.76	1.65	1.45	1.23	1.31	1.17	0.82
5. Services for elderly and disabled people	1.34	1.19	1.13	1.26	2.26	2.53	2.73	2.84	2.01
6. Survivors cash benefits	3.79	4.58	4.07	3.82	3.62	3.16	3.07	2.64	1.72
7. Family cash benefits	0.03	0.06	0.05	0.06	0.05	0.06	0.05	0.34	0.23
8. Family service	0.76	0.96	0.98	1.18	1.17	1.32	1.47	1.41	0.72
9. ALMP	1.49	1.27	1.66	1.82	1.29	1.40	1.49	1.94	4.47
10. Unemployment benefits	23.68	24.37	24.18	24.01	26.30	25.83	24.67	32.24	45.43
Unemployment compensation	0.00	0.00	0.00	0.00	0.00	0.00	0.05	0.27	1.66
Retirement pay	23.68	24.37	24.18	24.01	26.30	25.83	24.63	31.97	43.78
11. Public expenditure on health	41.19	37.16	36.26	35.35	33.41	33.73	36.33	31.88	21.89
12. Housing benefits	0.00	0.00	0.00	0.00	0.00	0.00	0.00	0.00	0.00
13. Other contingencies	4.42	3.86	3.05	2.88	2.39	2.36	2.60	2.49	1.80
Total	100	100	100	100	100	100	100	100	100
As % of GDP	3.9	3.8	4.2	4.4	4.7	5.1	5.3	6.8	6.9

Sources: Korea Institute for Health and Social Affairs 1998, and Koh et al. 2002.

charge of protecting the extreme and working poor, disabled, and elderly. In this regard, the Ministry of Health and Social Affairs was the only state office that concerned itself with implementing welfare policy. Critically, the ministry's welfare proposals were often cut off by the antiwelfare strategy of the economic offices such as the Economic Planning Board (1961–1992) and the Ministry of Finance and the Economy (1993–present).

Price controls and wage restraint were important instruments in the authoritarian regime's fight against inflation. Curbing inflation was a high priority for the government because this promoted investment and the expansion of production. Price controls were used for the dual purpose of lowering living costs for the working population and preventing wage drift from going beyond government guidelines. The government could exert discretionary power over public services and utilities such as public transportation, communication, electricity, fossil fuel, and basic commodities produced by public enterprises. The price control policy was relatively successful. It strengthened the government's position in implementing a wage policy that was first applied to the chaebol and large firms since these were principal sources of wage drift. Wage guidelines were not technically obligatory, but firms that exceeded the guidelines ran the risk of being investigated by the National Tax Office. Price controls were thus a powerful instrument for curbing wage drift as well as inflation over the period of high-speed growth. In strongly organized firms with a high capacity to pay above the wage guidelines, employers and unions acquired a means of avoiding direct confrontation with the state by agreeing upon the increase of company welfare benefits as a social wage. As a result, company welfare increased so dramatically after the labor dispute of 1987 that most firms began to suffer from high labor costs and a rapid decline of profitability. This stimulated capital outflows to low-wage regions.

The above description explains why Korean public welfare was underdeveloped until the mid-1990s. First, company welfare played a leading role in protecting employees and making up for the shortage of state welfare. Second, organized sectors could get more abundant benefits than unorganized ones through collective bargaining. Accordingly, unions did not pay attention to the poor levels of state welfare. During the authoritarian period the supreme goal of organized labor was to stimulate democracy rather than to promote state welfare. Third, and finally, the state and workers did not feel an urgent need to develop social safety nets. As a result of high-speed growth, there was no social emergency crisis, and the concept of universal social safety nets was unfamiliar. Safety nets were never regarded as a measure that could also be applied to professionals and other technically qualified workers should they find themselves in sudden distress. This precipitated the growth of corporations selling private welfare, a market that expanded very quickly. Today most members of the middle and upper class purchase various forms of insurance provided by private companies.[1]

The Politics of Democratization and Globalization

In state-led capitalist countries such as Korea's, the market is distorted by state intervention. Strategic industries and big business enjoyed tremendous benefits from the state in terms of cheap loans, tax exemptions, and tariff rebates. As democratization introduced new rules of the game in the political arena, the opening up of the market also encouraged greater competition in the national economy after 1987.[2]

The ambitious reform agenda of the Kim Young Sam government (1993–1997) contained two primary goals: political reform for democratic consolidation and economic reform to enhance the adaptability of the national economy to globalization. The first task was implemented relatively smoothly under the banner of small, clean, and efficient government. It included various actions such as purification of the military and political elites through the removal of those who had supported authoritarianism, introduction of local autonomy, amendment of election rules, and the restructuring of the party system. President Kim declared that he would dismantle the politics-business linkages popularly regarded as a principal source of corruption and decay. This goal helped pave the way for wage restraint, inducing the FKTU (Federation of Korean Trade Unions) to sign the wage agreement of April 1, 1993. The agreement between the FKTU and the KEF (Korean Employers Federation) contained government promises to complete social and economic reforms in exchange for wage concessions. The agreement was designed to improve the conditions for growth, thereby allowing the government to pursue further reforms. However, the political reform turned out to be unfruitful due to cleavages within the ruling party. The wage agreement also angered the KCTU (Korean Confederation of Trade Unions), a competing union movement that attacked it as elitist and exclusionary.

The Kim government shifted efforts of reform in the latter half of 1994 to structural adjustment of the national economy in response to globalization, strengthening market mechanisms, and deepening trade openness. The government committed itself to deregulation, reducing bureaucratic controls over trade and financial transactions. The state, business, and organized labor experienced structural change of the market and the national economy in two stages: economic liberalization from 1988 to 1993, and globalization from 1994 to the present. Although the distinction is subtle, people began to pay attention to the concept when the Kim Young Sam government promoted *Segyewha* (globalization) as a political slogan. Globalization came to their attention with the sudden collapse of socialist countries and the establishment of the WTO in 1993 as a consequence of the Uruguay Round. However, neither the Korean government nor Korean business was able to anticipate the changes in world markets, much less prepare for them. By 1994 it could be said that the Korean economy was fully incorporated into the global economy. As many scholars stress, globalization fundamentally changes the traditional relations between capital and labor since it enhances the flows of capital and services across nations. Business can take advantage of globalization as a means of avoiding challenges from unions and state regulation. Meanwhile, unions have to lower their demands to maintain job security in the face of a trend toward flexible production (Rodrik 1997; Betcherman 1995; Standing 1995).

The impacts of globalization on the Korean economy were striking. First, many workers lost their jobs and became unemployed due to shutdowns and bankruptcies of labor-intensive firms in sectors such as garments and textiles. Rising labor costs were the main reason for the bankruptcies and many Korean firms decided to move to less developed countries in Central America and Southeast Asia in search of cheaper labor. Capital flight and overseas investment devastated the national industrial parks and export-free zones where light manufacturing was concentrated. Second, chaebol firms began to downsize and release workers in order to deal with the financial crisis and economic recession. It was the first time that employees of big firms under the chaebol faced job insecurity in what had been a stable, lifelong employment system. Chaebol firms began to expand their business in other countries by taking out huge foreign loans. Unfortunately, this accelerated these firms' financial deficits which in a short time led to the foreign debt crisis that exploded in December 1997. Third, privatization of public enterprises and public services emerged as a hot issue when the Kim Young Sam government started to discuss the schedule for privatization of public enterprises in 1994. Public sector unions expressed strong and persistent opposition and announced a general strike. They constructed a joint committee to deter privatization and waged serious and violent struggles in 1994 and 1995. The confrontation continued unresolved until 1998 when the Kim Dae Jung government announced an official schedule for privatization as part of an emergency plan to overcome the financial crisis.

Labor market flexibility was a critical component of this reform agenda. Flexibility typically applies to three areas: employment, compensation, and skill sets. In the Korean case, this required fundamental change in seniority wages, job rotation, and the long-term employment system. The thrust for flexibility met with considerable discontent from workers who saw it as a threat to their job security and wage structure. Flexibility conferred high adaptability and profitability to employers but meant job insecurity and wage cuts to employees (Clarke 1992; McFate 1995). In May 1996 the Kim government announced the amendment of labor laws to reduce rising conflicts between unions and employers and to meet the challenges of globalization. A tripartite committee for the amendment of labor laws was established and an agenda for discussion formulated (Park 2000). The principal issue was whether to legalize layoffs and permit multiple unions. In an important political exchange, employers and organized labor accepted both; however, other important issues remained controversial and unresolved. The new labor laws, passed in the National Assembly at the end of 1996, exposed wage earners and industrial workers to greater market competition. In this sense the reform of industrial relations and labor laws fulfilled the structural requirements of globalization to a certain extent. But the new laws, revised by the state and passed without the consensus of organized labor, became the main source of industrial disputes and of political challenges from employers and unions alike.[3]

Efforts to reform social policy came only at the end of the government's tenure. Nonetheless, the Kim government did make an effort to improve the welfare system by expanding social insurance programs and drafting reform proposals. This effort provided the basis for welfare reforms led by the Kim Dae Jung government during the financial crisis.

Productive Welfare Programs

As a strategic response to globalization, the Kim Young Sam government announced in March 1995 that it would develop a comprehensive reform of social policy under the title of "productive welfare." The plan had a dual purpose: first, to satisfy popular expectations for an improvement in living conditions under democratic government, and second, to protect the working poor and wage earners through state subsidies and the encouragement of voluntary and private welfare as a complement to social welfare. In announcing "productive welfare," President Kim declared that democratic governments had a greater concern with people's living conditions and qualities of life. He also contended that the priorities in the authoritarian policy of "growth first and distribution later" were misplaced.

Productive welfare contained four basic principles: state support for a national minimum income floor, job opportunities and training for the poor and disabled, and the participation of voluntary and nonprofit organizations in welfare development. The principles stressed that the state would be a coordinator of a welfare system in which private firms, religious organizations, and working individuals formed the primary actors. In fact, this was equivalent to a minimalist strategy that aimed at maximizing effects by minimizing social expenditure (Koh 1998). Thus, productive welfare was neither substantive welfare nor workfare containing attractive work incentives.

Although productive welfare was not a paradigmatic change in social policy but rather a brilliant labeling of preexistent welfare institutions, one cannot deny that the Kim government made an effort to consolidate the foundation of welfare programs, especially of social insurance programs. First, the Kim government expanded the National Pension Program to farmers and fishermen and introduced unemployment insurance (1995) just before the debate on labor code reform. This completed implementation of the classic social insurance programs even though some of them did not cover the whole population. In addition to this achievement, the Kim government established a number of ad hoc committees for welfare reform. In 1996 the Welfare Policy Committee for the Disabled and the Medical Care Reform Committee were established under the prime minister. In 1997 the government established the Examining Committee for Social Security Policies to draft the Five-Year Welfare Development Plan (1997–2001). The plan outlined a comprehensive blueprint for reform covering social insurance, public assistance programs, health, housing, education, and employment. However, only a few of these were carried out during his term (Lee 1999). Although the Kim government showed a keen interest in welfare reform, this was ultimately inconsistent with the strategic emphasis placed on small and efficient government.

Financial Crisis as a Turning Point: Social Policy in Transition

The Birth of a Labor-Friendly Government

In light of the strong anti-labor ideology in Korea, it is surprising that a labor-friendly government (not pro-labor in the European sense) was inaugurated in the midst of the financial crisis.[4] President Kim Dae Jung was a well-known opposition leader who identified politically with the lower classes and in particular with industrial workers. During the presidential campaign he tried to transform his image to appear more moderate, appealing to the middle class and downplaying his past commitments to progressive positions. Nonetheless, his statement in the presidential campaign that organized labor would be allowed the right of political participation surprised the nation and caught the attention of capitalists and employers. His electoral victory did not depend upon convincing voters of his party's policy platform, but he was successful due to the economic disaster popularly blamed on the previous government's ineptness and corruption. Voters turned away from the ruling party in the expectation that the "prepared" president would reconstruct the national economy. Kim Dae Jung's victory was due largely to the regional coalition he put together and to the support of the lower classes in urban and rural areas. Organized labor and most social movement organizations strongly supported him in the hope that he might bring fundamental change. This might have been possible had the financial crisis not deprived him of policy autonomy. He found himself with no choice but to sign a technical agreement with the IMF in December 1997.

Following his victory he was faced with two urgent tasks: to overcome the financial crisis and complete democratic reform. These two tasks were an unwanted bequest from the previous government. The dilemma was in the short-run contradiction between the predictable economic impacts of the IMF's austerity policy and the goals of democratic consolidation. He could not betray the political support of the lower classes and industrial workers, but he recognized that the IMF's austerity policy, at least in the short run, would bring enormous hardship and suffering to wage earners in general and to industrial workers in particular. The IMF demanded five important actions as an initial response to the economic problems.[5] The thrust of the IMF's position was to let the market regulate the Korean economy, which until then had achieved economic growth through market-distorting methods (Lee 1998). Within a couple of months this reform package brought about disastrous consequences for economic and social life. By July 1998, interest rates had soared to 22 percent. As price controls were released, inflation also skyrocketed. Tens of thousands of firms under financial debt went bankrupt and the unemployed flooded into the streets. The Korean economy seemed to face a complete collapse. The income of workers and the middle class shrank substantially faster than that of the upper class with the result that income inequality in the first year of the crisis worsened from a Gini coefficient of 0.28 to 0.32. Several surveys show that the financial crisis undermined the middle class's economic foundation and forced one out of three into the lower class. It drove 1.5 million people out of work, raising the unemployment rate from 3 percent prior to the disaster to 8 percent within seven months. Above all, it raised the urban poverty rate from 7 percent in 1997 to 21 percent in 1998 (National Statistical Office 1999; Rew 2000; Jin 2002).

Not surprisingly, the lower classes, including industrial workers and the unemployed, expressed strong discontent toward the neoliberal policy promoted by the IMF and endorsed by the Kim government. Heated debates regarding the appropriateness of the IMF austerity policy occurred. Neoliberals agreed with the Kim government's policy choices, contending that restoring the market was the only road out of the disaster. In contrast, organized labor and other progressive intellectuals and opinion leaders argued that the neoliberal policies would ruin the foundation of the Korean economy and would only aggravate social displacement as income inequality, unemployment, and poverty rose.

The labor-friendly government was forced to implement what workers were most worried about in the IMF recommendations. Given the agreement with the IMF, the politics of crisis management involved implementing unattractive and unpopular policies. In his first speech after the electoral victory, Kim declared that "you elected me as president, but I have to set in motion what you dislike." Dislike proved to be a mild term as the government unveiled a paradox. Despite the fact that capitalists, bureaucrats, and politicians were the primary group responsible for the financial debt crisis and economic disaster, the costs of the labor-friendly government's policies fell primarily on the lower classes and industrial workers.

Politics of Crisis Management: The Tripartite Commission and Market Restoration

The political platform of a "democratic market economy" developed by President Kim Dae Jung contained a policy package that addressed social problems generated by economic openness. There was little opposition to Kim's decision to strengthen market processes in the national economy through a series of deregulatory measures and privatization policies but the questions of how far, in what ways, and in which direction caused strong debate both within and between government, business, and labor.

The democratic market economy had three focal points that distinguished it from previous reform attempts. It had as its goals finding a new balance between large and medium firms in the national economy, greater equity, and, perhaps paradoxically, heavier reliance on the market. Urged by the IMF, the Kim government set as its priorities four reform projects. These consisted of a reorganization of the chaebol's governance structure, reform of labor relations, rationalization of financial institutions, and privatization of public enterprises. Of these four targets, the government achieved relative success in the reform of financial institutions. One of the big banks was sold to foreign capital and a few succeeded in attracting foreign investors. But the process was accompanied by massive layoffs of employees from the financial sector, which lost 25 percent of its employment in a year. The Kim government faced formidable challenges dealing with the other three targets.

First, the Kim government strongly enforced reform measures on chaebol firms that included an obligatory reduction of the firms' debt ratios to 200 percent, transparency of transactions within and between chaebol firms, transformation of their governance structure by reducing owners' stock share, strengthening of management's responsibilities, and mandatory selling of troubled, unproductive firms to foreign capital. The chaebol strongly resisted this policy, contending that breaking chaebol firms into independent and small enterprises would seriously damage national competitiveness. For these reasons the restructuring of the chaebol is not yet complete.

Second, conservatives raised doubts about the compatibility between the commitment to progressive politics and the implementation of the IMF demands. Other critics stressed that greater reliance on the market frequently generated outcomes detrimental to equity, as evidenced in the American experience. President Kim attempted to find the answer in social safety nets, social integration, and a fundamental redesign of social insurance programs. However, the latter generated more turmoil than solutions, as will be described later.

Third, privatization provoked heated debates among intellectuals, policy makers, and public-sector employees regarding its impacts on the supply and price of public utilities such as electric power and telecommunication. To pacify the public sector unions—famous for their militancy, particularly under the leadership of the KCTU, the national center of democratic unions—the Kim government slowed the rate of privatization, setting the final schedule in mid-1998. By 2000, five public enterprises were sold and six larger enterprises were in the process of privatization in spite of severe resistance of public sector unions.

Finally, the government gave priority to the reform of labor relations and the employment system following the IMF recommendation that legalization of layoffs would be a necessary step in attracting foreign investment. Chaebol firms in need of downsizing welcomed legislation that would enable them to release redundant workers. The result was an explosion of massive unemployment. In the tripartite commission's social agreement of February 1998, unions agreed to legalization of layoffs in exchange for other reform items, political as well as economic.[6] Without such an agreement, workers' discontent could have exploded into massive turmoil and labor unrest. In this respect, the Kim government succeeded in incorporating organized workers into the politics of crisis management and in persuading them to be supportive of the restrictive economic policy that the IMF and the government had agreed to and signed in the technical agreement.

However, the success of this first phase of crisis management did not last long. The government was soon confronted with a serious dilemma intrinsic to the social agreement: it could not hold together. The business sector regretted that with soaring popular blame and under undue pressure from the government it had made hasty concessions and signed an agreement it did not like. Organized labor in turn was discontented because it felt that the government had adopted a passive attitude and had not pushed business to carry out its promises. As unemployment soared, labor unions began to raise demands for job security in accordance with the agreement. Despite the government's attempts to keep the spirit of the social agreement alive, the economic crisis and soaring unemployment made the tripartite commission fragile. A lack of mutual trust among the three parties and increasing discontent from the rank-and-file against union leadership and union concessions aggravated the problem.

The politics of crisis management was composed of two complementary sets of economic and social policy packages designed to facilitate implementation of the IMF's recommendations. The economic reforms placed an emphasis on restoring market functions, improving flexibility, and increasing the transparency of transactions and firms' financial structures. Social policy was introduced to reduce the cost of social displacement resulting from the neoliberal austerity policy, particularly in regard to poverty, unemployment, and inequality. As a result, social safety nets were implemented to help people in economic trouble. These safety nets were congruent with the IMF's recommendations since social disruption could endanger neoliberal and austerity policy; both scholars and government officials argued that economic reform could not be successfully undertaken without them.

The politics of crisis management resulted in a Janus-faced policy. Unlike some of the Latin American cases, the Kim Dae Jung government did not neglect the social consequences of neoliberal economic adjustment. In keeping with President Kim's promise to improve public welfare for wage earners, the unemployed, and the poor, the government undertook serious efforts to develop the institutional foundations for social welfare. In addition to addressing issues of unemployment, poverty, and inequality, the Kim government attempted to redesign the institutional and financial structure of social insurance programs. As a result, the politics of crisis management became a critical turning point in the development of the Korean welfare system.

Reform of Social Policy

As mentioned earlier, due to the political strategy of President Kim, politicians and bureaucrats began to pay attention to the importance of social policy in managing social problems. For the first time in modern Korean political history, social policy gained a status and importance of its own. The Kim government focused on four policy areas: labor market policy, poverty policy and public relief, inequality, and social insurance programs. Because of the rising unemployment rate, unemployment policy occupied center stage early on in the administration.

The bankruptcy of tens of thousands of firms due to the frozen credit market resulted in a massive increase in unemployment. The National Statistics Office announced that the number of unemployed practically tripled in the first year of the IMF bailout, rising to 1.8 million people at the end of 1998. The rate of unemployment rose from 3.1 percent in December 1997 to 4.5 percent in January, 5.9 percent in February, and 6.5 percent in March 1998, reaching its peak in August 1999. When underemployment (measured as 17 hours or less worked per week) is included, the rate rises to just over 10 percent. This was the highest rate of unemployment of the past four decades, and approximated the average in European countries. Inflation had been relatively stable throughout the 1990s, but the foreign debt crisis put an end to that. Inflation rose to 13 percent within a few months of the IMF bailout. Korea had received praise for achieving virtually full employment without resorting to rigorous labor market policy, but the 8.5 percent unemployment rate broke this pattern. However inevitable, the steep increase in unemployment caused social and political concern. More serious was the fact that the Korean government was unprepared for mass unemployment.

The Kim government's response was three-pronged: macroeconomic policy, labor market policy, and, relying on the unemployment insurance program of 1995, unemployment compensation. To keep the social agreement alive, it expanded interventionist measures of various kinds, procuring large budgets for them. The unemployment budget of 1998 amounted to eleven billion USD, one-third of which was aimed at paying unemployment compensation and living subsidies. Part of the budget was reserved for active labor market policy, including measures such as job creation, training, and job replacement. This budget was equivalent to approximately 13 percent of government spending; in 1999 the government increased the unemployment budget to sixteen billion USD. As far as budget size is concerned, the effect of the Kim government is notable. In terms of overall policy orientation, the government pursued a two-sided strategy: alleviation of firms' problems by legalizing layoffs, and protection of unemployed workers.

Due in large measure to government policies, the unemployment rate began to fall in the latter half of 1999, one and a half years after the foreign debt crisis. The decline was attributable more to economic recovery than to labor market policies. In fact, this economic recovery was in part due to a policy package that placed great emphasis on macro- and microeconomic policy, including financial support for small- and medium-sized firms and cheap long-term loans for venture capital and the creation of small business. Labor market programs were in general poorly designed and lacking in administrative infrastructure. Although the government quickly established local employment offices in large cities, these were not sufficient in number to meet demand. Despite these problems, the government effort was striking, for this was the first time a Korean government had carried out active labor market policy. The government allocated a large amount of resources to public relief for the unemployed in the form of public work programs, cheap loans to cover small business creation, and public assistance for the working poor. Unemployment insurance was expanded to firms with five or more employees in March 1998 and, in September 2000, it became a universal program covering all workers as well as part-time government workers. The government also extended the duration of unemployment benefits from a maximum of 60 to 210 days, depending on an individual's employment history.

Poverty policy was not new to the Korean government because it constituted the core of the preexisting welfare system. In the midst of waging war on social disruption, the government realized that the traditional institutions of poverty policy, that is, the Livelihood Protection Law and public assistance program of 1965, were not sufficient to cover the needs of the growing number of working poor. Thus, the government decided to redesign poverty policy by developing more comprehensive and generous forms of protection. The result was the introduction of the National Basic Livelihood Security Law of 1998. Although the new law resembled the old one in its aim of protecting the extremely poor and in its use of means-testing, the new law was more generous and gave cash benefits to the poor and the disabled instead of nonpecuniary support. Beneficiaries of the new law numbered approximately 1.5 million in contrast to 1 million under the old law.

National health insurance, introduced in 1977 and expanded to cover the whole population, was divided into four main parts (Kwon 2002a, 2002b). The disabled and the poor with incomes under the minimum wage were protected by the Health Assistance Program. The remaining economically active population belonged to three different programs according to occupation. Industrial Workers' Health Insurance covered regular employees in various industries (38 percent of the population), another program protected government employees and private school teachers (11 percent), and the self-employed and others belonged to the Regional Health Insurance Program (51 percent). These were financed by joint contributions from workers and employers. The government covered only administrative costs. In the hope of achieving greater financial and managerial efficiency, the Kim government wanted to integrate these various programs. Despite fierce resistance from each division, integration under the National Health Insurance Board is almost complete. But one disastrous reform regarding division of labor between prescription and medicine is worth mentioning. The Kim government started a rigorous reform separating prescriptions from the provision of medicine but ended up with social confusion and a serious financial deficit in the national health insurance program. The reform plan evoked fierce discontent among medical doctors and hospitals because it resulted in an abrupt decline of doctors' income (Song 2001).

Government plans to extend the National Pension Program to the self-employed in the urban sector in 1999 faced strong opposition from recipients concerning the amount of their individual contributions. The self-employed in urban areas were the last group excluded from the national pension scheme since its expansion to firms with five employees or more in 1992, and to farmers, fishermen, and the self-employed in rural areas in 1995. They had not been included in previous expansions of the pension program because of the difficulty in ascertaining their income. For this reason, the government decided to set individual contributions on the basis of individuals' two most important assets: their home and their car. The policy provoked a great deal of discontent from the urban self-employed, but the government nonetheless succeeded in incorporating them into the program. The national pension scheme is now a universal program, covering the whole population.

However, there is concern about the possible bankruptcy of the pension fund within twenty years because of the aging population (Kwon 1999). In fall 2000 the government presented the final draft of its pension reform, which would remedy the problem of future financial deficits by reducing benefits, increasing individual contributions, and tightening qualification criteria. The pension reform proposal ignited a serious challenge, particularly from the National Teachers' Union, but the challenge was ineffective in derailing the proposal.

The development of social safety nets is notable. The economic crisis generated tremendous numbers of people in trouble, so the government introduced public relief programs as an emergency means of helping the unemployed, the working poor, and the disabled. The programs were new to Korea, which had previously relied solely on the Livelihood Protection Law, and provided various state subsidies, including subsidized loans for rent, the start-up of a small business, and school expenses, as well as exemptions from taxes and contributions to the social insurance programs.

Finally, the government also announced plans to promote the "productive welfare system" through active labor market policy. Although the previous government had presented a draft but had not implemented any of the programs included in it, the Kim Dae Jung government declared in 1999 that it would improve living conditions by incorporating the unemployed into the labor market through work incentives. The plan was a Korean version of "welfare to work." While the Livelihood Protection Law aimed at protecting the extremely poor, the goal of the productive welfare system was to coordinate all existing welfare policies. The core of this project was the construction of an administrative infrastructure to expand and deliver welfare benefits. Beyond this, it also contained a diverse set of welfare benefits for particular target groups. How effective these programs have been in reducing inequality and relieving poverty is questionable. Although the government announced its intention to strengthen and consolidate policy instruments that serve ordinary citizens, people on the street and ordinary workers do not believe that the programs are working. If these programs do not produce a real effect, the government's policies might not amount to much more than political rhetoric, as was the case with the Kim Young Sam government.

Nonetheless, social expenditure did increase dramatically in 1998 and 1999 compared to previous years. When the eleven billion USD of the unemployment budget is included, social expenditure was 1.5 times greater in 1998 than in 1997. Social expenditure also grew in 2001 from 6 percent of GDP in 1999 to 10.2 percent in 2001. Substantial budgetary increases were not the only aspect of welfare expansion. Social policy gained special weight in government decisions. Analysts of social policy persuasively argue that the volume and speed of change in this area in the three years following the debt crisis was much greater than during previous decades. Contrary to the general view that globalization erodes the welfare state, Korean social policy developed substantially during the period of most intense opening and adjustment to the world economy (Lee 1999).

In all, the Kim government's efforts to develop social policy are characterized by three essential aspects: expansion, updating, and unequal protection. Expansion addresses enlargement of recipients and coverage, and updating implies incorporation of new welfare demand. But unequal protection has led to stronger and more generous conditions for the well-to-do workers than for the working poor. The state chose a safe route in constructing social welfare policies that alleviate financial burdens while also avoiding a financial crisis of the social insurance fund.

Behind this progress lies a serious conflict between what might be called the "distribution coalition" and the "growth coalition." The distribution coalition consists of industrial workers, farmers, and the low middle class who want greater institutional protection in the face of structural adjustment and fundamental reform of the national economy. The growth coalition consists mostly of business and the upper class, both resistant to welfare expansion. The growth coalition fiercely attacked the Kim government's labor-friendly position as reflected in the development of the tripartite commission and in a policy-making process favorable to industrial workers and the working poor. The growth coalition, consisting of business, economic ministries, and conservative intellectuals, emphasized the benefits of a market economy and defended the neoliberal argument that government intervention should be minimized to improve efficiency. However, the government's labor friendliness and the widely shared blame for the economic crisis, which was placed on the elites, helped the distributional coalition in its pursuit of welfare expansion.

Interestingly, social welfare expansion has not always been helpful to the government as it seeks to expand and consolidate political support. At times the political effects of welfare expansion and reform have been quite the opposite, provoking resistance and discontent rather than loyalty and satisfaction. Recent conflict surrounding health policy has provided evidence of this. In an environment where selling medication was one of the largest sources of profit for doctors and hospitals, the policy proposal that pharmacists be provided with the exclusive right to sell drugs met with strong opposition. Doctors participated in nationwide strikes from June to November 2000. The National Teachers' Union also demonstrated in opposition to pension reform. In pursuing welfare reform that adjusted individual contributions and benefits, integrated divided programs, and provided greater equity, the Kim government lost political support from the middle and upper-middle classes.

Conclusion

Welfare expansion in Korea has resulted from a combination of the politics of a neoliberal solution to the economic crisis with the inauguration of democratic and labor-friendly government. Even though welfare expansion has occurred not through rupture but through gradual change, clear differences are observable between the Kim Young Sam and Kim Dae Jung governments. While the former relied upon passive measures in labor market intervention and offered limited protection for the disabled and the extremely poor, the latter introduced active labor market measures and expanded welfare benefits to the working poor and the unemployed. The latter also introduced social safety nets in the form of a public relief system. Although the active measures of the Kim Dae Jung government resulted from a political agreement legalizing layoffs in exchange for social protection, this agreement paved the way institutionally for further progress in social policy.

Progress, however, was not assured. Although the tripartite commission has been very active, bureaucrats and the National Assembly have tended to ignore the commission's proposals when they conflict with other interests. The commission is not a politically strong institution relative to the National Assembly and the Federation of Korean Industry (FKI); it just produces policy recommendations that are easily discarded by government, the National Assembly, and even the national center of labor unions. The commission remains at its core a talking shop for discussing and setting policy agendas that are considered to be important for reducing conflict between capital and labor. Nonetheless, the very establishment of the tripartite commission is a striking development in a country where exclusion and repression of labor had long been the norm. It is also significant that social policy has obtained a status independent from economic policy, and that the government has become aware of the need for social policy packages.

However, it should be stressed that the Korean welfare system does not go beyond the lowest level of OECD countries. In fact, social protection in Korea is still far poorer than in the most advanced countries of Latin America, despite the obvious advantage of Korea's overall level of economic development. As the ratio of social expenditure to GDP clearly indicates, Korea has a long way to go until it reaches the average of OECD countries and its welfare system is equipped with well-designed and deeply rooted institutional provisions. The rapid increase of social expenditure and the development of social insurances under the Kim Dae Jung government indicate a "catching-up" effort toward the advanced welfare states.

This is also true of other East Asian countries, including Japan, where company welfare remains predominant. Popular demand for public welfare has increased rapidly with the decline of company welfare in the wake of economic malaise. Where the economically active population is principally protected through company benefits, governments focus their policy efforts on satisfying the welfare demands of target groups such as retirees, the disabled, and women. In 2000, for example, the Japanese government submitted a proposal for protection of the elderly in terms of hospitalization and long-term care. This policy will reduce the burden on women of providing care for older family members. It is highly likely that the growth of public welfare in this region will be closely related to the decline of company welfare. Insofar as the decline in company welfare is the result of firms' strategies toward global competition, the growth of public welfare is closely associated with globalization. As companies recede from welfare provisions, the state begins to emerge.

What light, then, does the Korean case shed on the effects of globalization on social policy? It seems likely that the progress in social protection is attributable not only to economic openness and globalization but also to democratization. Democratic governments in Korea have had to reform and expand the social policy regime in order to improve social performance, viewed as important for the consolidation of democracy (O'Donnell and Valenzuela 1992; Schmitter and Karl 1991; Choi 1997; Im 1994). Democracy is more easily sustained when it is accompanied by policies that improve the standard of living and income equality, and which eliminate structural and regional discrimination in the society (Diamond and Plattner 1991; Diamond and Gunther 2001). The gradual expansion of social policy in Korea is a joint result of the maladjustment to globalization that resulted in the financial crisis, and the timely emergence of democratic government, which permitted the rise to power of a progressive and labor-friendly leadership.

9

Conclusion
Politics Matters

MIGUEL GLATZER AND DIETRICH RUESCHEMEYER

In this concluding essay, we return to the questions raised in the opening chapter. We will closely review each of the studies that form the main body of this project. But at the same time, we will try to come to broader conclusions about the impact of globalization on welfare state development and will do so by exploring the social and economic mechanisms through which economic openness may affect social welfare policy. Of particular importance is how different aspects of economic globalization are related to the domestic factors that shape welfare state development.

A First Look at the Results

The studies assembled in this volume portray a great variety of social policy developments in countries experiencing increased economic openness. What stands out is, first of all, the relative immunity to the undermining effects of economic globalization displayed by the welfare states of northwestern Europe. Questions remain about the consequences of greater capital mobility for macroeconomic policy options and, more generally, for the balance of power in these societies as well as for the particular "coordinated" versions of capitalism that have been associated with their social welfare systems. Nonetheless, with the exception of Britain these countries have largely retained their overall patterns of social protection. This in spite of the serious problems they face for reasons other than economic openness, problems that derive from a changing age structure, increases in the cost of medical care, high levels of unemployment, and the emergence of new problems related to changing family patterns and increasing levels of immigration. The welfare states of northwestern Europe were the point of departure for our comparative analysis (see Stephens, this volume; Huber and Stephens 2001a). They defined the dimensions of vulnerability and resilience on which the examination of the middle-income countries in different regions focused.

Among the countries and regions examined in this project, the strongest negative impact of economic globalization on social welfare policies is found in Latin America. Here the protectionist policies of import substitution industrialization (ISI) were prolonged in the 1970s with the help of easy credit, which derived from the massive gains of the oil-producing countries organized into the OPEC cartel. This led abruptly into the debt crisis of the 1980s, when interest rates rose and the international banks stopped making new loans as Mexico, Argentina, and Brazil faced serious repayment difficulties. The debt crisis opened most Latin American countries to very strong pressures from the international financial institutions urging austerity and market-oriented reform. As conditions for restructuring loans they insisted on severe budget cuts as well as a drastic opening to international trade, which many enterprises did not survive.[1] If the 1980s became "the lost decade" for most of Latin America, the 1990s saw some economic recovery; but this decade also witnessed new inflows and outflows of short-term capital that were held responsible for the financial crises of Mexico and Argentina in 1994–1995 and of Brazil in 1998–1999. The broad picture of change in Latin America during the last generation is clear: States were weakened in their capacity to intervene on behalf of the weaker strata. Among the more important social and economic outcomes was an increase in the informal economy, removing more people not only from taxation but also from social regulation and support, as well as persistently high levels of unemployment, poverty, and income inequality. The results in social policy were decade-long cuts in social expenditures and policy reforms that emphasized privatization and targeted help for the poor rather than universal programs.

Yet the differences among Latin American countries are as instructive as this overall picture. Costa Rica as well as Uruguay and Panama increased their already high level of social spending as a share of the gross domestic product even during the 1980s. "Costa Rica and Uruguay . . . were consistently different from the other Latin American countries in spending efforts and outcomes, and . . . they were also different in some aspects of their traditional systems of social protection and in their approach to social policy reform" (Huber, this volume). In contrast to Chile, where neoliberal transformation of social policy led to privatization, reductions of universalistic benefits, more means-tested programs, and an overall decline in social expenditures by more than a quarter, Costa Rica did not opt for a similar individualization and privatization of social policy; instead, it strengthened the universalistic character of its pension and health policies and sought to put them on a sounder financial basis.[2] Evelyne Huber traces these differences convincingly to the structure and capacity of the state and to the balance of social and political power. And these factors not only account for the differences between the extreme cases but are shown to shape the more mixed policy developments in other countries as well.

Spain and Portugal offer the clearest evidence that a social policy trajectory very different from neoliberal minimalism can be associated with increased economic openness. Since the 1970s, both countries significantly opened their economies to international trade and capital flows. Yet at the same time they developed comprehensive welfare states, taking off from the rather austere foundations that were the legacy of the previous authoritarian corporatist regimes.

Post-Communist Eastern Europe presents a very different picture from the other regions. Until the collapse of Communism in 1989–1990, countries under Soviet control had comprehensive—if in their absolute levels of provision, austere—social welfare systems. These systems were, however, tied to a centrally planned economy. With the rapid disintegration of that economy and with the policy of establishing market economies in a very short period of time, the Communist welfare systems ran into mounting difficulties. The old social welfare provisions were cut loose from their institutional moorings in industrial enterprises; centrally provided benefits such as pensions became too expensive, and new problems such as unemployment had to be dealt with. At the same time, the expectations engendered by the old system made cutbacks and restructuring politically difficult. In Russia, these difficulties led in the Yeltsin period to a stalemate between the reformist presidential executive, advised by the World Bank, and the Communist-dominated Parliament (Cook, this volume). In east-central Europe there were a variety of policy responses until the middle 1990s, when policies began to converge in response to increasing budgetary constraints and guided by the World Bank and other international institutions (Orenstein and Haas, this volume). As in Latin America, the international financial institutions urged a policy direction defined by privatization and strict targeting of social supports. Another similarity is, however, equally noteworthy: After initially neglecting social policy altogether, the international financial institutions became concerned with the disruptive potential of a lack of social protection for economic openness and for market-oriented reform in general.

The political economies of Japan and the more recent industrializing countries of East Asia are in still other ways set off from the advanced capitalist countries of Europe and the English-speaking settler countries. These differences are evidenced in the social problems generated by a capitalist economy; in the rapid economic growth these countries experienced since the 1950s and 1960s, respectively; and in their emerging social policy patterns.[3] Among the major similarities relevant for social welfare policy in East Asian countries were the following: widespread poverty after the Second World War and the Korean War, which was, however, combined with low income inequality; an education system of high quality; a strong policy priority given to fast income growth rather than special social policies; low unemployment; encouragement of corporate welfare; and adoption of the classic social programs with little emphasis on generous funding.

Song's chapter sees South Korea as a laggard in social welfare policies that finds itself now at a crossroads. During the 1960s and 1970s, rapid economic growth substituted for social welfare policies beyond education, health care, and pension programs for privileged groups (the military, government employees, and teachers). Unions were politically constrained and limited to single enterprises; not unexpectedly they supported corporate welfare programs in the larger chaebol, which were also strongly encouraged by the military government. Democratization since the late 1980s, even though less than complete in the freedom provided for self-organization of society,[4] encouraged the institutional rounding out of the classic social welfare programs, though these remain still at a low level of spending. At the same time, Korea's economy opened itself to freer import trade and later to an open capital account. The financial crisis of 1997–1998 made increases in social spending both for general assistance and, above all, for unemployment compensation imperative. Whether a more democratic and economically open Korea will move toward stronger welfare state development on the basis of tripartite political cooperation is at this point an open question. If it does, it will join the Iberian countries in a social policy trajectory in which democratization and economic opening jointly encourage rather than undermine welfare state development. But a much more limited version of social welfare policy seems equally possible.

Geoffrey Garrett and David Nickerson offer a cross-national examination of relevant indicators for a large number of middle-income countries. They focus on the compensation and efficiency hypotheses that defined one of the primary themes of our project. The conclusion that middle-income countries with more open economies have larger public economies extends earlier work (Cameron 1978; Rodrik 1997). Garrett and Nickerson show that capital mobility is positively associated with public spending. Their analysis strongly suggests that there may be a positive effect of globalization on social policy worth investigating. They distinguish between level of openness to capital mobility and increases in capital mobility and find different effects of the two: while the former is associated with higher levels of public spending, the latter correlates negatively with growth in public spending. Their chapter, then, points to fascinating complexities in the relationship between openness and size of government. These complexities as well as the important variation among middle-income countries make a good case for the comparative case studies that comprise the bulk of this volume.

The conclusions that can be reached from this set of interregional comparisons are inherently tentative because of the recurrent problem of macro-comparative social analysis—too many potentially important factors, too few cases. Careful causal tracing within countries, based on many observations, can ease these problems. Furthermore, since welfare state development has been the subject of much theoretical and empirical comparative work during the past twenty years, we can approach the limited number of cases and comparisons with quite specific theoretical expectations and interpretations and thus improve the plausibility of our conclusions.

Our cases share important similarities: All the mid-income countries and regions saw in the last generation significant advances in democratization, though the realities of democratic politics varied considerably from country to country. All increased their openness to the international economy, though there were important variations in this dimension as well. These latter variations included differences in the pace of opening to both trade and capital mobility and, importantly, the incidence of economic crises that were related to a country's greater integration into the international markets for goods, services, and capital. Yet with the possible exception of the latter—an issue to which we will return—it seems that these differences in exposure to the international economy do not offer the key for understanding the variety of outcomes in social policy.

The results of our cross-regional inquiries suggest two first-order conclusions: The very variability of outcomes implies that the advances of international economic integration during the past two decades do not constitute a development that defines the future of social welfare policy worldwide. Equally important is another strongly supported claim: Politics makes a decisive difference for the consequences of economic globalization for social policy in a given country. "Politics" here, of course, must not be understood as a matter of sheer political will. What politics can accomplish is always mediated by the historical background of political and economic structures, by the resultant balance of power within a country, and by a country's insertion into its geopolitical environment and the structures of the international political economy. Yet within those constraints politics does indeed seem to make a decisive difference.

What does the pattern of findings in our cross-regional comparison of mid-income countries suggest about the two opposed master hypotheses on the relation between economic openness and social welfare policies? Those hypotheses are the compensation thesis, which claims that economic openness induces social protection measures, and the efficiency thesis, which holds that welfare state policies make economies less efficient in international competition.

Neither of the two broad arguments can account for the whole set of outcomes. However, there is an important asymmetry in the implications our cases have for the two views, and this entails a third preliminary result: The radical formulations of the efficiency view are simply mistaken. It is impossible to maintain in the face of our results that expanding free trade and free flows of capital always undermine social welfare policies.

The compensation view, to begin with, does not have a radical version that could be falsified by a few instances. While the compensation view does not explain the cases where severe cutbacks in social provisions came about in response to international economic pressures, it can point to important other instances where increasing opening to the international economy did not lead to such cutbacks but actually went along with extensive welfare state building.

Even more significant is another asymmetry. The efficiency view is basically at odds with our claim that politics matters. In its pure—or perhaps better, fundamentalist—form, the efficiency hypothesis denies that politics can truly modify the impact of market forces. Advocates of the efficiency view often assume that market forces are by far the more powerful and that in conflict with social needs and policies market forces always win out in the end. By contrast, the compensation view inherently involves politics, at least implicitly, unless one assumes in functionalist fashion that policy responses will come forth uniformly and succeed regularly in compensating for the impact of international market forces. Our understanding of the impact of economic globalization on social welfare policies will be deepened if we examine the causal mechanisms underlying the outcomes claimed by the two views. These more detailed underlying mechanisms give us insight into the conditions under which one or the other takes place.

These more specific hypotheses relating economic globalization to social welfare policies must also be integrated with the body of earlier work seeking to explain the rise and consolidation of welfare states. Remarkably, this earlier work has largely focused on internal, domestic factors—on the logic of industrialism, the power resources of contending groups and classes, the autonomy and capacity of states and, more recently, on the more or less coordinated character of the political economy of a country. Bringing the consideration of internal and external factors shaping social policy development together seems to hold significant promise for both sides, though it is our contention that such an integration will have a more decisive impact on the views about the consequences of economic openness.

Causal Mechanisms Shaping Social Policy

What are the more detailed causal hypotheses that have been advanced on the link between openness to the international economy and the extent of social welfare policy? The efficiency view provides a robust and fairly detailed theory that is plausible but not broadly corroborated by empirical evidence. The compensation view, by contrast, is supported by multiple correlation results but relies for their interpretation on rather underspecified and sometimes functionalist ideas.

The Efficiency Theory

The causal mechanisms associated with the efficiency theory need only a brief review. International markets, more than local and national ones, are beyond the control of national governments, while limiting a country's participation in free trade often means foregoing important economic gains. A first causal mechanism invoked by the efficiency view involves the effects of competition from countries with lower costs. Low-cost and especially low-wage competition can force wage and benefit cuts or lead to the elimination of jobs and unemployment in the affected sectors. The threat of such competition may, however, be balanced by productivity advantages of more advanced capitalist countries and especially of countries with effective welfare states policies. If high earnings and workers' benefits are not compensated by productivity levels that leave the labor costs per unit low, low-wage competition can be an effective pressure for lowering welfare benefits.

Increased capital mobility has multiple consequences. It gives capital owners a wider choice of profitable investment, and it lowers the cost of capital in countries with scarce savings. Rapid changes in the availability and price of capital can lead to devastating financial crises, as happened in the 1980s in Latin America and again in the 1990s in Latin America, East Asia, and Russia. More fundamentally, increased capital mobility is likely to increase the power of capital in relation to labor and government, both of which are inherently less mobile. Specifically, some claim that capital mobility reins in the space for governmental action because it constrains national macroeconomic policy as well as, albeit more indirectly, subsidized investment and above-average levels of taxation and public expenditures. These results are, however, contingent on the extent to which increased mobility of capital results in a truly international capital market with homogeneously shaped interest rates. Furthermore, it is important to remember in this context that the productivity-enhancing consequences of public expenditures may be attractive to investors as well as labor, though they may be irrelevant to the interests of capital owners seeking short-term interest gains. As already mentioned, Garrett and Nickerson (this volume) found in their examination of middle-income countries that recent increases in capital mobility were indeed associated with lower public expenditures, but that the levels of openness to capital mobility and public expenditures were positively correlated with each other.[5]

While overall there is only very limited support for the claim that economic openness as such is at odds with generous social provisions, there is a special constellation in which economic opening does seem to have a strong negative impact on social welfare policy. Sudden opening—to trade or capital flows or both—constitutes such a constellation and can produce wrenching change that destroys previously well-established policies and institutions. Where institutional arrangements had been built on insulation from market forces with which they would be incompatible, a sudden economic opening can wreck them, while new ones are not easily built. This has been identified as a major cause of the radical restructuring of the welfare state of New Zealand (Huber and Stephens 2001a; Stephens, this volume). If we allow for different kinds of institutional dislocations with various implications for social policy, it seems that this causal mechanism pertains to a wide range of circumstances: Most severe cutbacks appear to be associated with radical institutional dislocations due to sudden opening—Latin America's extended and then abruptly ended ISI; the disruption of privileged trade flows in the antipodes; even the post-Communist countries of east-central Europe fit here.[6] This may well be the most important direct negative effect of economic openness on social welfare policy.

While the causal mechanisms primarily associated with the efficiency view do not involve politics, it is important to realize that politics enters the picture nevertheless. This is obvious in the case of social dumping—a politically induced variety of low-cost trade competition and similar competitive moves designed to attract foreign direct investment. Furthermore, the negative impact of openness on social welfare policies involves political choice and requires political enforcement; the build-down of welfare states is clearly a matter of politics.[7] Multinational corporations and other strong corporate actors give political "voice" to pro-market pressures (in contrast to the "voiceless" working of competitive markets), though it must be kept in mind that corporate actors are not uniformly opposed to social welfare policies. The political element in the spread of neoliberal policies is most obvious when policy ideas are imposed as conditions for credits by the IFIs and private banks. Finally, the views that set international markets against politics overlook another important fact. The expansion of an open international economy is itself the product of political action by many states, albeit states of quite varied power resources. The international market needs infrastructural guarantees as much as any national market, and these requisite elements of the rule of law are ultimately based on the coercive power of states. Thus, even a closer look at the efficiency view provides important evidence for the claim that "politics matters," contradicting the inclination of its advocates to give politics only a marginal role.

The Compensation Hypothesis

The compensation hypothesis, as already indicated, puts politics at the center of attention. It must do so unless one assumes in naively functionalist fashion that all needs arising from an opening to the international economy will invariably call forth protective responses. It is true, however, that the ways in which domestic factors shape political responses remain rather shadowy.

The compensation hypothesis is supported by positive correlations repeatedly found in different sets of countries between trade and public expenditures, including expenditures on social protection (Cameron 1978; Rodrik 1997). In their examination of mid-income countries, Garrett and Nickerson (this volume) report that the same relationship holds for capital mobility and public expenditures. Furthermore, they found that democracy increased the association. These correlations are just that—statistical associations between numerical indicators, not causal accounts, but they are significant empirical findings that need explanation. The compensation view seeks to provide that.

The Hypothetical Sequence Model

A hypothetical sequence model makes clear that compensation policies must not be taken for granted and conceived as an automatic or modal response. Inspecting this model suggests that there will be great variability in possible compensatory responses. Response and nonresponse as well as different kinds of responses are determined at various critical points: the diagnosis of risk; the definition and articulation of affected interests; the conception of possible policies against the background of existing policies and institutional arrangements (even at the level of conceiving possible responses, this background will make for a variety of responses across countries); the relative power of interests (including the role of a state more or less autonomous from dominant interests and more or less responsive to weaker interests) in defining the situation; and finally the relative power of interests in deciding about diverse compensatory measures and implementing them.

International exposure is likely to lead to compensating policy responses through the following sequence.

- Actual or anticipated exposure to international markets for goods, services, and capital
- Anticipation of social and economic risks
- Actual changes in the market position of different economic sectors
- Job losses, unemployment, job insecurity, and income volatility in the different branches affected
- Various actors—affected groups and their organizations, political parties, governments—assess risks, ascertain outcomes, and promote policies. Since other actors have interests opposed to these policies, the balance of power among the contending sides shapes diagnosis, decision making, and implementation of policies
- These policies may concern unemployment compensation, retraining, and active labor market policies, but they may also take quite different forms,

for instance increasing income streams not related to market developments such as minimum pensions, welfare in the narrow sense, or generous child support

Given this variability of compensating reactions, one might be tempted to conclude that the compensation hypothesis faces so many contingencies that it has little value as a master hypothesis. But that conclusion runs into an empirical stumbling block already mentioned repeatedly—the correlations between economic openness and public spending. These correlations are only correlations, but they do exist, and any explanation of social policy developments must account for them.

Two other implications of the hypothetical model are equally important. First, the very contingent character of compensatory responses underlines the decisive role played by the internal balance of power and the capacity to act responsively. Balance of power and the capacity to act have also been identified as the most important factors in the advancement of social welfare policies generally.

Second, quite a few measures that might be considered compensatory may in fact already be in force for other reasons grounded in internal politics. Many features of established welfare states as well as of less established, but domestically rooted social policy projects are "preemptively compensatory." This probably explains why Miguel Glatzer (this volume) found in his causal tracing of welfare state development in Portugal and Spain few indications of a direct link between exposure to the international economy and social policy proposals.

By contrast, the lower level of social welfare policy in the United States and in particular the much more limited protection against job loss in North America explain why any expansion of free trade runs here into vocal opposition and generates demands for special provisions. Similarly, the fact that small farmers have in many countries—including the United States, Germany, France, and Italy— rather poor social security provisions goes hand in hand with the exemption of farming from most free trade agreements (Rieger and Leibfried 2000, 87–88; see also Rieger and Leibfried 2001). Last but not least, a similar reasoning made the IFIs pay attention to social policy issues after initial neglect in Latin America and Eastern Europe (Huber, and Orenstein and Haas, this volume).[8] The neoliberal character of the policies they recommend should not obscure the fact that these are conceived as compensatory if minimalist social welfare policies. In short, welfare policies are most manifestly compensatory in character where the alternative is no or only a weak social protection against the risks of dislocation.

The compensation view can also invoke two other causal mechanisms. The first is the by now familiar idea that certain social welfare provisions such as high-quality public education, retraining programs, and other active labor market interventions improve the competitiveness of a political economy. Again, these measures may not have evolved as direct responses to international competition, though it is interesting to see that in the United States, a political economy with poorer provisions, education is being discussed as one of the more promising long-term responses to competitive pressures from the international market.

The other causal mechanism worth mentioning in connection with the compensation view is that more openness to the international economy promises—and often delivers—wealth increases that can pay for more generous systems of social security. This certainly is a major reason why the leaders of all advanced welfare states do not seriously consider retreating from economic openness.

Integration with the Classic Theories of the Welfare State

Finally, it is time to link the causal mechanisms associated with the compensation view and the efficiency view to the classic analyses of the welfare states of advanced capitalist political economies. To simplify, these can be said to have followed three different, though arguably complementary, approaches—the logic of industrialism approach, the state-centered approach, and the power resources approach.[9]

National social policies address in different ways a broad spectrum of risks that became more serious as the capitalist economy intensified its creative destruction of established economic and social patterns, were less amenable to self-help solutions due to changes in family and community structures, and could be tackled with increased economic resources available for collective security projects. These three considerations inform the logic of industrialism approach to explaining the growth of welfare states, though they are quite compatible with the state-centered and power resources approaches as well. Analysts looking at the state as an independently important causal factor focus on the structure of political decision making (for example, checks and balances versus concentration of power in democracies), on the autonomy of the state from—and its responsiveness to—various interests in society, and on the capacity of the state to extract resources and to devise and implement policies. This research has identified important constraints and opportunities for social policy developments. Its interest in the autonomy of the state from dominant interests in society overlaps with the perspective of the power resources approach. The latter, however—concentrating in particular on the balance of class power and detailing the role of unions, parties, and governing political coalitions—has contributed most to the explanation why different forms of social provisions developed in different advanced capitalist countries.

The power resources framework for understanding social welfare policies has been challenged more recently by what some call the "institutional turn" of comparative political economy. This literature emphasizes intraclass divisions of interest and interclass alliances against too simplistic versions of class analysis, and it focuses on the coordinating capacities of business, government, and labor. More broadly, it sees advanced welfare state systems as indivisible parts of advanced capitalist political economies rather than as protective and redistributing responses of social policy to economic developments from which they remain separate.[10] This certainly has added an important nuance to the balance of class power perspective, emphasizing that the beneficiaries of policies are not necessarily their initiators, that the beneficiaries of social protection are not homogeneous in their interests, and that policy outcomes are almost always affected by the powerful interests of employers and capital owners. These considerations are particularly important for the analysis of welfare policies that have become a fully institutionalized feature of a political economy, and they are therefore especially useful in studying the politics of downward pressure on established social welfare systems.

The three classic approaches worked nearly exclusively with domestic factors, and yet they arrived at impressive accounts of welfare state development. The more recent emphasis on the institutional capacity for coordination is partly inspired by the challenges of international openness, though it, too, focuses on internal institutional patterns. This suggests that it would be a big mistake to discuss the impact of economic openness on social policy in isolation from internal factors. A number of considerations stand out when we look at the impact of international openness on social policy against the background of the domestic roots of systems of social provision.

First, the risks created by international openness are only one subset of the broader spectrum of risks addressed by social welfare policies. Thus, the problems of old age, illness, and disability, which together account for the bulk of social expenditures in all welfare systems, are unrelated to international involvement.

Furthermore, protection against some of the internal risks also protects against international market risks. Dislocation and creative destruction of established economic activities are not only due to international openness but derive from the internal working of capitalism as well. Thus, the problems of job insecurity and income volatility may in a given country well have been addressed independent of international economic openness. However, there appears to be a significant difference between external and internal risks when it comes to perceiving and evaluating them as problems requiring governmental action. This is not only due to the greater difficulty of regulating international markets. Both the fact that foreign competition comes from outside the political community and that boundary maintenance is one of government's established responsibilities tend to make the pressure for protectionist or compensatory state action stronger. This might very well be considered a specific mechanism supporting the compensation view especially, as noted above, in conditions where social policy measures dealing with dislocation and unemployment are as yet nonexistent or weak.

The classic welfare state policies also have important consequences for improving an economy's ability to move toward high remuneration, high-quality production and thus preserve its international competitiveness. Education and public health measures are most relevant here. Income maintenance and transfer policies are less immediately pertinent, though they may affect inequality and poverty levels and thus shape skill levels in the long run. Measures to improve labor force participation occupy a middling position.

Compensation policies require a willingness and capacity to respond to external risks. That is, they require economic resources, a favorable power constellation, and an adequate organizational capability that make a compensatory response possible and effective. Where these conditions exist, social policy responses to internal risks are likely to develop as well. That means that compensatory responses to external risks will often have been preempted by internally motivated policies or take the form of some rounding out of existing measures rather than a de novo policy development.

Where international competition does put downward pressure on welfare state measures, the same domestic factors that the classic studies of welfare state development identified will be important for the consequences. The balance of power, now affected by typically broad popular support for existing policies, is important for resisting these pressures, for developing policy adjustments aimed at the systemic maintenance of social protection, as well as for policies of retrenchment. State capacity is a critical factor as well because it defines options for redesigning social policy as well as tax policy and the financing of social welfare policies. Defense of existing protection, expansion of social policy, and retrenchment rely on the state's capacity for innovation and adaptation. Responses to downward pressures are likely affected by the degree of coordination among the economic, social, and political institutions of a country. Finally, advances or reductions in the available economic resources may be crucial for decisions to cut back welfare provisions or can, in turn, enable a state to finance countermeasures, bridge transition periods, and tackle new problems.

In sum, neither the efficiency hypothesis nor the compensation hypothesis seems by itself to be a major determinant of welfare state development. Both identify potential pressures and outcomes, but these tendencies must be seen in the context of domestic conditions shaping social welfare policies. The actual trajectories of social policy development will rely primarily on conditions within countries. Welfare states are in the first instance shaped by the wealth of nations, by state-society and state-economy relations, and by power relations within countries. If these factors are fundamentally changed by international openness of the economy, we should expect fundamental changes in social welfare policy. The impact of increased capital mobility on the freedom of action of states and the balance of power within societies may have such potential.

The Cases Revisited: Openness and Domestic Conditions

At this point it may be useful to briefly revisit our cases and examine the interplay of international openness and domestic conditions in shaping social policy developments. Are the domestic factors identified by classic welfare state theories as central in the causal accounts of these national and regional developments as they emerged in the preceding discussion of the causal mechanisms underlying social welfare policies?

Latin America

Latin America has seen the greatest negative impact of economic globalization on social policy, and it came about in the wake of sudden and deep economic crises. Both the long-term background and the factors shaping current developments reveal that domestic factors played a critical role in shaping the social policy developments in response to these crises.

Prominent among the long-term conditions are factors—prevalent in many Latin American countries—that do not bode well for compensatory policies or a vigorous defense of existing social protection: a smaller working class in the formal sector; weaker self-organization of subordinate interests in unions and parties; in some countries (for instance, Argentina and Mexico) unions dependent on parties not devoted to subordinate interests; unevenly efficient state bureaucracies that frequently use what autonomy they enjoy to favor particular and often well-to-do groups and strata and often treat subordinate interests with neglectful inefficiency; and finally a legacy of social policies that were overall quite limited and often favored particular interests with special programs.[11] The exceptional cases exemplified by Costa Rica prove the rule: They responded to increased openness with an expansion of social welfare policies, and their long-term historical background is characterized by more effective and more universalistically oriented state organizations and by a balance of social and political power more favorable to subordinate popular interests.

Domestic factors were also decisive in current developments. The apparent paradox that the spread of formal democracy went hand in hand with a deterioration of social protection finds its explanation in changes that are typical of the majority of Latin American countries: A consequence of deindustrialization, marketization, and the privatization of productive assets is a weakening of unions and popular social and political participation as well as a concentration of economic power. These changes are also related to, and reinforced by, a de facto weakening of parliaments and parties in comparison to executives, a development Guillermo O'Donnell (1994) has aptly called "delegative democracy" (Huber, Rueschemeyer, and Stephens 1997; see also Weyland 1996). Again, the exceptional cases with different social policy developments as well as the details of policy changes in countries that did retrench their social protection confirm that the current balance of social and political power and the structure and capabilities of the state are of critical importance for developments in social policy (Huber, this volume).

Spain and Portugal

Spain and Portugal developed comprehensive welfare states after opening to the international economy in the 1970s. In both countries, the baseline of these developments over the course of the last generation was a rejection of past authoritarian regimes. The democratization of these countries went hand in hand with their new economic and social policies and the balance of power shifted in favor of subordinate interests. Competing unions saw a rapid expansion of their membership, and union power was leveraged by politically instituted extensions of collective bargaining to whole industries. In addition, state elites also were receptive to building a more comprehensive welfare state. In part this seems related to the rejection of the old regime; in Portugal, the threat of Communism played a significant role, and the western European countries offered attractive models as well as supportive advice. The balance of power was favorable for building comprehensive welfare states, and the international political context supported the same policy thrust.

Eastern Europe and Russia

The post-Communist countries of Eastern Europe present a very different picture, though in one formal respect there is an interesting similarity: the current phase of their political and economic histories opened with a radical regime change—the breakdown of East European Communism. Among the cases we considered (and perhaps in all of recorded economic history), this was by far the greatest sudden dislocation of whole political economies. Orenstein and Haas (this volume) emphasize the radical changes the transition entailed. They point to the dramatic differences in economic development and social policy between east-central Europe and the countries of the former Soviet Union. They show that the political economies of east-central Europe became at the same time most internationally integrated and emerged with the most generous new social welfare programs. They describe how during the first years small groups of experts, primarily located in the executive branch, responded to chaotic conditions and uncertain prospects with idiosyncratic policy decisions that had long-term consequences.[12] And they emphasize that international policy influences, including the prospect of joining the European Union as well as very forceful and direct interventions by the World Bank, brought about some convergence in the most recent years even though the influence of European models and requirements stand in some tension with the thrusts of World Bank advice.

The difference between east-central Europe and the countries of the former Soviet Union (on Russia, see Cook, this volume) seems to an important extent related to the greater international involvement of the Polish, Czech, and Hungarian economies; but it also reflects the longer history of capitalist development that preceded the Communist period in these countries as well as the presence of far more efficient state apparatuses and more propitious state-society relations than are characteristic of today's Russia, Ukraine, and Belarus. The Europe effect, to use Orenstein and Haas's term, as well as the "strong agenda-setting influence" of the World Bank (Orenstein and Haas, this volume) represent a powerful impact of globalization on the East European transition. However, as Orenstein (2001) points out, the abiding orientation of the east-central European countries toward western Europe must not be taken for granted; it has to be seen as a long-term state project whose pursuit gives continuity to post-Communist policy making. Similarly, the pervasive influence of the neoliberal policy ideas of the World Bank cannot be understood simply as an imposition from abroad but has strong roots in the experience with the failing state socialist economy. In Russia, while economic policies and social policy proposals were heavily influenced by international advice, the dilapidated condition of the Russian state, the limited economic recovery from the shock of transition, and the prolonged stalemate between the executive branch and parliament about the restructuring of social welfare policy all point to the major role of internal factors. Overall, there is little doubt that historical experience, the previous structures of the economy and the state, as well as current power relations are playing a major part in shaping the impact of economic globalization on the transitions of post-Communist political economies.

South Korea

Contrary to conventional views, South Korea opened itself late to foreign imports and free capital flows, even though its phenomenal economic development was due to state-managed export-led growth. The later opening to economic globalization coincided with a democratization of its military dictatorship. In the course of these dual developments, South Korean social policy changed from a growth and power maintenance orientation to the provision of an austere but comprehensive system of social protection. Some of this transformation responded to dislocations associated with import competition and capital outflows. That was very clear in the case of policies dealing with unemployment and impoverishment in the wake of the financial crisis of 1997–1998. The transformation as a whole, however, is hardly conceivable without the concurrent process of democratization, which opened the door to some advances in the power of labor. At the same time, it seems that the legacy of segmented social provisions for privileged parts of the population and the as yet limited transformation of the balance of class power may well mean that the recent welfare policies along compensatory lines will converge more with the residual welfare state of the United States than with the continental European welfare systems.

A second look at the developments in middle-income countries, then, confirms that internal, domestic factors are critical for the consequences of the impact of economic globalization. It also specifies that—and how—politics matters. The critical background factors determining the role of politics seem to be four: the balance of power in society, the capacity for effective state action, the condition and the prospects of the economy, and the legacy effects of earlier social policies. These four conditioning factors accord precisely with the classic theories of welfare state development that were worked out in the European context. The Latin American experience as well as current Korean developments suggest that democratization as such does not seem to favor unequivocally a deepening of social welfare policy. It does so only if it is accompanied by a change in the social and political balance of power in society.

That politics matters and that it in turn is shaped by the background factors identified is strongly backed up by the northwestern European experience. This not only emerges from the overview of John Stephens (this volume; see also Huber and Stephens 2001a). Examining the advanced welfare states in greater detail and more skeptically, Scharpf and Schmidt (2000) arrive at a similar conclusion in their important study of advanced welfare states: differences among these political economies and among their policies matter decisively for the ways in which they adjust to the challenges of a changed economic environment (see also Scharpf 2000).

Some Broader Reflections

The compensation hypothesis and the efficiency hypothesis are offsprings of broader conceptions about the role of the market. In its radical version, the efficiency hypothesis derives from the view that the workings of the market are not only more powerful than political action but also provide the best answers to virtually all problems in economy and society. This "market fundamentalism" is not the dominant position among sophisticated economists, but it does prevail in neoliberal policy circles. Beliefs in the market as the primary ordering principle of social and economic life were famously challenged by Karl Polanyi (1957/1944) in his analysis of the decline of the international liberal economic order of the late nineteenth century. And the conception of an "embedded liberalism" (Ruggie 1982; Katzenstein 1985), which we discussed in the introduction, developed these insights further.[13] Neoliberal market fundamentalism represents in our view the intellectually weaker position. We set out with the conviction that the ideas of embedded liberalism offered a more fruitful framework for understanding the interrelations between market functioning, social practices and institutions, and political policy initiatives. We see these initial hunches reinforced by the interregionally comparative chapters as well as by our examination of the social and economic mechanisms that seem to underlie the claims of the compensation and the efficiency view.

Yet if market fundamentalism and the unqualified versions of the efficiency hypothesis are flawed intellectually, we cannot conclude that the worldwide outlook of social welfare policies is on balance positive. At least for the foreseeable future, one may well argue the opposite. In many low- and middle-income countries, the distribution of social and economic power is not favorable for the further development of social welfare policies or even for the maintenance of rather meager provisions. And that is often reinforced by various factors we have discussed earlier, prominent among them the increased mobility of capital and the strength of neoliberal policy ideas in the dominant rich countries and the transnational financial institutions. Similarly, the character of the state is in many countries such that one cannot expect the efficient pursuit of even rather elementary state tasks, not to mention the complex challenges raised by the deep interventions in social life that the creation of strong welfare policies entails. Finally, many countries do not have a policy history that encourages the active pursuit of social welfare, as was the case in the northwestern European countries that now have comprehensive welfare states.

One conclusion of earlier research on social welfare policies is strongly confirmed by our comparative examination of middle-income countries. Long-lasting structural features of society and politics, which typically have deep roots in history, shape and constrain current political action. Prominent among these characteristics of political economies that define the chances of social welfare policies are the long-term balance of power, the capacity of government for effective action, institutional arrangements that help social and economic actors to overcome collective action problems and realize joint "win-win" solutions, the history of past social welfare policies, and the favorable or problematic insertion of the national political economy into the international division of labor.

We have treated these structural constraints as the major qualification of our claim that politics matters: Politics must not be understood as the exertion of sheer political will but as a matter of collective choice that is made in an environment of givens. From a different perspective, emphasizing these constraints rather than political action, one might be tempted to conclude that the future is largely determined by the limits they set on political choice. This, however, overlooks one of the most salient political experiences anywhere: To the chagrin of politicians and their commentators the future is far less predictable that the determinists claim.

To put this argument differently, within the constraints we have repeatedly identified, there is a role for agency, for political imagination, and for innovations in social policy that transcend the sheer reproduction of past patterns. This is most clearly expressed in the retrospective views of politicians (Broadbent 1999; Russell 1999; see also Birnbaum 2001).

The interaction of political agency and structural constraints becomes particularly visible in major crises. By definition, crises destroy some of the structural constraints and opportunities that were inherited from the past, and this provides openings for new departures. For the prospects of social welfare policies, the outcomes may be ambiguous. We have argued that sudden and crisis-induced shifts toward greater economic openness created the most important conditions for austere neoliberal social policies in much of Latin America, in New Zealand and Australia, as well as in the former Soviet Union. By contrast, the Great Depression of the 1930s dramatically advanced social welfare policies in the United States, and something similar seems to be happening in today's South Korea in response to the financial crisis of 1997–1998. In all of these cases, however, political agency and policy ideas gained in importance, even though their success still depended on powerful structural conditions, both those remaining despite the crisis and those radically altered by it.

Our conclusions about the structural constraints and opportunities shaping the prospects of social welfare policies leave us with a number of critical questions about the long-term effects of economic globalization: Does globalization change the underlying structural conditions favoring and obstructing social welfare policies? Does it change the balance of power within nations and between them? Does it affect the capacity of states to make decisions about social policy and to implement them? Does economic globalization transform the structure of political economies and thereby affect the prospects of social policy? Does it enhance or constrain the ability to fund measures of social protection? This volume leaves us without definite answers to these questions, but the answers will determine whether the impact of globalization on social welfare policies will be negative, neutral, or even positive in the long run.

Rather than leaving these questions dangling without any further thought, we will offer a few responses that—however speculative—may be helpful in thinking about the future and, perhaps, in orienting further research. Among the structural changes that can reasonably be anticipated, the most favorable for advances in social welfare policies is probably the likely increase in economic resources. Despite major setbacks in Africa and in the former Soviet bloc that go beyond cyclical ups and downs, most countries will experience long-term economic growth, and this is very likely to be enhanced by economic openness. Even if in many countries this greater openness is not accompanied by reductions in economic inequality (and in some may actually lead to a larger gap between the well-off and the poor), the overall increase in production very likely makes more funds available for public expenditures, a point that has been forcefully made by Sen (1999).

The balance of power issue is probably the most difficult structural condition to reasonably anticipate. The enhanced mobility of capital, which could be somewhat reduced in the future but is unlikely to be radically curtailed as it was from the Great Depression through the 1960s, certainly represents by itself a major shift in power vis-à-vis other interests. But two important qualifications must not be forgotten. First, as we have noted repeatedly, the interests of capital owners are not unambiguously opposed to social welfare policies because these policies are associated with significant direct and indirect productivity gains. The fact that the bulk of international investment goes to countries with substantial social welfare provisions is partly explained by these interests, which transcend simplistic bipolar class images. The second qualification derives from an apparently ineluctable consequence of capitalist development—a long-term shift in social power that favors the many.[14] This is an uneven and in many ways contingent process that relies primarily on an increasing self-organization of society and in particular on the organization of subordinate interests. Contrary to much wishful thinking, which sees free markets and democracy as two sides of the same coin, this self-organization is not enhanced but rather obstructed by neoliberal marketization and the social policies accompanying it. However, in the long run, it is possible and even likely that capitalist development will transform social structures so as to enhance the social and economic power of the many.

The balance of power within countries is inevitably affected by shifts in power across nations. The concentration of geopolitical power in one country, the United States, and the rise of transnational institutions certainly have favored neoliberal policy ideas and undercut the prospects of more comprehensive welfare policies. But it is an open question whether this is a stable constellation. Ideologies and policy ideas are notoriously responsive to short- and medium-term developments in the world economy, and the single superpower as well as the international financial institutions under its sway may face increasing attempts at containment in the future. Certainly, the high degree of autonomy that they currently enjoy represents a worldwide deficit in democracy. One might see here an analogy to the tensions between European states and their societies during the nineteenth century that engendered the rise of modern national democracies, though it is difficult to imagine what form a worldwide equivalent of national democratization might take.

Many hold that globalization spells the end of the national state as we know it. A decisive weakening of the states' roles would indeed affect the future of social welfare radically, since states are central to the past development of social policy. States are a major feature of the national landscape of power; they represent the arena in which politics is fought out; and their control is the prize of domestic politics. If national decision making becomes sharply constrained, the factors that shaped welfare state development in the past are similarly reduced in importance.

The main basis for the claim of the demise of the nation-state is the vast increase in the power of capital owners in a unified global capital market and the development of transnational economic institutions, from global corporations to the IFIs. Yet it seems that these claims simply extrapolate trends that may or may not continue along the same lines as they developed during the past generation. At present, there are many indications that capital markets are still far away from a worldwide integration. It seems reasonable to conclude for now that the jury is still out on the question of whether capital mobility constrains the degree of freedom of state action sufficiently to affect the potential for social welfare policies.

Furthermore, many overlook a particular leverage states have for influencing the international economy and its institutions. The very legal and institutional framework that underpins international economic transactions as well as the so-called transnational organizations rests on a system of law and regulation that ultimately requires coercive foundations. These are still provided by different ensembles of nation-states. It is true that the power and autonomy of the cooperating nation-states vary tremendously, but even small and medium powers have to make their contribution to let international transactions proceed smoothly. It is obviously hazardous to make predictions about the capacity of states for effective action. Yet it may not be unreasonable to see in their very participation in the international economic system an opportunity to advance organizational effectiveness, as Evans (1985) argued when it was fashionable to identify only negative consequences from international dependence and interdependence.

Will an increasingly integrated and competitive international economy lead to a decline of the forms of coordinated capitalism that have distinguished the continental and Scandinavian political economies from their Anglo-American counterparts? The argument that these more coordinated market economies articulate well with the wage and tax policies undergirding comprehensive welfare states is widely accepted.[15] Deriving from this, pessimistic predictions about the welfare states of northwestern Europe as well as about the chances for social policy in less rich countries may be premature. We are inclined to think that welfare states tend to be overdetermined in their causal conditions, resting, so to speak, on more than one or a few pillars of support. Furthermore, it is not obvious that the cross-class cooperation arising from and reinforcing such economic coordination will be easily abandoned if it has proved advantageous in the past. Finally, even a superficial glance around the political economies of the world quickly encounters other varieties of capitalism that seem to have very sturdy powers of survival. Some of these—for instance, the political economies of Japan and Korea—might also be dubbed "coordinated market economies," but it is significant to note that they are not accompanied by generous and comprehensive systems of welfare.

On the Value of Comprehensive Welfare States

The past century has seen huge and horrible disasters of collective human effort, whether those efforts were in large measure coerced or based on voluntary enthusiasm. Intentional transformation of societies has so often and so grossly failed in the past that, for many, grand political projects are now in thorough disrepute. James Scott's *Seeing Like a State* (1998) seeks to describe and explain "how certain schemes to improve the human condition have failed," as the subtitle puts it. Against this background of state-sponsored horrors, the rise of welfare states stands out as an astounding counterpoint: Comprehensive welfare policies represent profound and sustained transformations of whole societies through state action. Yet these are transformations that have been, and continue to be, embraced by vast majorities of the populations involved.

For Europe and more broadly for the Atlantic community of nations, social welfare policies supported social peace and democracy at critical junctures. This was true of the United States during the Great Depression. Equally important, social policy secured external and internal peace in Europe after the devastations of the Second World War (Broadbent 1999). A consequence of the democratizing shift of power in society, social welfare policy proved in turn to be the foundation of a stable democracy.

The strong grounding welfare state policies find in popular expectations provokes further reflection. We deem this to be a phenomenon of profound significance. Narrowly conceived, the "naturalization" of social welfare programs expressed in popular expectations that consider established benefits to be elementary rights may be construed as rigidities that make restructuring and adaptation of welfare provisions to new conditions and problems difficult. This is indeed the case where overall increases in social revenues are politically problematic, while social change creates new demands or expands old ones. Yet at the same time, such strongly supportive expectations are a critical ingredient in the resiliency of established welfare states. It is significant that Huber and Stephens (2001a) found that while the development of European welfare states was pushed forward in partisan fashion by some political forces against the resistance of others, this partisan effect weakened radically in the subsequent period of stagnation, restructuring, and maintenance.

This can be denounced as the "tyranny of the status quo," as Milton Friedman did in an interview with the German news magazine *Der Spiegel* (October 9, 2000). But such labeling does not explain which status quo is stable and why. The decline of partisanship regarding established systems of social protection represents the resilience of an established pattern even in the face of difficulties. It may indicate something even more fundamental than the conclusion that social welfare provisions are popular and that the politics of stagnation, retrenchment, and maintenance differ from the politics of welfare state building for this reason (Pierson 1994).

The decline of partisanship in the politics of welfare state maintenance can be taken as an indication of the "objective interests" of people. To argue that something is in the objective interest of people is to make a difficult claim, but it is clear that the pursued interests are not only subject to change and influence but experience transformations that are not easily turned back.[16] Huber and Stephens speak of a "ratchet effect" of welfare state policy:

> Once the policy was instituted, its constituency expanded as its benefits became apparent to the citizenry. In countries such as the Nordic ones, this initiated a path-dependent interactive process in which the policy ratchet effect, labor movement counterhegemony, transformation of social consciousness, policy transformation, left governance, and consequent policies facilitating organization fed each other. As our analyses of the development of women's movements and gender-egalitarian legislation showed, an exactly parallel path-dependent process developed later between women's organization, policy developments, and consciousness transformation. (2001a, 343)

We believe that a plausible case for an approximation of actual interests to objective interests can be made if broad populations, and not only narrow segments of past beneficiaries, opt for the security that welfare states offer against risks that are beyond people's control, provided that they have had the experience of risk as well as security and that they have the chance to consider and express their options.

These fundamental considerations about the resilience of established welfare states in a variety of countries also make us confident that the appeal of social welfare provisions transcends cultural boundaries. Even if the actual prospects for successful social policy are not good for many middle-income countries, not to mention their poorer developing counterparts, we are convinced that the idea of politically sponsored social welfare will remain on the global agenda for the indefinite future.

Notes

Chapter 1. An Introduction to the Problem

1. See, for instance, Wilensky and Lebaux (1965).

2. Some did see Scandinavian social democracy as potentially transcending capitalism in a radical way, while not abandoning democracy; see Stephens (1979). But the expected transformation of property relations did not come to pass. While later works view social democratic welfare politics as in tension with the market (Esping–Andersen 1985), they speak of Scandinavian social democracy as one version of "welfare capitalism" (Esping-Andersen 1990).

3. See, for instance, Rueschemeyer, Stephens, and Stephens (1992, chaps. 1 and 7) and the classic formulation by Marshall (1950).

4. Available research offers an inconclusive picture, if one takes reduced income inequality as a rough indicator of successful social welfare policies. Some cross-national statistical comparisons found no correlation between democracy and social inequality. One disputed study yielded a correlation when it related democracy to inequality nearly a generation later. And reflections on contemporary developments suggest that democratization in the 1990s had frequently only weak foundations in the mobilization of subordinate strata and groups that might gain from greater political equality. Democratization thus often represented only a thin veneer on modes of collective decision making that otherwise remained largely unchanged, if it did not actually fall short of the minimal standards of formal political democracy. See Bollen and Jackman (1985) for the negative result. Muller (1988) found that a long experience with democracy was associated with lower inequality independent of level of development, position in the world system, and the age structure of the population. These findings were challenged with new evidence by Weede (1989), but defended with yet further evidence by Muller (1989). For a reflection on the contemporary scene, see Huber, Rueschemeyer, and Stephens (1997).

5. This volume builds upon Esping-Andersen's *Welfare States in Transition* (1996), one of the first books to encompass a similar degree of diversity. While the Esping-Andersen volume offers analytic accounts of welfare state developments in different

regions, this book has a different focus. Its primary concern is to evaluate competing views of how globalization has affected social welfare policy and politics in regions with different histories of integration in the world economy.

6. While it is true that the early innovations in social security programs occurred in the late nineteenth and early twentieth centuries, the massive budgetary expansion and universal coverage of these programs came about after the Second World War, at the same time that economic openness prevailed in the Atlantic economies after depression and war.

7. As demonstrated by the famous U-turn away from socialist policies in 1982, when France ran into capital flight difficulties.

8. For an overview of different approaches, see Skocpol and Amenta (1986). For the balance of class power approach, see Stephens (1979), Korpi (1983), Esping-Andersen (1990), and Huber and Stephens (2001a).

9. See Keynes (1936) and Thomas J. Biersteker (1992); a more guarded assessment is offered by Biersteker and Kearney (2000).

10. For a more nuanced as well as more skeptical assessment that is in our view nevertheless compatible with the judgments expressed in the text, see Scharpf (2000).

11. Welfare states in Australia and New Zealand differed radically from their northern counterparts because they depended on trade protection rather than economic openness and operated through wage policy rather than transfers and services. Furthermore, Australia and New Zealand (at the time of the reforms) used the Westminster system of single member districts. In contrast to the electoral rules of most European countries, this provided minorities with majority power in parliament and the concomitant ability to enact change quickly.

12. This is likely to be the case for two reasons: First, social welfare policies have other determinants than the relations to the international economy. Second, successes as well as failures of social policy may well be "overdetermined"—the result of more than one sufficient causal condition.

Chapter 2. Globalization, Democratization, and Government Spending in Middle-Income Countries

1. The World Bank divides countries into four income groups based upon GDP per capita: high income, upper middle income, lower middle income, and low income. We select our cases by combining the upper and lower middle-income groups (see table 2.1 for a complete listing).

2. Garrett (2001a) also finds that globalization has not increased inequality in middle–income countries, perhaps reflecting the fact that less skilled labor is abundant in these countries relative to the OECD. That is, lost manufacturing jobs in the United States and Europe have been translated into manufacturing jobs and higher standards of living for workers in middle-income countries.

3. See Garrett (1998a) for a more detailed presentation of these two perspectives.

4. See Garrett (2000) for a discussion of the causes of globalization.

5. Hungary would also fall into the big spending group were it not for its low general government consumption score.

Chapter 3. Economic Internationalization and Domestic Compensation

I would like to thank the University of North Carolina for the research and study leave which provided me the time to write this paper, and Duane Swank for the data on direct foreign investment and foreign borrowing. Miguel Glatzer, Evelyne Huber, Jonah Levy, Dietrich Rueschemeyer, and Duane Swank provided helpful comments on an earlier draft.

1. The main product of this research is Huber and Stephens (2001a). Also see Huber, Ragin, and Stephens (1993), Stephens (1976), Huber and Stephens (1998, 2001b), and Stephens, Huber, and Ray (1999).

2. Although open to trade, their capital markets were, in some cases, quite closed, as we will see below.

3. In my 1979 book, I presented a similar causal chain linking size of the domestic economy and economic concentration to union organization, social democratic strength, and so on. In my analysis I did include measures of union and bargaining centralization, but I did not measure and test for direct effects of trade openness.

4. Wilensky (1976) is the earliest test of the effect of corporatism on social spending, but Wilensky presented corporatism as an alternative to left government rather than as part of a causal complex that included left government. The latter conception dominated the explanations of social expenditure advanced by subsequent quantitative analysts, above all the work of Hicks and Swank (Hicks 1999; Hicks and Swank 1992; Hicks and Misra 1993; Swank 1988, 1998, 1999).

5. The neoliberal argument is also concerned with the low levels of wage dispersion and labor market "rigidities" (for example, senior hiring rules, high levels of severance pay, and so on) characteristic of European economies. Since this chapter is primarily concerned with the welfare state proper, I leave these aside now, but will return to them below.

6. Note that factors several steps removed in the causal chain may not be that strongly correlated. Thus, Cameron (1978, 1256) hypothesizes the following causal chain: openness —> economic concentration —> unionization —> left government. As one can see from table 3.1, at each immediate link in the chain, the correlations are quite strong, but openness is only modestly correlated to unionization or left government.

7. The link of divisions on the right to country size here is complex: The large countries of Europe had strong landed elites, as the large landlord-state alliance was a militarily strong one (Tilly 1975). The small countries, where small farming dominated, only avoided being gobbled up by reasons of geography and the European system of states. The large landholding countries tended to produce unified parties of

the right led in part by agrarian elites (see Stephens 1989; Rueschemeyer, Stephens, and Stephens 1992, chap. 4, for an elaboration).

8. In the analyses in Huber and Stephens (2000a, 2001a), women's labor force participation is a stand-in for women's organization. Huber and I subsequently developed a measure of women's organization with much greater face validity, which is even more strongly related to the dependent variables. Results are available from the author upon request.

9. Time varying measures of corporatism are almost always based on union or wage-setting centralization measures, or both, developed from the Golden-Lange-Wallerstein data set. These do not vary greatly from year to year.

10. In table 3.2, the countries are grouped by welfare state type. Austria is clearly a Christian Democratic welfare state in terms of its social policy configuration, but is quite similar to Norway, Finland, and Sweden in the pattern of its political economy. Denmark deviates from the social democratic type of political economy in many respects though it is similar to the other Nordic countries in fiscal policy and wage formation. See Huber and Stephens (1998) for an extended discussion.

11. The following few paragraphs summarize our arguments in Huber and Stephens (2001b, 2001a, chap. 7). See those writings for more detailed discussion and statistical documentation.

12. Another part of the reason is competition from non-OECD countries for investment funds (Rowthorn 1995) and the worldwide debt build-up in the wake of the two oil shocks.

13. I want to underline that my remarks here about the negative effects of globalization apply only to financial market deregulation, and even there I would not defend just any regulation as being positive. In the case of trade, I do think the benefits of free trade far outweigh the costs.

14. It should be pointed out that the United States' unemployment performance in the eighties, with 7.5 percent of the labor force unemployed, was hardly outstanding, and liberal welfare states as a group registered higher levels of unemployment than the Christian Democratic welfare states, so it is not surprising that the liberal welfare states were not looked to as a model. The U.S. unemployment performance only began to look attractive once the conjunctural features discussed in the following paragraphs kicked in during the nineties.

15. See Czada (1998) for a discussion of the enormous impact of unification on the German production regime and welfare state.

16. See Huber and Stephens (1998) for a more detailed analysis.

17. A case can be made for a greater role of tripartite agreements in implementing retrenching reforms, particularly of popular universalistic programs. In this case, unions agreed to the cutbacks (or increases in employee contributions) in return for government, and in some cases employer efforts to increase employment. See Ebbinghaus and Hassel (1999) and Rhodes (2001).

18. I see two problems in this literature. First, it neglects aspects of labor organi-

zation other than the degree of bargaining centralization. In particular, the degree of organization and, relatedly, the diversity of the organized set the Nordic countries apart from Germany. White-collar workers are much better organized in the Nordic countries, as are private and public sector services. Thus, it is much easier for the metal workers' union to exercise wage leadership in Germany. Second, this literature misses important nuances in the bargaining systems that can have large impacts on the ability to coordinate bargaining. For instance, Iversen (1996, 1998) classifies the current Danish and Swedish bargaining systems as sector-level bargaining, but this overlooks the strong role of the mediator in the Danish system, which greatly increases the capacity of the system to avoid free riding. In fact, the increased centralization suggested by the Swedish LO (Trade Union Confederation) in the recent "Alliance for Growth" discussions with the Swedish Employers Association (SAF) was a move to the current Danish system, not a return to the pre-1983 Swedish system.

Chapter 4. Globalization and Social Policy Developments in Latin America

I would like to thank Miguel Glatzer, Robert Kaufman, Dietrich Rueschemeyer, and John Stephens for helpful comments, and Jenny Pribble for research assistance.

1. For a more extensive treatment of the emergence, nature, crisis, and reforms of systems of social protection in Latin America, see Huber (1996).

2. These figures are drawn from Mesa-Lago (1994, 22); he does not provide figures for Trinidad and Tobago nor for any of the small Caribbean countries. Coverage figures vary widely among different sources, depending on whether legal entitlements or actual contributions are taken as the criterion. Mesa-Lago is the most prolific researcher and writer on social security in Latin America, and his figures can be accepted for the purposes of classification here.

3. The figures are based on employment in industry as a percentage of total employment, and they include mining, quarrying, manufacturing, electricity, gas and water, and construction (CEPAL, 1994-1998, 2002).

4. There are no good comparative studies of the distributive impact of Latin American social insurance (Musgrove 1985, 187–208). Most case studies point to a regressive or neutral effect (Mesa-Lago 1983, 95), with the exception of the health care system.

5. The literature on the debt crisis and structural adjustment is voluminous; among the best treatments are Haggard and Kaufman (1992); Stallings and Kaufman (1989); Handelman and Baer (1989); see also Williamson (1990).

6. For an analysis with similar results but data for more restricted periods, see Cominetti (1996).

7. As will become clear immediately, the Chilean reforms actually took place in the early 1980s, but they are discussed here in the context of the general reforms of social policy in Latin America, most of which took place in the 1990s.

8. For a discussion of the Chilean and other pension reforms, see Barrientos

(1998), Borzutzky (1998), and Mesa-Lago and Arenas de Mesa (1998); for reviews of Chilean social policy more broadly, see Raczynski (1994, 1997).

9. For a more extensive treatment of the nature, determinants, and consequences of pension reforms in Latin America, see Huber and Stephens (2000b), Madrid (2002, 2003), and Müller (2003).

10. It is important to note in this context that the economic collapse in Argentina also devastated the private pension companies. They had been pressured to buy government bonds and did so from highly indebted provinces. These bonds ultimately became worthless. Legislation that would allow people to return from the private to the public pension scheme passed the Chamber of Deputies and as of July 2004 was stalled in the Senate.

11. See Teichman (2001) for an analysis of networks connecting domestic technocrats and IFI officials.

12. As Kay (1998) points out, employers in Argentina lobbied very strongly for a reduction of contributions to social security.

13. See Korzeniewicz and Smith (1998) for a comprehensive analysis of the evolution of the development discourse and prescriptions of the IFIs and core governments.

14. Nancy Birdsall was at the time executive vice president of the Inter-American Development Bank.

15. Kay (1998) makes a very similar argument about pension reforms in Argentina, Brazil, and Uruguay, which is well supported by his evidence. He argues that external pressures provided strong incentives for executives to propose privatizing pension reforms, but that the strength of interest groups opposing the reforms and the extent to which political institutions enabled veto players shaped the final outcome of pension reform attempts. Madrid (2003) makes a somewhat different argument for pension reforms in Latin America. He claims that governments in countries with very high pension expenditures opted only for partial privatization because of the high costs of transition, and that insufficiency of domestic capital sources and the hope that pension privatization would increase domestic savings were prime motivations for privatization. However, he also recognizes the importance of domestic political actors and institutions.

16. Even in Uruguay, the military, police, bank employees, professionals, and notaries were able to exempt themselves from reforms that would have curbed their privileges.

17. The Brazilian case demonstrates clearly that power dispersion can be a mixed blessing indeed, insofar as it not only retards radical neoliberal reforms but also social policy reforms aimed at eliminating extremely expensive and inegalitarian privileges and making universalistic and solidaristic schemes financially viable.

18. Haggard and Kaufman (1995) emphasize fragmentation and polarization of the party system, the latter defined as presence of left-wing or populist parties, as obstacles to economic reform.

19. Figures for Brazil are missing after 1985 in this series. The figures for Argentina

for 1989 given in IDB (1996, 370) for total revenue and total expenditure are higher than the ones cited here, but the series there does not go back farther than 1986 and thus does not allow the comparisons I am making here.

20. Lecture by Albert Fishlow, Princeton University, May 1999.

21. Actually, he lists a further source that I am not including because it seems too far out of line with the rest.

22. Mexico under Presidents de la Madrid and Salinas would belong here also if one was willing to classify it as a democracy, which I am not.

23. To underline the point about overbearing executives, it is worth pointing out that Menem revoked one of the most important concessions to labor by presidential decree a few months after the passage of the reform (Kay 1998; Madrid 2003).

24. Figures for current revenue are higher than for the total tax burden because current revenue also includes revenue arising from government ownership of property in the form of dividends, interest, rents, royalties, and entrepreneurial income, as well as administrative fees, charges, fines, and forfeits levied by the government (IDB 1996, 379).

25. Kitschelt et al. (1999) make this point convincingly for Europe.

Chapter 5. Revisiting "Embedded Liberalism"

Research for this paper was supported by a grant from FLAD (the Luso-American Development Foundation), whose support is gratefully acknowledged.

1. The EMS allowed the currencies of member countries to vary within a narrow band.

Chapter 7. Globalization and the Politics of Welfare State Reform in Russia

Research for this paper was supported by a grant from the National Council for Eurasian and East European Research. The council's support is gratefully acknowledged.

1. According to McAuley's classic study, in the Soviet period "public assistance, or minimal financial aid to those who do not fit into one of the benefit categories but are still without means of support, was almost entirely lacking" (McAuley 1979).

2. Above I described most of these services as provided by the state. In the provision of social services the division between the Soviet state and its enterprises was blurred, but most analysts agree that at least part of enterprise provision was not reflected in budgetary social expenditure data.

3. It should be noted, however, that the enforcement and effectiveness of IMF conditionality generally has been questioned, and the Fund's treatment of Russia may not be as exceptional as it is often characterized (see, for example, Killick 1996).

4. While Deacon shows that other organizations have exercised dominant influence in some countries, he asserts, "The scale of the Bank's work in the region outstrips everything else" (1997, 99).

5. Comment made at the Conference of the Social Cohesion Study Group of the Russia Initiative, sponsored by the Carnegie Corporation of New York, Moscow, June 6, 2000.

6. The Left was joined in its opposition by many liberal deputies who did not necessarily oppose reforms as such, but distrusted the government to carry them out honestly or effectively.

7. The support of the World Bank is documented in the publications on Russia's housing policy that are listed in the bibliography. The U.S.-based Urban Institute was also heavily involved in Russian housing reform.

Chapter 8. Globalization and Social Policy in South Korea

1. The chaebol like to operate at least one insurance company since they are an effective and legal instrument for mobilizing capital. The chaebol are not allowed to own banks.

2. Parts of this section are derived from Song (2002).

3. Brady and Mo (1997) contend that the amendment of labor laws in 1996 helped consolidate democracy. But a careful examination reveals the opposite. The amendment generated more tension than resolution.

4. Parts of this section are also derived from Song (2002).

5. These were: termination of bank loans to financially distressed firms, a shutdown of bankrupt firms, the implementation of a restrictive monetary policy through interest rate hikes, a shutdown of financial institutions that could not fulfill regulation criteria, and the lifting of the ceiling on foreign capital investment.

6. In January 1998, shortly after his electoral victory, President Kim announced the establishment of a tripartite commission that, as a political instrument of crisis management, would deal with urgent issues and develop reform agendas. After three weeks of heated debate, the commission reached a dramatic compromise on ten major issues of reform, including ninety specific items, regarding social protection of workers, economic restructuring, economic policy, industrial relations, and labor law. More specifically, the social compact contained the following agreement: Government and employers would construct nationwide organizations and prepare a policy package for unemployment. All parties in the tripartite committee would make an effort to improve job security by introducing work sharing and would try to minimize layoffs and revive financially troubled firms. All parties would make progress in eliminating unfair labor practices and would establish bodies to monitor compliance. The policy-making process would be open to labor unions, which would participate both in the making and implementation of important policies affecting wage earners' standards of living. All parties would have input in the restructuring of chaebol firms. Reform of public enterprises would occur through agreements between labor and management, the teachers' union would be legalized, and all parties would make an effort to improve worker participation in management. Labor laws were amended shortly after this agreement.

Chapter 9. Conclusion

1. The "conditionalities" of the IFIs had important counterparts in personnel developments. The World Bank funded a large number of consultants working for Latin American countries on social policy reforms. In addition, there was and is a pattern of rotation of Latin American officials in and out of international financial institutions, which results in very similar mindsets in the IFIs and among high-level reformers in Latin America. We thank Evelyne Huber for underlining these supplementary mechanisms in the impact of globalization on social policy development, which have weaker counterparts in east-central Europe and in Russia.

2. Social expenditures in Chile declined from 21.6 percent of GDP in 1982 to 13.3 percent in 1997 (see Huber, this volume).

3. For recent treatments of Japanese social policy, see Calder (1988), Milny (1999), and, in a broader context, Pempel (2002).

4. For long after 1987 unions were not allowed to cooperate with political parties or to establish more than one union in an enterprise.

5. Multinational corporations represent a special mode of international investment. Their distinctive corporate identity, often buttressed by a strong market position, potentially makes them into powerful actors in economic and social politics. Yet with the partial exception of Latin America and Korea (Huber, Song, this volume), our case studies did not assign special importance to them.

6. We are, of course, aware that these three disruptive changes differed greatly in character. The New Zealand system of social provision was built around well-established export streams to Britain. When the country lost its privileged access to the British market due to the entry of the United Kingdom into the European Common Market, severe problems of budget deficits and inflation developed, and the government followed radical neoliberal policies that significantly reduced the system of social security. Evelyne Huber argues in comments on this chapter that in Latin America the sudden opening took place in a context of a generalized economic crisis, which made the social welfare institutions all the more susceptible to attack. Significant changes in social policy took place in response to the debt crisis that began in 1982 and before the massive trade opening began in most countries. For the post-Communist countries of east-central Europe a similar qualification holds with even greater force. Here the main forces dislocating earlier social welfare policies derived from the transformation of the centrally planned economy into a market-oriented one, though this also involved a rapid turning away from the managed trade that linked Communist European countries to each other to a focus on both the United States and western Europe.

7. Some of the more dramatic instances occurred under especially favorable political circumstances. A prominent example is the neoliberal policy in Chile under Pinochet's military dictatorship. Huber and Stephens (2001) have also noted that both New Zealand and the United Kingdom have electoral laws that permit govern-

ments supported by a minority of the population to carry out unpopular cutbacks; the United Kingdom is not, however, a case where strong international economic pressures have urged reduced social welfare policies, except for the power of neoliberal ideas.

8. Unemployment protection constitutes an exception to the observation that social policy was neglected in the first years after the collapse of Communism. Since unemployment was extremely low or absent before 1989–1990, it was treated early on as a major problem potentially threatening the transition to a different economic regime.

9. The following references by no means describe this literature in full. They are representative of and point to a large body of work. The logic of industrialism approach is most closely associated with the work of Wilensky (1975). Skocpol and Amenta (1986) present and review the state-centered approach. Stephens (1979) and Korpi (1983) are important early formulations of the power resources approach, which was reviewed by Shalev (1983) and restated by Huber and Stephens (2001a).

10. See the recent review by Pierson (2000). Important examples of this literature are Soskice (1999), Manow (2001), Crouch and Streeck (1997), and Hollingsworth and Boyer (1997). Esping-Andersen (1990) began to address these issues early.

11. The capacity of states for effective action is inevitably intertwined with unequal relations to different types of interests. Partiality and incapacity must be kept separate conceptually. In reality, they are often not easy to distinguish, and they clearly impact on each other: capacity tends to be less developed in areas of no or little concern and vice versa.

12. That it was the executive branch that offered both the early expert groups and the later policy designs of the World Bank a powerful point of entry is reminiscent of O'Donnell's (1994) concept of "delegative democracy." For east-central Europe, the parallel has probably more value for the first years of transition and is losing relevance now.

13. In the view of Polanyi as well as the embedded liberalism theorists, a liberal economic order has to be buttressed by social regulations and provisions if it is to be politically sustainable. These views had, of course, even earlier roots as well as many parallel proponents. The German Verein für Sozialpolitik advanced many of these ideas in the last quarter of the nineteenth century, and the "Ordo-Liberalism"—so called after the Ordo yearbook—that informed the "social market economy" conceptions of social and economic policy in West Germany after the Second World War was similarly based on the idea that a strong role of the market in the economy must be combined with measures protecting the weakest strata as well as the institutions of family, community, and wider social solidarity.

14. This was formulated in theories of modernization as the concept of a broad "social mobilization" (see, for example, Deutsch 1961 and Huntington 1968). More closely articulated with a theory of social class, this idea informed Lenski (1966) as well as Rueschemeyer, Stephens, and Stephens (1992).

15. See, in addition to the literature cited in note 10, Hall and Soskice (2001) as well as Huber and Stephens (2001b).

16. Many social scientists have reservations about any reference to objective interests because such discourse often substitutes in paternalistic fashion the judgment of the observer for the actually pursued goals of people. Furthermore, it is argued, speaking of objective interests moves one out of the realm of empirical analysis and into inevitably divergent philosophical positions. Yet while the concept is clearly a difficult one, it can be approximated empirically, as Lukes (1974) has successfully argued in a different context.

Bibliography

Adserà, Alícia, and Carles Boix. 2001. "Trade, Democracy and the Size of the Public Sector." *International Organization* 56, no. 2: 229–62.

Aedo, Cristián, and Osvaldo Larrañaga. 1994. "The Chilean Experience." In *Social Service Delivery Systems: An Agenda for Reform,* edited by Cristián Aedo and Osvaldo Larrañaga, 13–50. Washington, DC: Inter-American Development Bank.

Alexandrova, Anastassia. 2000. Operations officer, Social Protection, Social and Human Development Programs, Moscow Office, World Bank. Interview by Linda J. Cook, Moscow, June 9.

Alvarez, R. Michael, Geoffrey Garrett, and Peter Lange. 1991. "Government Partisanship, Labor Organization, and Macro-Economic Performance." *American Political Science Review* 85: 539–56.

Aslund, Anders. 2002. *Building Capitalism: The Transformation of the Former Soviet Bloc.* New York: Cambridge University Press.

———. 1995. *How Russia Became a Market Economy.* Washington, DC: The Brookings Institution.

Astapovich, A. Z., C. A. Afontsev, and A. A. Blokhin. 1998. *Obzor ekonomicheskoi politiki vRossii za 1997 g.* Moscow: Biuro ekonomicheskogo analiza.

Aven, Petr. 1994. "Problems in Foreign Trade Regulation in the Russian Economic Reform." In *Economic Transformation in Russia,* edited by Anders Aslund, 80–93. New York: St. Martin's Press.

Avtonomov, Alexie. 1999. Director of Legal Department, Foundation for the Development of Parliamentarism in Russia. Interview by Linda J. Cook, Moscow, February 1.

Balcerowicz, Leszek. 1995. *Socialism, Capitalism, Transformation.* Budapest: Central European University Press.

Barbado, Amparo Almarcha, ed. 1993. *Spain and EC Membership Evaluated.* New York: St. Martin's Press.

Barr, Nicholas. 1994. "Income Transfers: Social Insurance." In *Labor Markets and Social Policy in Central and Eastern Europe: The Transition and Beyond,* edited by Nicholas Barr, 192–225. Oxford: Oxford University Press.

Barreto, Jose, and Naumann, Reinhard. 1998. "Portugal: Industrial Relations under Democracy." In *Changing Industrial Relations in Europe*, edited by Anthony Ferner and Richard Nyman, 394–425. Oxford: Blackwell.

Barrientos, Armando. 1998. *Pension Reform in Latin America*. Aldershot: Ashgate.

Baumann, Renato. 2002. "Trade Policies, Growth and Equity in Latin America." In *Models of Capitalism: Lessons for Latin America*, edited by Evelyne Huber, 53–80. University Park, PA: The Pennsylvania State University Press.

Beck, Nathaniel, and Jonathan Katz. 1996. "Nuisance versus Substance: Specifying and Estimating Time-Series-Cross-Section Models." *Political Analysis* 6: 1–36.

Belkina, Tatyana. 1998. Department head, Institute of National Economic Forecasting, Russian Academy of Sciences. Interview by Elena Vinogradova, Moscow, November 17.

Berger, Suzanne, and Ronald Dore, eds. 1996. *National Diversity and Global Capitalism*. Ithaca, NY: Cornell University Press.

Bermeo, Nancy. 1994. "Comments." In *The Political Economy of Policy Reform*, edited by John Williamson, 197–206. Washington, DC: Institute for International Economics.

Bermeo, Nancy, with Jose Garcia-Duran. 1994. "Spain: Dual Transition Implemented by Two Parties." In Stephan Haggard and Steven Webb, *Voting for Reform*. New York: Oxford University Press, 89–127.

Betcherman, Gordon. 1995. "Globalization, Labor Markets and Public Policy." In *States against Markets: The Limit of Globalization*, edited by Robert Boyer and Daniel Drache, 250–69. London: Routledge.

Biersteker, Thomas J. 1992. "The 'Triumph' of Neo-Classical Economics in the Developing World: Policy Convergence and Bases of Governance in the International Economic Order." In *Governance without Government: Order and Change in World Politics*, edited by J. N. Rosenau and E. O. Czempiel, 102–31. Cambridge: Cambridge University Press.

Biersteker, Thomas J., and Christine Kearney. 2000. "Global Economic Doctrines: Still the Triumph of Liberal Orthodoxy in Latin America?" Paper presented at the Conference on Economic Doctrines in Latin America: Their Evolution, Transmission and Power. Latin America Centre, St. Antony's College, Oxford.

Birdsall, Nancy, and Frederick Jaspersen. 1997. "Lessons from East Asia's Success." In *Pathways to Growth: Comparing East Asia and Latin America*, edited by Nancy Birdsall and Frederick Jaspersen, 1–12. Washington, DC: Inter-American Development Bank.

Birnbaum, Norman. 2001. *After Progress: American Social Reform and European Socialism in the Twentieth Century*. Oxford: Oxford University Press.

Blanchard, Olivier, and Juan Jimeno. 1995. "Structural Unemployment: Spain versus Portugal." *American Economic Review* 85: 212–18.

Blanchard, Olivier, Rudiger Dornbusch, Paul Krugman, Richard Layard, and Lawrence Summers. 1991. *Reform in Eastern Europe*. Cambridge, MA: MIT Press.

Block, Fred. 1977. "The Ruling Class Does Not Rule: Notes on the Marxist Theory of the State." Reprinted in *The Political Economy: Readings in the Politics and Economics of American Public Policy,* edited by Thomas Ferguson and Joel Rogers, 32–46. Armonk, NY: M. E. Sharpe, 1984.

Bochkareva, Valentina. 1998. Senior researcher, Institute for Social and Economic Problems of the Population, Russian Academy of Sciences. Interview by Elena Vinogradova, Moscow, June 25.

Bollen, Kenneth A., and Robert Jackman. 1985. "Political Democracy and the Size Distribution of Income." *American Sociological Review* 50: 438–57.

Borzutzky, Silvia. 1998. "Chile: The Politics of Privatization." In *Do Options Exist: The Reform of Pension and Health Care Systems in Latin America,* edited by María Amparo Cruz-Saco and Carmelo Mesa-Lago, 35–55. Pittsburgh, PA: University of Pittsburgh Press.

Boyer, Robert, and Daniel Drache, eds. 1996. *States against Markets: The Limits of Globalization.* London: Routledge.

Brady, D., and J. Mo. 1997. "Politics of Labor Reform in Korea: In Search of a Final Settlement." Paper presented at the Seventeenth World Congress of the International Political Science Association, Seoul, August 18–19.

Braga de Macedo, Jorge. 1990. "External Liberalization with Ambiguous Public Response: The Experience of Portugal." In *Unity with Diversity in the European Economy: The Community's Southern Frontier,* edited by Christopher Bliss and Jorge Braga de Macedo, 310–54. Cambridge: Cambridge University Press.

Braithwaite, Jeanine. 1999. "Targeting and the Longer-Term Poor in Russia" (draft). Washington, DC: World Bank.

———. 1997. "The Old and New Poor in Russia." In *Poverty in Russia: Public Policy and Private Responses,* edited by Jeni Klugman, 29–64. Washington, DC: World Bank.

Braithwaite, Jeanine, Christiaan Grootaert, and Branko Milanovic. 1999. *Poverty and Social Assistance in Transition Countries.* New York: St. Martin's Press.

Brenton, Paul, and Daniel Gros. 1997. "Trade Reorientation and Recovery in Transition Economies." *Oxford Review of Economic Policy* 13, no. 2: 65–76.

Broadbent, Edward. 1999. "Social Justice and Citizenship: Dignity, Liberty, and Welfare." In *Governing Modern Societies,* edited by R. V. Ericson and N. Stehr, 276–95. Toronto: University of Toronto Press.

Brune, Nancy, Geoffrey Garrett, Alexandra Guisinger, and Jason Sorens. 2001. "The Political Economy of Capital Account Liberalization." Unpublished manuscript, Yale University.

Cain, Michael J. G., and Aleksander Surdej. 1999. "Transitional Politics or Public Choice? Evaluating Stalled Pension Reforms in Poland." In *Left Parties and Social Policy in Postcommunist Europe,* edited by Linda J. Cook, Mitchell A. Orenstein, and Marilyn Rueschemeyer, 145–74. Boulder, CO: Westview Press.

Calder, Kent. 1988. *Crisis and Compensation: Public Policy and Political Stability in Japan.* Princeton: Princeton University Press.

Calmfors, Lars, and John Driffil. 1988. "Bargaining Structure, Corporatism and Macroeconomic Performance." *Economic Policy* 6: 14–47.

Cameron, David. 2001. "The Return to Europe: The Impact of the EU on Political and Economic Reform in the Post-Communist Countries." Paper prepared for the annual meeting of the American Political Science Association, San Francisco, August 29–September 2.

———. 1984. "Social Democracy, Corporatism, Labour Quiescence, and Representation of Economic Interest in Advanced Capitalist Society." In *Order and Conflict in Contemporary Capitalism: Studies in the Political Economy of Western European Nations,* edited by John Goldthorpe, 143–78. Oxford: Clarendon Press.

———. 1978. "The Expansion of the Public Economy: A Comparative Analysis." *American Political Science Review* 72, no. 4: 1243–61.

Casas, Antonio, and Herman Vargas. 1980. "The Health System of Costa Rica: Toward a National Health Service." *Journal of Public Health Policy* 1 (September): 258–79.

Castles, Francis G. 1985. *The Working Class and Welfare.* Sydney: Allen and Unwin.

———. 1978. *The Social Democratic Image of Society.* London: Routledge and Kegan Paul.

Castles, Francis G., Rolf Gerritsen, and Jack Vowles, eds. 1996. *The Great Experiment: Labour Parties and Public Policy Transformation in Australia and New Zealand.* Sydney: Allen and Unwin.

Castles, Francis G., and Deborah Mitchell. 1993. "Worlds of Welfare and Families of Nations." In *Families of Nations: Public Policy in Western Democracies,* edited by Francis G. Castles, 93–128. Brookfield, VT: Dartmouth Press.

Cavaco Silva, Anibal. 1995. *As Reformas da Decada.* Venda Nova: Bertrand Editora.

CEPAL (Economic Commission for Latin America and the Caribbean). 2002. *Social Panorama of Latin America.* Santiago, Chile: United Nations Economic Commission for Latin America and the Caribbean.

———. 1998. *Social Panorama of Latin America.* Santiago, Chile: United Nations Economic Commission for Latin America and the Caribbean.

———. 1997. *Social Panorama of Latin America.* Santiago, Chile: United Nations Economic Commission for Latin America and the Caribbean.

———. 1996. *Social Panorama of Latin America.* Santiago, Chile: United Nations Economic Commission for Latin America and the Caribbean.

———. 1995. *Social Panorama of Latin America.* Santiago, Chile: United Nations Economic Commission for Latin America and the Caribbean.

———. 1994. *Economic Panorama of Latin America 1994.* New York: United Nations.

Choi, Jang-Jip. 1997. *The Vision and Condition of Korean Democracy* [in Korean]. Seoul: Nanam.

Cichon, Michael, Krzysztof Hagemejer, and Markus Ruck. 1997. "Social Protection and Pension Systems in Central and Eastern Europe." ILO-CEET report no. 21. Budapest: International Labor Organization.

Clarke, Oliver. 1992. "Employment Adjustment: An International Perspective." In *Employment Security and Labor Market Flexibility: An International Perspective*, edited by Kazutoshi Koshiro, 218–44. Detroit: Wayne State University Press.

Cohen, Michael D., James G. March, and J. P. Olsen. 1972. "A Garbage Can Model of Organizational Choice." *Administrative Science Quarterly* 17: 1–25.

Cominetti, Rossella. 1996. "Social Expenditure in Latin America—An Update." Santiago, Chile: CEPAL. Unpublished document.

Commander, Simon, Qimiao Fan, and Mark E. Schaffer. 1996. *Enterprise Restructuring and Economic Policy in Russia*. Washington, DC: World Bank.

Connor, Walter. 1996. *Tattered Banners: Labor, Conflict and Corporatism in Postcommunist Russia*. Boulder, CO: Westview Press.

Cook, Fay Lomax, and Edith J. Barrett. 1992. *Support for the American Welfare State*. New York: Columbia University Press.

Cook, Linda J. 1997. *Labor and Liberalization: Trade Unions in the New Russia*. New York: Twentieth Century Fund.

———. 1993. *The Soviet Social Contract and Why It Failed: Welfare Policy and Workers' Politics from Brezhnev to Yeltsin*. Cambridge, MA: Harvard University Press.

Cook, Linda J., and Mitchell A. Orenstein. 1999. "The Return of the Left and Its Impact on the Welfare State in Russia, Poland, and Hungary." In *Left Parties and Social Policy in Postcommunist Europe*, edited by Linda J. Cook, Mitchell A. Orenstein, and Marilyn Rueschemeyer, 47–108. Boulder, CO: Westview Press.

Cook, Linda J., Mitchell A. Orenstein, and Marilyn Rueschemeyer, eds. 1999. *Left Parties and Social Policy in Postcommunist Europe*. Boulder, CO: Westview Press.

Cornelius, Wayne, Ann L. Craig, and Jonathan Fox. 1994. "Mexico's National Solidarity Program: An Overview." In *Transforming State-Society Relations in Mexico*, edited by Wayne Cornelius, Ann L. Craig, and Jonathan Fox, 3–28. San Diego: University of California Center for U.S.-Mexican Studies.

Crouch, Colin, and Wolfgang Streeck, eds. 1997. *Political Economy of Modern Capitalism: Mapping Convergence and Diversity*. Beverly Hills, CA: Sage Publications.

Czada, Roland. 1998. "Vereinigungskrise und Standortdebatte: Der Beitrag der Wiedervereinigung zur Krise des westdeutschen Modells." *Leviathan* 26, no. 1: 24–59.

———. 1988. "Bestimmungsfaktoren und Genese politischer Gewerkschaftseinbindung." In *Staatstätigkeit: International und historisch vergleichende Analysen*, edited by Manfred G. Schmidt, 178–95. Opladen: Westdeutscher Verlag.

Deacon, Bob. 2001. "Social Policy in a Global Context." In *Inequality, Globalization and World Politics*, edited by Andrew Hurrell and Ngaire Woods, 211–47. Oxford: Oxford University Press.

Deacon, Bob, with Michelle Hulse and Paul Stubbs. 1997. *Global Social Policy: International Organizations and the Future of Welfare*. London: Sage Publications.

Dehesa, Guillermo de la. 1994. "Spain." In *The Political Economy of Policy Reform*, edited by John Williamson, 123–40. Washington, DC: Institute for International Economics.

Deutsch, Karl W. 1961. "Social Mobilization and Political Development." *American Political Science Review* 55: 493–511.

Diamond, Larry, and Richard Gunther, eds. 2001. *Political Parties and Democracy*. Baltimore: The Johns Hopkins University Press.

Diamond, Larry, and Marc F. Plattner, eds. 1991. *The Global Resurgence of Democracy*. Baltimore: The Johns Hopkins University Press.

Diamond, Peter, and Salvador Valdés-Prieto. 1994. "Social Security Reforms." In *The Chilean Economy: Policy Lessons and Challenges*, edited by Barry P. Bosworth, Rudiger Dornbusch, and Raúl Labán, 257–328. Washington, DC: The Brookings Institution.

Díaz, Alvaro. 1993. "Restructuring and the New Working Classes in Chile: Trends in Waged Employment, Informality and Poverty 1973–1990." Discussion paper 47. Geneva: United Nations Research Institute for Social Development.

Dornbusch, Rudiger. 1989. "The Latin American Debt Problem: Anatomy and Solutions." In *Debt and Democracy in Latin America*, edited by Barbara Stallings and Robert Kaufman, 7–22. Boulder, CO: Westview Press.

Draibe, Sonia Miriam. 1997. "The System of Social Protection in Brazil." Paper prepared for the Conference on Social Policies for the Urban Poor in Latin America: Welfare Reform in a Democratic Context, Kellogg Institute, University of Notre Dame, September 12–14.

Drake, Paul W. 1996. *Labor Movements and Dictatorships: The Southern Cone in Comparative Perspective*. Baltimore: The Johns Hopkins University Press.

———. 1994. "Introduction: The Political Economy of Foreign Advisers and Lenders in Latin America." In *Money Doctors, Foreign Debts, and Economic Reforms in Latin America from the 1890s to the Present*, edited by Paul W. Drake, xi–xxxiii. Wilmington, DE: Scholarly Resources.

Easterly, William, and H. Yu. Global Development Network Growth Database. Washington, DC: World Bank, 1999.

Ebbinghaus, Bernhard, and Anke Hassel. 1999. "The Role of Tripartite Concertation in the Reform of the Welfare State." *Transfer* 5, nos. 1–2: 64–81.

Ebbinghaus, Bernhard, and Philip Manow. 1998. "Studying Welfare State Regimes and Varieties of Capitalism: An Introduction." Paper prepared for the Conference on Varieties of Welfare Capitalism, Max Planck Institute for the Study of Societies, Cologne, June 11–13.

Ebbinghaus, Benhard, and Jelle Visser. 2000. *Trade Unions in Europe since 1945*. London: Macmillan.

Echenike, Elena. 1999. Social Reform Foundation. Interview by Elena Vinogradova, Moscow, June.

Edwards, Sebastian, and Nora Lustig. 1997. "Introduction." In *Labor Markets in Latin America: Combining Social Protection with Market Flexibility*, edited by Sebastian Edwards and Nora Lustig, 1–24. Washington, DC: The Brookings Institution.

Eichengreen, Barry, and Richard Kohl. 1998. "The External Sector, the State and Development in Eastern Europe." Working Paper 125, The Berkeley Roundtable on the International Economy. http://www.ciaonet.org.

Eichengreen, Barry, and David Leblang. 2003. "Capital Account Liberalization and Growth: Was Mr. Mahathir Right?" National Bureau for Economic Research Working Paper 9427.

Ekiert, Grzegorz, and Jan Kubik. 1999. *Rebellious Civil Society: Popular Protest and Democratic Consolidation in Poland*. Ann Arbor: University of Michigan Press.

Esping-Andersen, Gøsta. 1999. *Social Foundations of Postindustrial Economies*. New York: Oxford University Press.

———. 1996. "After the Golden Age? Welfare State Dilemmas in a Global Economy." In *Welfare States in Transition*, edited by Gøsta Esping-Andersen. London: Sage.

———. 1990. *The Three Worlds of Welfare Capitalism*. Princeton, NJ: Princeton University Press.

———. 1985. *Politics against Markets*. Princeton, NJ: Princeton University Press.

Esping-Andersen, Gøsta, ed. 1996. *Welfare States in Transition*. London: Sage.

Esping-Andersen, Gøsta, Duncan Gallie, Anton Hemerijck, and John Myles. 2002. *Why We Need a New Welfare State*. New York: Oxford University Press.

Estevez-Abe, Margarita, Torben Iversen, and David Soskice. 2001. "Social Protection and the Formation of Skills: A Reinterpretation of the Welfare State." In *Varieties of Capitalism*, edited by Peter Hall and David Soskice, 145–83. Oxford: Oxford University Press.

Evans, Peter B. 1985. "Transnational Linkages and the Economic Role of the State: An Analysis of Developing and Industrialized Nations in the Post–World War II Period." In *Bringing the State Back In*, edited by Peter Evans, Dietrich Rueschemeyer, and Theda Skocpol, 192–226. Cambridge: Cambridge University Press.

Fidrmuc, Jarko. 2000. "Restructuring European Union Trade with Central and Eastern European Countries." *Atlantic Economic Journal* 28, no. 1: 83–92.

Field, Mark G., and Judyth L. Twigg. 2000. *Russia's Torn Safety Nets: Health and Social Welfare during the Transition*. New York: St. Martin's Press.

Filgueira, Carlos, and Fernando Filgueira. 1997. "Taming Market Reform: The Politics of Social State Reform in Uruguay." Paper presented at the Conference on Social Policies for the Urban Poor in Latin America: Welfare Reform in a Democratic Context, Kellogg Institute, University of Notre Dame, September 12–14.

Filgueira, Fernando. 1995. "A Century of Social Welfare in Uruguay: Growth to the Limit of the Batllista Social State." Working Paper 5, Kellogg Institute, University of Notre Dame, Democracy and Social Policy Series.

Fligstein, Neil. 1998. "Is Globalization the Cause of the Crisis of Welfare States?" Paper presented at the annual meeting of the American Sociological Association, Toronto, Canada, August 1997.

Fox, Louise. 1997. "Pension Reform in the Post-Communist Transition Economies." In *Transforming Post-Communist Political Economies*, edited by Joan M. Nelson, Charles Tilly, and Lee Walker, 370–84. Washington DC: National Academy Press.

Franzese, Robert J., and Peter A. Hall. 2000. "The Institutional Interaction of Wage Bargaining and Monetary Policy." In *Unions, Employers and Central Banks: Wage Bargaining and Macroeconomic Regimes in an Integrating Europe*, edited by Torben Iversen, Jonas Pontusson, and David Soskice, 173–204. Cambridge: Cambridge University Press.

Friedman, Milton. 2000. "Alle Steuern sind zu hoch" (All taxes are too high). *Der Spiegel* 9 (October). http://www.spiegel.de.

Frye, Timothy. 2003. "State Spending and Globalization(s) in the Post-Communist World." Manuscript, Ohio State University.

———. 2001. "Economic Openness and State Spending in the Post-Communist World." Paper presented to the Conference on State-Building in Post-Communist States, Yale University, April 27–28.

Ganghof, Steffen. 2001. "Global Markets, National Tax Systems and Domestic Politics: Rebalancing Efficiency and Equity in Open States' Income Taxation." MPIfG Discussion Paper 01/09, Max Planck Institute for the Study of Societies.

Garretón, Manuel Antonio. 1986. "The Political Evolution of the Chilean Military Regime and Problems in the Transition to Democracy." In *Transitions from Authoritarian Rule: Latin America*, edited by Guillermo O'Donnell, Philippe C. Schmitter, and Laurence Whitehead, 95–122. Baltimore: The Johns Hopkins University Press.

Garrett, Geoffrey. 2001a. "The Distributive Consequences of Globalization." Manuscript, Yale University.

———. 2001b. "Globalization and Government Spending around the World." *Studies in Comparative International Development* 35, no. 4: 3–29.

———. 2000. "The Causes of Globalization." *Comparative Political Studies* 33: 941–91.

———. 1998a. "Global Markets and National Politics: Collision Course or Virtuous Circle?" *International Organization* 52: 787–824.

———. 1998b. *Partisan Politics in the Global Economy*. New York: Cambridge University Press.

Garrett, Geoffrey, and Deborah Mitchell. 2001. "Globalization, Government Spending and Taxation in the OECD." *European Journal of Political Research* 39, no. 2:145–77.

Garrett, Geoffrey, and Jonathan Rodden. 2001. "Globalization and Fiscal Decentralization." Manuscript, Yale University.

Gereffi, Gary. 1995. "Global Production Systems and Third World Development." In *Global Change, Regional Response: The New International Context of Development*, edited by Barbara Stallings, 100–142. Cambridge: Cambridge University Press.

Gimpelson, Vladimir. 2002. Director, Centre for Labour Market Studies, Higher School of Economics. Interview by Linda J. Cook, Moscow, June 26.

Glyn, Andrew. 1995. "The Assessment: Unemployment and Inequality." *Oxford Review of Economic Policy* 11, no. 1: 1–25.

Godfrey, Martin, and Peter Richards. 1997. *Employment Policies and Programmes in Central and Eastern Europe.* Geneva: International Labour Office.

Gomulka, Stanislaw. 1998. "Output: Causes of the Decline and the Recovery." In *Emerging from Communism: Lessons from Russia, China, and Eastern Europe,* edited by Peter Boone, Stanislaw Gomulka, and Richard Layard, 13–42. Cambridge, MA: MIT Press.

Goskomstat. 1997/2001. *Sotsialnoe polozhenie i uroven' zhizni naseleniia Rossii: Ofitsialnoe Izdanie.* Moscow: Goskomstat Rossii.

———. 1998a. *Russia in Figures: Concise Statistical Handbook.* Moscow: Goskomstat.

———. 1998b. *Statisticheskii Biulleten,* no. 3 (42), June.

Gould-Davies, Nigel, and Ngaire Woods. 1999. "Russia and the IMF." *International Affairs* 75, no. 1: 1–22.

Graham, Carol. 1994. *Safety Nets, Politics, and the Poor: Transitions to Market Economies.* Washington, DC: The Brookings Institution.

Greskovits, Bela. 1998. *The Political Economy of Protest and Patience: East European and Latin American Transformations Compared.* Budapest: Central European University Press.

Grosse, Robert. 2002. "Investment Promotion Policies in Latin America. In *Models of Capitalism: Lessons for Latin America,* edited by Evelyne Huber, 103–26. University Park, PA: The Pennsylvania State University Press.

Gustafson, Thane. 1989. *Crisis Amid Plenty: The Politics of Soviet Energy under Brezhnev and Gorbachev.* Princeton, NJ: Princeton University Press.

Hagemejer, Krzysztof. 1999. "The Transformation of Social Security in Central and Eastern Europe." In *Transformation of Social Security: Pensions in Central-Eastern Europe,* edited by Katharina Müller, Andreas Ryll, and Hans-Jurgen Wagener, 31–60. Heidelberg: Physica-Verlag.

Haggard, Stephan, and Robert R. Kaufman. 2001. "Introduction." In *Reforming the State: Fiscal and Welfare Reform in Post-Socialist Countries,* edited by János Kornai, Stephan Haggard, and Robert R. Kaufman, 1–24. Cambridge: Cambridge University Press.

———. 1995. *The Political Economy of Democratic Transitions.* Princeton, NJ: Princeton University Press.

Haggard, Stephan, and Robert R. Kaufman, eds. 1992. *The Politics of Economic Adjustment.* Princeton, NJ: Princeton University Press.

Hall, Peter A. 1998. "Organized Market Economies and Unemployment in Europe: Is It Finally Time to Accept the Liberal Orthodoxy?" Paper delivered at the Eleventh International Conference of Europeanists, Baltimore, February 26–28.

Hall, Peter A., and David Soskice, eds. 2001. *Varieties of Capitalism: The Institutional Foundations of Comparative Advantage*. Oxford: Oxford University Press.

Handelman, Howard, and Werner Baer, eds. 1989. *Paying the Costs of Austerity in Latin America*. Boulder, CO: Westview Press.

Hernández, Diego. 2002. "Pension Reform in Uruguay and Argentina." Master's thesis, Department of Political Science, University of North Carolina, Chapel Hill.

Hicks, Alexander. 1999. *Social Democracy and Welfare Capitalism*. Ithaca, NY: Cornell University Press.

Hicks, Alexander, and Joya Misra. 1993. "Political Resources and the Growth of Welfare in Affluent Capitalist Democracies, 1960–1982." *American Journal of Sociology* 99, no. 3: 668–710.

Hicks, Alexander, and Duane Swank. 1992. "Politics, Institutions, and Welfare Spending in Industrialized Democracies, 1960–1982." *American Political Science Review* 86, no. 3: 658–74.

Hollingsworth, J. Rogers, and Robert Boyer, eds. 1997. *Contemporary Capitalism: The Embeddedness of Institutions*. Cambridge: Cambridge University Press.

Hollman, Otto. 1996. *Integrating Southern Europe: EC Expansion and the Transnationalization of Spain*. London: Routledge.

Huber, Evelyne. 1996. "Options for Social Policy in Latin America: Neoliberal versus Social Democratic Models." In *Welfare States in Transition: National Adaptations in Global Economies*, edited by Gøsta Esping-Andersen, 141–91. London: Sage Publications.

Huber, Evelyne, Charles Ragin, and John D. Stephens. 1997. Comparative Welfare States Data Set, Northwestern University and University of North Carolina. http://www.lis.ceps.lu/compwsp.htm.

———. 1993. "Social Democracy, Christian Democracy, Constitutional Structure and the Welfare State." *American Journal of Sociology* 99, no. 3: 711–49.

Huber, Evelyne, Dietrich Rueschemeyer, and John D. Stephens. 1997. "The Paradoxes of Contemporary Democracy: Formal, Participatory, and Social Dimensions." *Comparative Politics* 29, no. 3: 323–42.

Huber, Evelyne, and John D. Stephens. 2001a. *Development and Crisis of the Welfare State: Parties and Policies in Global Markets*. Chicago: University of Chicago Press.

———. 2001b. "Welfare State and Production Regimes in the Era of Retrenchment." In *The New Politics of the Welfare State*, edited by Paul Pierson, 107–45. Oxford: Oxford University Press.

———. 2000a. "Partisan Governance, Women's Employment and the Social Democratic Service State." *American Sociological Review* 65: 323–42.

———. 2000b. "The Political Economy of Pension Reform: Latin America in Comparative Perspective." Occasional Paper #7. Geneva: United Nations Research Institute for Social Development.

———. 1998. "Internationalization and the Social Democratic Model." *Comparative Political Studies* 31, no. 3: 353–97.

———. 1993. "The Swedish Welfare State at the Crossroads." *Current Sweden*, no. 394 (January).

Huntington, Samuel. 1991. *The Third Wave: Democratization in the Late Twentieth Century*. Norman: University of Oklahoma Press.

———. 1968. *Political Order in Changing Societies*. New Haven, CT: Yale University Press.

Hunya. 2000. "Home Country Patterns of Foreign Direct Investment in Central and East European Countries." *Russian and East European Finance and Trade* 36, no. 2: 87–104.

Im, Hyuk Back. 1994. *Market, State, and Democracy* [in Korean]. Seoul: Nanam.

Ingham, Geoffrey K. 1974. *Strikes and Industrial Conflict: Britain and Scandinavia*. London: Macmillan.

Inter–American Development Bank. 1997. *Economic and Social Progress in Latin America: 1997 Report*. Washington, DC: Inter-American Development Bank.

———. 1996. *Economic and Social Progress in Latin America: 1996 Report*. Washington, DC: Inter-American Development Bank.

———. 1991. *Economic and Social Progress in Latin America: 1991 Report*. Baltimore: The Johns Hopkins University Press, for the Inter-American Development Bank.

International Labour Office. 1998. *World Labour Report, 1997–1998: Industrial Relations, Democracy and Social Stability*. Geneva: International Labour Office.

———. 1984. *The Cost of Social Security: Twelfth International Inquiry, 1981–83*. Geneva: International Labour Office.

International Monetary Fund. 2002. *World Economic Outlook 2002*. www.imf.org.

———. 2001. *Russian Federation: Report on Post-Program Monitoring Discussions*, May 17. Washington, DC: International Monetary Fund.

———. 2000. *World Economic Outlook 2000*. www.imf.org.

———. 1999. *Russian Federation: Recent Economic Developments*. IMF Country Staff Report No. 99/100, September. Washington, DC: International Monetary Fund.

Iversen, Torben. 1998. "Wage Bargaining, Central Bank Independence and the Real Effects of Money." *International Organization* 52, no. 3: 469–504.

———. 1996. "Power, Flexibility and the Breakdown of Centralized Wage Bargaining: The Cases of Denmark and Sweden in Comparative Perspective." *Comparative Politics* 28 (July): 399–436.

Janoski, Thomas, and Alexander Hicks. 1994. *The Comparative Political Economy of the Welfare State*. Cambridge: Cambridge University Press.

Jelinek, Tomas, and Ondrej Schneider. 1999. "An Analysis of the Voluntary Pension Fund System in the Czech Republic." In *Transformation of Social Security: Pen-*

sions in Central-Eastern Europe, edited Katharina Müller, Andreas Ryll, and Hans Jurgen Wagener, 259–74. Heidelberg: Physica.

Jenkins, Robert. 1999. "The Role of the Hungarian Nonprofit Sector in Postcommunist Social Policy." In *Left Parties and Social Policy in Postcommunist Europe,* edited by Linda J. Cook, Mitchell A. Orenstein, and Marilyn Rueschemeyer, 175–206. Boulder, CO: Westview Press.

Jin, Ho Chung, et al., eds. 2002. *Income Inequality, Poverty, and Policy Suggestion* [in Korean]. Seoul: Korean Labor Institute.

"June Draft Legislative Package." 1997. Russian Duma. Photocopy.

Kapstein, Ethan B., and Branko Milanovic. 2003. *Income and Influence: Social Policy in Emerging Market Economies.* Kalamazoo, MI: W. E. Upjohn Institute for Employment Research.

———. 2000. "Dividing the Spoils: Pensions, Privatization and Reform in Russia's Transition." Policy Research Working Paper 2292. Washington, DC: The World Bank.

Karagodin, Maksim Mikhailovich. 2002. Deputy department head, Ministry of Economics of the Russian Federation, Department of Labor, Employment, and Social Policy. Interview by Linda J. Cook, Moscow, June 25.

Katzenstein, Peter. 1985. *Small States in World Markets.* Ithaca, NY: Cornell University Press.

Kay, Stephen James. 1998. "Politics and Social Security Reform in the Southern Cone and Brazil." Ph.D. dissertation, University of California, Los Angeles, Department of Political Science.

Kenworthy, Lane, and Alexander Hicks. 1999. "Neocorporatism, Income Distribution, and Macroeconomic Performance." Paper delivered at the Eleventh Annual Meeting on Socio-Economics, University of Wisconsin, Madison, July 8–11.

Keynes, John Maynard. 1936. *The General Theory of Employment, Interest and Money.* London: Macmillan.

Kierzkowski, Henryk. 2000. "Challenges of Globalization: The Foreign Trade Restructuring of Transition Economies." *Russian and East European Finance and Trade* 36, no. 2 (March-April): 8–41.

Killick, Tony. 1996. "Principles, Agents, and the Limitations of BWI Conditionality." *World Economy* 19, no. 2: 211–29.

Kitschelt, Herbert, Peter Lange, Gary Marks, and John D. Stephens, eds. 1999. *Continuity and Change in Contemporary Capitalism.* New York: Cambridge University Press.

Klugman, Jeni, ed. 1997. *Poverty in Russia: Public Policy and Private Responses.* Washington, DC: World Bank.

Koh, Kyong Wha, et al. 2002. *Korea's Social Expenditure: A Comparative Analysis with OECD Countries.* Seoul: Korea Institute for Health and Social Affairs.

———. 1998. *Korea's Social Expenditure: A Comparative Analysis with OECD Countries* [in Korean]. Seoul: Korea Institute for Health and Social Affairs.

Kolodko, Grzegorz. 1999. "Ten Years of Post-Socialist Transition: Lessons for Policy Reform." World Bank Policy Research Working Paper 2095 (April).

Kopstein, Jeffrey, and David A. Reilly. 2000. "Geographic Diffusion and the Transformation of the Postcommunist World." *World Politics* 53, no. 1: 1–37.

Korea Institute for Health and Social Affairs. 1999. *Health and Welfare Indicators in Korea* [in Korean]. Seoul: KIHSA.

———. 1998. *Health and Welfare Indicators in Korea* [in Korean]. Seoul: KIHSA.

Korea Labor Institute. 1999. *Employment Policy* [in Korean]. Seoul: KLI.

Korpi, Walter. 1989. "Power, Politics, and State Autonomy in the Development of Social Citizenship." *American Sociological Review* 54: 309–28.

———. 1983. *The Democratic Class Struggle*. London: Routledge and Kegan Paul.

Korpi, Walter, and Joakim Palme. 1998. "Redistribution and Strategies of Equality in Western Countries." *American Sociological Review* 63, no. 5: 661–87.

Korzeniewicz, Roberto Patricio, and William C. Smith. 1998. "Searching for the High Road to Economic Growth: Overcoming the Legacy of Persistent Poverty and Inequality in Latin America." Paper presented at the Twenty-first International Congress of the Latin American Studies Association, Chicago, September 24–26.

Kosareva, Nadezhda, and Raymond J. Struyk. 1997. "Reforming Russia." In *Restructuring Russia's Housing Sector: 1991–1997*, edited by Raymond J. Struyk, 1–6. Washington, DC: Urban Institute.

Kozmina, Maya. 1998. Co-founder and co-leader, Association "Senior Generation." Interview by Elena Vinogradova, Moscow, June.

Kulczycki, Andrzej. 1995. "Abortion Policy in Postcommunist Europe: The Conflict in Poland." *Population and Development Review* 21, no. 3: 471–505.

Kuraishi, Mari. 1999. Corporate Strategy Group, Strategy and Resource Management, World Bank. Interview by Linda J. Cook, Washington, DC, April 16.

Kuron, Jacek. 1991. *Moja Zupa* (My soup). Poland: Polska Oficyna Wydawnicza BGW.

Kwon, Huck-ju. 1999. "Inadequate Policy or Operational Failure? The Potential Crisis of the Korean National Pension Program." *Social Policy and Administration* 33, no. 1: 20–38.

Kwon, Soonman. 2002a. "Globalization and Health Policy in Korea." *Global Social Policy* 2: 3.

———. 2002b. "Achieving Health Insurance for All: Lessons from the Republic of Korea." ESS Paper No. 1. Geneva: International Labor Office.

Lee, Eddy. 1998. *The Asian Financial Crisis: The Challenge for Social Policy*. Geneva: International Labor Office.

Lee, H. K. 1999. "Globalization and the Emerging Welfare State—The Experience of South Korea." *International Journal of Social Welfare* 8: 23–37.

Lehmbruch, Gerhard. 1984. "Concertation and the Structure of Corporatist Networks." In *Order and Conflict in Contemporary Capitalism*, edited by John H. Goldthorpe, 60–80. Oxford: Clarendon.

Leibfried, Stephan, and Paul Pierson, eds. 1995. *European Social Policy: Between Fragmentation and Integration*. Washington, DC: The Brookings Institution.

Lenski, Gerhard E. 1966. *Power and Privilege*. New York: McGraw-Hill.

Levy, Jonah. 1999. "Vice into Virtue? Progressive Politics and Welfare Reform in Continental Europe." *Politics and Society* 27, no. 2: 239–73.

Lindbeck, Assar. 1994. "The Welfare State and the Employment Problem." *American Economic Review* (May): 71–75.

———. 1992. *The Welfare State*. London: Elgar.

———. 1975. "Business Cycles, Politics, and International Economic Dependence." *Skandinaviska Eskilda Bank Quarterly Review* 2: 53–68.

———. 1974. *Swedish Economic Policy*. Berkeley and Los Angeles: University of California Press.

Lindblom, Charles E. 1977. *Politics and Markets*. New York: Basic Books.

Lipsmeyer, Christine S. 2000. "Reading between the Welfare Lines: Politics and Policy Structure in Post-Communist Europe." *Europe-Asia Studies* 52, no. 7: 1191.

Lopes, Jose da Silva. 1996. "A Economia Portuguesa desde 1960." In *A Situacao Social em Portugal, 1960–1995*, edited by Antonio Barreto. Lisbon: Instituto de Ciencias Sociais da Universidade de Lisboa.

Lo Vuolo, Rubén M. 1997. "Retrenchment of the Welfare State in Argentina." Paper prepared for the Conference on Social Policies for the Urban Poor in Latin America: Welfare Reform in a Democratic Context, Kellogg Institute, University of Notre Dame, September 12–14.

Lukes, Steven. 1974. *Power: A Radical View*. London: Macmillan.

Madrid, Raúl L. 2003. *Retiring the State: The Politics of Pension Privatization in Latin American and Abroad*. Stanford, CA: Stanford University Press.

———. 2002. "The Politics and Economics of Pension Privatization in Latin America." *Latin American Research Review* 37, no. 2: 159–82.

———. 1997. "The Politics of Social Security Privatization." Paper prepared for the meeting of the Latin American Studies Association, Guadalajara, Continental Plaza Hotel, April 17–19.

Mainwaring, Scott, and Timothy R. Scully, eds. 1995. *Building Democratic Institutions: Party Systems in Latin America*. Stanford, CA: Stanford University Press.

Malloy, James M. 1979. *The Politics of Social Security in Brazil*. Pittsburgh: University of Pittsburgh Press.

Manow, Philip. 2001. "Comparative Institutional Advantages of Welfare State Regimes and New Coalitions in Welfare State Reforms." In *The New Politics of the Welfare State*, edited by Paul Pierson, 146–64. Oxford: Oxford University Press.

Manow, Philip, and Eric Seils. 2000. "Adjusting Badly: The German Welfare State, Structural Change, and the Open Economy." In *Welfare and Work in the Open Economy*. Volume 2, *Diverse Responses to Common Challenges*, edited by Fritz W. Scharpf and Vivien A. Schmidt, 264–307. Oxford: Oxford University Press.

Maravall, Jose Maria. 1993. "Politics and Policy: Economic Reforms in Southern Europe." In *Economic Reforms in New Democracies: A Social Democratic Approach,* edited by Luiz Carlos Bresser Pereira, Jose Maria Maravall, and Adam Przeworski, 77–131. Cambridge: Cambridge University Press.

March, James G., and Herbert A. Simon. 1958. *Organizations.* New York: Wiley.

Mares, Isabela. 2001. "Firms and the Welfare State: When, Why and How Does Social Policy Matter to Employers?" In *Varieties of Capitalism: The Institutional Foundations of Comparative Advantage,* edited by Peter A. Hall and David Soskice, 184–212. New York: Oxford University Press.

Marshall, Thomas. 1950. *Citizenship and Social Class and Other Essays.* Cambridge: Cambridge University Press.

Martin, Cathie Jo. 2000. *Stuck in Neutral: Business and the Politics of Human Capital Investment Policy.* Princeton, NJ: Princeton University Press.

McAuley, Alastair. 1979. *Economic Welfare in the Soviet Union: Poverty, Living Standards, and Inequality.* Madison: University of Wisconsin Press.

McFate, Katherine. 1995. "Trampolines, Safety Nets, or Free Fall: Labor Market Policies and Social Assistance in the 1980s." In *Poverty, Inequality and the Future of Social Policy,* edited by Katherine McFate, Roger Lawson, and William Julius Wilson, 631–64. New York: Russell Sage Foundation.

McGuire, James W. 1996. "Union Strength and Human Development in East Asia and Latin America." Paper presented at the Ninety-second Annual Meeting of the American Political Science Association, San Francisco, CA, August 28–September 1.

Mesa-Lago, Carmelo. 1994. *Changing Social Security in Latin America: Toward Alleviating the Social Costs of Economic Reform.* Boulder, CO: Lynne Rienner.

———. 1991. "Social Security and Prospects for Equity in Latin America." World Bank Discussion Papers 140. Washington, DC: World Bank.

———. 1989. *Ascent to Bankruptcy: Financing Social Security in Latin America.* Pittsburgh: University of Pittsburgh Press.

———. 1983. "Social Security and Extreme Poverty in Latin America." *Journal of Development Economics* 12: 83–110.

———. 1978. *Social Security in Latin America: Pressure Groups, Stratification, and Inequality.* Pittsburgh: University of Pittsburgh Press.

Mesa-Lago, Carmelo, and Alberto Arenas de Mesa. 1998. "The Chilean Pension System: Evaluation, Lessons, and Challenges." In *Do Options Exist? The Reform of Pension and Health Care Systems in Latin America,* edited by María Amparo Cruz-Saco and Carmelo Mesa-Lago, 56–84. Pittsburgh: University of Pittsburgh Press.

Mikhalev, Vladimir. 1996. "Social Security in Russia under Economic Transformation." *Europe-Asia Studies* 48, no. 1: 5–25.

Milanovic, Branko. 1999. "The Role of Social Assistance in Addressing Poverty." In *Poverty and Social Assistance in Transition Countries,* edited by Jeanine Braithwaite, Christiaan Grootaert, and Branko Milanovic, 99–156. New York: St. Martin's Press.

———. 1998. *Income Inequality and Poverty during the Transition from Planned to Market Economy.* Washington, DC: World Bank.

———. 1995. "Poverty, Inequality, and Social Policy in Transition Economies." World Bank Policy Research Working Paper 1530 (November).

Milny, Deborah J. 1999. *Poverty, Equality and Growth: The Politics of Economic Need in Postwar Japan.* Cambridge, MA: Harvard University Asia Center.

Mintrud (Ministry of Labor). 1998. "Mintrud schitaet neobkhodimym otkorrektirovat Programmu pensionnoi reformy" (Mintrud considers it necessary to correct the program of pension reform). *Chelovek I Trud* 9: 31–33.

Misikhina, S. G. 1999. *Sotsial'nye posobiya, l'goty i vyplaty v Rossiiskoi Federatsii: Raspredelenie po gruppam naseleniya s razlichnym urovnen dokhoda: Problemy i resheniya* (Social benefits, privileges, and payments in the Russian Federation: Distribution among groups of the population by levels of income: Problems and solutions). Moscow: TACIS.

Morley, Samuel A. 1995. *Poverty and Inequality in Latin America: The Impact of Adjustment and Recovery in the 1980s.* Baltimore: The Johns Hopkins University Press.

Morrison, Rodney J. 1981. *Portugal: Revolutionary Change in an Open Economy.* Boston: Auburn House.

Mosley, Layna. 2003. *Global Capital and National Governments.* New York: Cambridge University Press.

Mozzicafreddo, Juan. 1997. *Estado Providencia e Cidadania em Portugal.* Oeiras: Celta Editora.

Mudrakov, V. I. 1998. "Programma pensionnoi reformy v Rossiiskoi Federatsii vstupila v silu" (The program of pension reform in the Russian Federation enters into force). *Pensiia* 6, no. 21: 2–4.

Muller, Edward N. 1989. "Democracy and Inequality: Reply to Weede." *American Sociological Review* 54, no. 5: 868–71.

———. 1988. "Democracy, Economic Development, and Income Inequality." *American Sociological Review* 53: 50–68.

Müller, Katharina. 2003. *Privatising Old Age Security: Latin America and Eastern Europe Compared.* Cheltenham: Edward Elgar.

———. 1999. *The Political Economy of Pension Reform in Central-Eastern Europe.* Cheltenham: Edward Elgar.

Musgrove, Philip. 1985. "The Impact of Social Security on Income Distribution." In *The Crisis of Social Security and Health Care: Latin American Experiences and Lessons,* edited by Carmelo Mesa-Lago, 185–208. Latin American Monograph and Document Series, no. 9. Pittsburgh: University of Pittsburgh Center for Latin American Studies.

Myagkov, Mikhail, and Peter Ordeshook. 2001. "The Trail of Votes in Russia's 1999 Duma and 2000 Presidential Elections." *Communist and Post-Communist Studies* 34: 353–70.

Myles, John. 2002. "How to Design a 'Liberal' Welfare State: A Comparison of Canada and the United States." In *Models of Capitalism: Lessons for Latin America*, edited by Evelyne Huber, 339–66. University Park, PA: The Pennsylvania State University Press.

Myles, John, and Paul Pierson. 2001. "The Political Economy of Pension Reform." In *The New Politics of the Welfare State*, edited by Paul Pierson, 305–33. Oxford: Oxford University Press.

National Statistical Office. 1999. Korean Statistical Database [in Korean]. www.nso.go.kr.

Nelson, Joan. 2001. "The Politics of Pension and Health-Care Reforms in Hungary and Poland." In *Reforming the State: Fiscal and Welfare Reform in Post-Socialist Countries*, edited by Janos Kornai, Stephan Haggard, and Robert R. Kaufman, 235–66. Cambridge: Cambridge University Press.

Oates, Sarah. 2000. "1999 Russian Duma Elections." *Problems of Post-Communism* 47, no. 3: 3–15.

O'Donnell, Guillermo. 1999. "Horizontal Accountability and New Polyarchies." In *The Self-Restraining State: Power and Accountability in New Democracies*, edited by Andreas Schedler, Larry Diamond, and Mark Plattner, 29–51. Boulder, CO: Lynne Rienner.

———. 1994. "Delegative Democracy." *Journal of Democracy* 5, no. 1: 55–69.

O'Donnell, Guillermo, Scott Mainwaring, and Samuel Valenzuela, eds. 1992. *Issues in Democratic Consolidation: The New South American Democracies in Comparative Perspective*. Notre Dame, IN: University of Notre Dame Press.

OECD (Organization for Economic Co-operation and Development). 2001. *Social Crisis in the Russian Federation*. Paris: OECD.

———. 2000. *Economic Surveys: Russian Federation, March 2000*. Paris: OECD

———. 1997. *Economic Surveys: Russian Federation 1997*. Paris: OECD.

———. 1996. *The Changing Social Benefits in Russian Enterprises*. Paris: OECD.

———. 1995. *Historical Statistics 1960–93*. Paris: OECD.

———. 1994. *The OECD Jobs Study*. Paris: OECD.

———. Various years. *Economic Surveys Portugal*. Paris: OECD.

———. Various years. *Economic Surveys Spain*. Paris: OECD.

Orenstein, Mitchell. 2001. *Out of the Red: Building Capitalism and Democracy in Postcommunist Europe*. Ann Arbor: University of Michigan Press.

———. 2000. "How Politics and Institutions Affect Pension Reform in Three Post-communist Countries." Policy Research Working Paper 2130. Washington, DC: The World Bank.

Park, Se Il. 2000. *Reforming Labor Management Relations: Lessons from the Korean Experience: 1996–97*. Seoul: KDL Press.

Pempel, T. J. 2002. "Labor Exclusion and Privatized Welfare: Two Keys to Asian Capitalist Development." In *Models of Capitalism: Lessons for Latin America*, edited by Evelyne Huber, 277–300. University Park, PA: The Pennsylvania State University Press.

Perez-Diaz, Victor, and Juan Carlos Rodriguez. 1995. "Inertial Choices: An Overview of Spanish Human Resources, Practices and Policies." In *Employment Relations in a Changing World Economy,* edited by Richard Locke, Thomas Kochan, and Michael Piore, 165–96. Cambridge, MA: MIT Press.

Petrov, Valdimir. 1999. Assistant to the president, Russian Pensioners' Party. Interview by Elena Vinogradova, Moscow, June.

Pfaller, Alfred, Ian Gough, and Goran Therborn, eds. 1991. *Can the Welfare State Compete?* Hampshire: Macmillan.

Pierson, Paul. 2001. "Post-Industrial Pressures on Mature Welfare States." In *The New Politics of the Welfare State,* edited by Paul Pierson, 80–106. Oxford: Oxford University Press.

———. 2000. "Three Worlds of Welfare State Research." *Comparative Political Studies* 33, no. 6/7: 791–821.

———. 1998. "Irresistible Forces, Immovable Objects: Post-Industrial Welfare States Confront Permanent Austerity." *Journal of European Public Policy* 5/4: 539–60.

———. 1996. "The New Politics of the Welfare State." *World Politics* 48, no. 2: 143–79.

———. 1994. *Dismantling the Welfare State: Reagan, Thatcher and the Politics of Retrenchment.* Cambridge: Cambridge University Press.

Pierson, Paul, ed. 2001. *The New Politics of the Welfare State.* Oxford: Oxford University Press.

Poik, Valentin. 1998. "Postroenie novoi pensionnoi sistemy: zadacha natsionalnogo masshtaba" (The construction of a new pension system: A task on a national scale). *Chelovek I Trud* 4: 65–71.

Polanyi, Karl. 1957/1944. *The Great Transformation.* Boston: Beacon Press.

Posner, Paul. 1997. "Pacted Democratization and the Urban Poor in Chile." Ph.D. dissertation, Department of Political Science, University of North Carolina.

Pryor, Frederic. 1973. *Property and Industrial Organization in Communist and Capitalist Countries.* Bloomington: Indiana University Press.

Przeworski, Adam, Michael Alvarez, Jose Cheibub, and Fernando Limongi. 2000. *Democracy and Development.* New York: Cambridge University Press.

Pushkina, Tamara, and Maria Turovskya. 1999. "Negosudarstvennym pensionnym fondam trebuetsia gosudarstvennaia podderzhka" (Non-state pension funds demand state support). *Chelovek I Trud* 4: 36–37.

Puzanov, Alexander S. 1999. Project manager and board member, Institute for Urban Economics. Interview by Linda J. Cook, Moscow, February 5.

Quinn, Dennis, and Carla Inclan. 1997. "The Origins of Financial Openness: A Twenty-one Country Study of Its Determinants, 1950–1988." *American Journal of Political Science* 41: 771–813.

Raczynski, Dagmar. 1994. "Social Policies in Chile: Origin, Transformations, and Perspectives." Working Paper 4, Democracy and Social Policy Series. Notre Dame, IN: Kellogg Institute, University of Notre Dame.

———. 1997. "Social Policies in Chile: Origin and Transformations." Paper prepared for the Conference on Social Policies for the Urban Poor in Latin America: Welfare Reform in a Democratic Context, Kellogg Institute, University of Notre Dame, September 12–14.

Rein, Martin, Barry L. Friedman, and Andreas Wörgötter, eds. 1997. *Enterprise and Social Benefits after Communism*. Cambridge: Cambridge University Press.

Remington, Thomas. 2001 *The Russian Parliament: Institutional Evolution in a Transitional Regime, 1989–1999*. New Haven, CT: Yale University Press.

Remington, Thomas F., and Steven S. Smith. 1995. "The Development of Parliamentary Parties in Russia." *Legislative Studies Quarterly* 20, no. 4: 457–89.

Rew, Jung Soon. 2000. "Estimation of Population in Poverty and Livelihood of Poor Households." In *Poverty after IMF in Korea* [in Korean], edited by Kim Dong Choon. Seoul: Nanam.

Rhodes, Martin. 2001. "The Political Economy of Social Pacts: 'Competitive Corporatism' and European Welfare Reform." In *The New Politics of the Welfare State*, edited by Paul Pierson, 165–96. Oxford: Oxford University Press.

Rieger, Elmar, and Stephan Leibfried. 2003. *Limits to Globalization*. Cambridge: Polity Press.

———. 2000. "Wohlfahrtsmerkantilismus: Wechselwirkungen zwischen demokratischer Sozialpolitik und Welthandelsordnung." *Aus Politik und Zeitgeschichte* 48: 12–22.

Ringold, Dena. 1999. "Social Policy in Postcommunist Europe: Legacies and Transition." In *Left Parties and Social Policy in Postcommunist Europe*, edited by Linda J. Cook, Mitchell A. Orenstein, and Marilyn Rueschemeyer, 11–46. Boulder, CO: Westview Press.

Rodrik, Dani. 1999. *The New Global Economy and Developing Countries: Making Openness Work*. Washington, DC: Overseas Development Council.

———. 1998. "Why Do More Open Economies Have Bigger Government?" *Journal of Political Economy* 106: 997–1032.

———. 1997. *Has Globalization Gone Too Far?* Washington, DC: Institute for International Economics.

Rokkan, Stein. 1970. *Citizens, Elections, Parties*. Oslo: Universitetsforlaget.

Rose, Richard, Neil Munro, and Stephen White. 2001. "Voting in a Floating Party System: The 1999 Duma Election." *Europe-Asia Studies* 53, no. 3: 419–44.

Rowthorn, Robert. 1995. "Capital Formation and Unemployment." *Oxford Review of Economic Policy* 11, no. 1: 29–39.

Roxborough, Ian. 1989. "Organized Labor: A Major Victim of the Debt Crisis." In *Debt and Democracy in Latin America*, edited by Barbara Stallings and Robert Kaufman, 91–108. Boulder, CO: Westview Press.

Rueschemeyer, Dietrich, Evelyne H. Stephens, and John D. Stephens. 1992. *Capitalist Development and Democracy*. Cambridge: Polity Press.

Ruggie, John Gerard. 1982. "International Regimes, Transactions and Change: Embedded Liberalism in the Postwar Economic Order." *International Organization* 36: 379–415.

Russell, Peter, ed. 1999. *The Future of Social Democracy*. Toronto: University of Toronto Press.

Russian Economic Trends. 2002. Russian-European Centre for Economic Policy and the Working Centre for Economic Reform, Government of the Russian Federation. April 15.

Rys, Vladimir. 1998. "From the Communist Welfare State to Social Benefits of Market Economy: The Determinants of the Transition Process in Central Europe." In *Challenges to the Welfare State: Internal and External Dynamics for Change*, edited by Henry Cavanna, 138–53. Cheltenham: Edward Elgar.

Sachs, Jeffrey. 1995. "Postcommunist Parties and the Politics of Entitlements." *Transition Newsletter*. Development Economics Group, World Bank. http://www.worldbank.org/html/prddr/trans/mar95/pgs1–4.htm.

Scharpf, Fritz W. 2000. "Economic Changes, Vulnerabilities, and Institutional Capabilities." In *Welfare and Work in the Open Economy*, vol. 1, edited by F. W. Scharpf and V. A. Schmidt, 21–124. Oxford: Oxford University Press.

Scharpf, Fritz W., and Vivien A. Schmidt. 2000. Introduction and Conclusion to *Welfare and Work in the Open Economy*, vol. 1, edited by F. W. Scharpf and V. A. Schmidt, 1–20, 310–36. Oxford: Oxford University Press.

Schmitter, Philippe, and Terry Lynn Karl. 1991 "What Democracy Is . . . And Is Not." In *The Global Resurgence of Democracy*, edited by Larry Diamond and Marc F. Plattner, 49–62. Baltimore: The Johns Hopkins University Press.

Schwartz, Herman. 2000. "Internationalization and Two Liberal Welfare States: Australia and New Zealand." In *Welfare and Work in the Open Economy*, vol. 2, edited by F. W. Scharpf and V. A. Schmidt, 69–130. Oxford: Oxford University Press.

———. 1998. "Social Democracy Going Down or Down Under: Institutions, Internationalized Capital and Indebted States." *Comparative Politics* 30, no. 3: 253–72.

———. 1994a. "Public Choice Theory and Public Choices: Bureaucrats and State Reorganization in Australia, Denmark, New Zealand, Sweden in the 1980s." *Administration and Society* 26: 48–77.

———. 1994b. "Small States in Big Trouble: The Politics of State Organization in Australia, Denmark, New Zealand, and Sweden." *World Politics* 46: 527–55.

Scott, James C. 1998. *Seeing Like a State: How Certain Schemes to Improve the Human Condition Have Failed*. New Haven, CT: Yale University Press.

Sederlof, Hjalte. 1999. Program team leader, Social and Human Development Programs, Europe and Central Asia Region, World Bank. Interview by Linda J. Cook, Providence, RI, April 29.

Sen, Amartya. 1999. *Development as Freedom*. New York: Alfred A. Knopf.

Shalev, Michael. 1983. "The Social Democratic Model and Beyond: Two 'Generations' of Comparative Research on the Welfare State." *Comparative Social Research* 6: 315–51.

Shishkov, Iu. 1996. "Russia's Thorny Path to the Global Economy." *Russian Social Science Review* 37, no. 6: 3–20.

Shleifer, Andrei, and Daniel Treisman. 2000. *Without a Map: Political and Economic Reform in Russia*. Cambridge: MIT Press.

Skocpol, Theda, and Edwin Amenta. 1986. "States and Social Policies." *Annual Review of Sociology* 12: 131–57.

Slay, Ben. 2002. "The Russian Economy: How Far from Sustainable Growth?" In *Russia's Uncertain Economic Future*, U.S. Congress Joint Economic Committee. Washington, DC: GPO.

Smith, W. Rand. 1998. *The Left's Dirty Job: The Politics of Industrial Restructuring in France and Spain*. Pittsburgh: University of Pittsburgh Press.

Song, Ho Keun. 2002. "Labour Unions in the Republic of Korea: Challenge and Choice." In *Organized Labour in the Twenty-First Century*, edited by A.V. Jose, 199–237. Geneva: ILO, International Institute for Labor Studies.

———. 2001. *What Doctors Wanted to Say* [in Korean]. Seoul: Samsung Economic Institute.

———. 1996. *Company Welfare in Korea: An Empirical Study* [in Korean]. Seoul: FKTU.

Soskice, David. 2000. "Macroeconomic Analysis and the Political Economy of Unemployment." In *Unions, Employers and Central Banks: Wage Bargaining and Macroeconomic Regimes in an Integrating Europe*, edited by Torben Iversen, Jonas Pontusson, and David Soskice, 38–76. Cambridge: Cambridge University Press.

———. 1999. "Divergent Production Regimes: Coordinated and Uncoordinated Market Economies in the 1980s and 1990s." In *Continuity and Change in Contemporary Capitalism*, edited by H. Kitschelt, G. Marks, and J. D. Stephens, 101–34. Cambridge: Cambridge University Press.

Stallings, Barbara, and Robert Kaufman, eds. 1989. *Debt and Democracy in Latin America*. Boulder, CO: Westview Press.

Stallings, Barbara, and Wilson Peres. 2000. *Growth, Employment, and Equity: The Impact of the Economic Reforms in Latin America and the Caribbean*. Washington, DC: Brookings Institution Press.

Standing, Guy. 1995. "Labor Insecurity through Market Regulation: Legacy of the 1980s, Challenge for the 1990s." In *Poverty, Inequality and the Future of Social Policy*, edited by Katherine McFate, Roger Lawson, and William Julius Wilson, 153–96. New York: Russell Sage Foundation.

Standing, Guy, and Daniel Vaughan-Whitehead. 1995. *Minimum Wages in Central and Eastern Europe: From Protection to Destitution*. Budapest: Central European University Press.

Stephens, John D. 2000. "Is Swedish Corporatism Dead? Thoughts on Its Supposed Demise in the Light of the Abortive 'Alliance for Growth' in 1998." Paper presented at the Twelfth International Conference of Europeanists, Council of European Studies, Chicago, March 30–April 1.

———. 1996. "The Scandinavian Welfare States." In *Welfare States in Transition*, edited by Gøsta Esping-Andersen, 32–65. London: Sage.

———. 1991. "Explaining Crossnational Differences in Union Organization: Why Are Small Countries More Organized than Large Ones?" *American Political Science Review* (September).

———. 1989. "Democratic Transition and Breakdown in Europe, 1870–1939: A Test of the Moore Thesis." *American Journal of Sociology* 94, no. 5: 1019–77.

———. 1986/1979. *The Transition from Capitalism to Socialism*, 2nd ed. Urbana: University of Illinois Press.

Stephens, John D., Evelyne Huber, and Leonard Ray. 1999. "The Welfare State in Hard Times." In *Continuity and Change in Contemporary Capitalism*, edited by Herbert Kitschelt, Peter Lange, Gary Marks, and John D. Stephens, 164–93. New York: Cambridge University Press.

Stiglitz, Joseph E. 2002. *Globalization and Its Discontents*. New York: W. W. Norton.

Streeck, Wolfgang. 1997. "German Capitalism: Does It Exist? Can It Survive?" *New Political Economy* 2: 237–56.

———. 1995. "From Market Making to State Building? Reflections on the Political Economy of European Social Policy." In *European Social Policy: Between Fragmentation and Integration*, edited by Stephan Leibfried and Paul Pierson, 389–431. Washington, DC: The Brookings Institution.

Struyk, Raymond J., ed. 1997. *Restructuring Russia's Housing Sector, 1991–1997*. Washington, DC: Urban Institute.

Struyk, Raymond J., Alexander S. Puzanov, and Lisa A. Lee. 1997. "Monitoring Russia's Experience with Housing Allowances." *Urban Studies* 34, no. 11: 1789–1818.

Swank, Duane. 2002. *Global Capital, Political Institutions, and Policy Change in Developed Welfare States*. New York: Cambridge University Press.

———. 1999. "Diminished Democracy?" Paper delivered at the Eleventh Annual Meeting on Socio-Economics, University of Wisconsin, Madison, Wisconsin, July 8–11.

———. 1998. Funding the Welfare State: Globalization and the Taxation of Business in Advanced Market Economies. *Political Studies* 46, no. 4: 671–92.

———. 1988. "The Political Economy of Governmental Domestic Expenditure in Affluent Democracies, 1960–1980." *American Journal of Political Science* 32: 1121–50.

Swenson, Peter. 2002. *Capitalists against Markets: The Making of Labor Markets and Welfare States in the United States and Sweden*. Oxford: Oxford University Press.

———. 1991. "Bringing Capital Back In, or Social Democracy Reconsidered: Employer Power, Cross-Class Alliances, and Centralization of Industrial Relations in Denmark and Sweden." *World Politics* 43, no. 4: 513–44.

Szacki, Jerzy. 1995. *Liberalism after Communism*. Translated by Chester A. Kisiel. Budapest: Central European University Press.

Teichman, Judith A. 2001. *The Politics of Freeing Markets in Latin America: Chile, Argentina, and Mexico*. Chapel Hill, NC: University of North Carolina Press.

Tilly, Charles. 1975. Reflections on the History of European State-Making. In *The For-*

mation of National States in Western Europe, edited by C. Tilly, 3–83. Princeton, NJ: Princeton University Press.

Trejos, Juan Diego, Leopoldo Garnier, Guillermo Monge, and Roberto Hidalgo. 1994. "Enhancing Social Services in Costa Rica." In *Social Service Delivery Systems: An Agenda for Reform,* edited by Cristián Aedo and Osvaldo Larrañaga, 51–90. Washington, DC: Inter-American Development Bank.

UNICEF. 1994. *Crisis in Mortality, Health, and Nutrition.* Economies in Transition Studies Regional Monitoring Report 2.

Urban, Joan Barth, and Valerii D. Solovei. 1997. *Russia's Communists at the Crossroads.* Boulder, CO: Westview Press.

Uthoff, Andras. 1995. *Reformas a los sistemas de pensiones en América Latina y el Caribe.* Santiago, Chile: CEPAL.

Varas, Augusto. 1995. "Latin America: Toward a New Reliance on the Market. In *Global Change, Regional Response: The New International Context of Development,* edited by Barbara Stallings, 272–308. New York: Cambridge University Press.

Vecernik, Jiri. 2000. "Social Problems and Policies in the Czech Republic after 1989: Transition Costs and Social Structure." Prague: Institute of Sociology. Unpublished manuscript.

———. 1999. "The Middle Class in the Czech Reforms: The Interplay between Policies and Social Stratification." *Communist and Post-Communist Studies* 32: 397–416.

Vecernik, Jiri, et al. 1999. *Ten Years of Rebuilding Capitalism: Czech Society after 1989.* Prague: Academia.

Vinals, Jose. 1996. "Job Creation in Spain: A Macroeconomic View." In *The Social Challenge of Job Creation,* edited by Jordi Gual, 91–118. Cheltenham: Edward Elgar.

Vinogradova, Elena. 1999. "Provision of Social Benefits by Russian Enterprises: Managers' Behavior and Motivations." Paper presented at the Workshop on Labor and Privatization, Watson Institute, Brown University, Providence, RI, March 6.

Visser, Jelle. 1991. "Union Organization: Why Countries Differ." Paper presented at the meeting of the International Industrial Relations Association, Sydney, Australia, August 30-September 3.

Vujacic, Veljko. 1996. "Gennadiy Zyuganov and the 'Third Road.'" *Post-Soviet Affairs* 12, no. 2: 118–54.

Wade, Robert. 1996. "Globalization and Its Limits." In *National Diversity and Global Capitalism,* edited by Suzanne Berger and Ronald Dore, 60–88. Ithaca, NY: Cornell University Press.

Wallerstein, Michael. 1991. "Explaining Crossnational Differences in Union Organization: Why Are Small Countries More Organized than Large Ones?" *American Political Science Review* 85: 41–49.

———. 1989. "Union Organization in Advanced Industrial Democracies." *American Political Science Review* 83: 481–501.

Walton, John. 1989. "Debt, Protest, and the State in Latin America." In *Power and*

Popular Protest: Latin American Social Movements, edited by Susan Eckstein, 299–328. Berkeley and Los Angeles: University of California Press.

Weede, Erich. 1989. "Democracy and Income Inequality Reconsidered: Comment on Muller." *American Sociological Review* 54: 865–68.

Western, Bruce. 1991. "A Comparative Study of Corporatist Development." *American Sociological Review* 56: 283–94.

Westin, Peter. 1999. "Foreign Direct Investments in Russia." *Russian Economic Trends* 1: 36–43.

Weyland, Kurt G. 2002. *The Politics of Market Reform in Fragile Democracies: Argentina, Brazil, Peru, and Venezuela.* Princeton, NJ: Princeton University Press.

———. 1998. "Swallowing the Bitter Pill: Sources of Popular Support for Neoliberal Reform in Latin America." *Comparative Political Studies* 31, no. 5: 539–68.

———. 1996. *Democracy without Equity: Failures of Reform in Brazil.* Pittsburgh: University of Pittsburgh Press.

Wilding, Paul. 1997. "Globalization, Regionalism and Social Policy." *Social Policy and Administration* 31, no. 4: 410–28.

Wilensky, Harold. 1976. *The "New Corporatism," Centralization, and the Welfare State.* Beverly Hills, CA: Sage.

———. 1975. *The Welfare State and Equality: Structural and Ideological Roots of Public Expenditure.* Berkeley and Los Angeles: University of California Press.

Wilensky, Harold, and Charles Lebeaux. 1965. *Industrial Society and Social Welfare.* New York: The Free Press.

Williamson, John, ed. 1990. *Latin American Adjustment: How Much Has Happened?* Washington, DC: Institute for International Economics.

Wood, Adrian. 1994. *North-South Trade, Employment and Inequality.* Oxford: Clarendon Press.

World Bank. 2000. *Balancing Protection and Opportunity: A Strategy for Social Protection in Transition Economies.* Technical paper, Social Protection Team, Human Development Sector Unit, Europe and Central Asia Region. Washington, DC: World Bank.

———. 1999a "Russia's Social Policy Malaise: Key Reform Priorities as a Response to the Present Crisis." Photocopy, "Work in Progress," dated March 18.

———. 1999b. *World Development Indicators.* Washington, DC: World Bank.

———. 1998. *Russian Federation Housing and Utility Services: Policy Priorities and the Next Stage of Reforms.* Report No. 17483-RU. Washington, DC: World Bank.

———. 1997. "Report and Recommendation of the President of the I.B.R.D. to the Executive Directors on a Proposed Social Protection Adjustment Loan." June 5. Washington, DC: World Bank.

———. 1996a. *Fiscal Management in Russia.* Washington, DC: World Bank.

———. 1996b. *Russian Federation: Enterprise Housing Divestiture Project.* Staff Appraisal Report No. 15112-RU. Washington, DC: World Bank.

———. 1996c. *Russian Federation: Toward Medium-Term Viability.* Washington, DC: World Bank.

———. 1996d. *From Plan to Market: World Development Report.* Washington, DC: World Bank.

———. 1995a. *Poverty in Russia: An Assessment.* World Bank Report No. 14110-RU. Washington, DC: World Bank.

———. 1995b. *Russia: Housing Reform and Privatization.* Vol. 1, *Main Report,* No. 14929-RU. Washington, DC: World Bank.

———. 1995c. *Russian Federation Housing Project.* Staff Appraisal Report No. 13022–RU. Washington, DC: World Bank.

———. 1995d. *Understanding Poverty in Poland.* Washington, DC: World Bank.

———. 1994a. *Averting the Old Age Crisis: Policies to Protect the Old and Promote Growth.* New York: Oxford University Press.

———. 1994b. *World Development Indicators.* Washington, DC: World Bank.

World Development Indicators. 2000. Washington, DC: World Bank.

Yannopoulos, George, ed. 1989. *European Integration and the Iberian Economies.* London: Macmillan.

"Za Nashu sovetskuiu rodinu" (For our Soviet homeland). 1995. Pre-electoral platform of the KPRF. *Pravda Rossii,* no.16 (30), September 7: 2.

Contributors

Linda Cook is professor of political science at Brown University. She has published two books on Soviet/Russian labor and social policy, *The Soviet Social Contract and Why It Failed: Welfare Policy and Workers' Politics from Brezhnev to Yeltsin* and *Labor and Liberalization: Trade Unions in the New Russia*. Additional publications include *Left Parties and Social Policy in Postcommunist Europe* (co-edited with Mitchell Orenstein and Marilyn Rueschemeyer) and *Privatization and Labor: Responses and Consequences in Global Perspective* (co-edited with Marsha Pripstein Posusney).

Geoffrey Garrett is dean and vice provost of the International Institute, director of the Burkle Center for International Relations, and professor of political science at UCLA. He is author of *Partisan Politics in the Global Economy* and is currently completing *Globalization Fact and Globalization Fiction*.

Miguel Glatzer is a visiting lecturer in the Department of Political Science at the University of Massachusetts-Dartmouth and the Department of History, Philosophy, and Social Science at the Rhode Island School of Design. His research interests lie in comparative social policy and civic education in divided societies and new democracies. He has written on labor market reforms and the relationship of welfare states to nonprofit organizations and is co-editor of *Portugal: Strategic Options in a European Context* (with Angelo Cardoso, Fatima Monteiro, and Jose Tavares).

Martine Haas is assistant professor of organizational behavior at the School of Industrial and Labor Relations at Cornell University. Her research focuses on the dissemination of information and ideas within and between organizations, with particular attention to the power and status of the actors involved and the implications for international development.

Kyung Zoon Hong is associate professor of social welfare at Sungkyunkwan University. His research interests include Korea's welfare regime, welfare politics, and poverty. He is the author of *The Social Welfare Regime in Korea* (in Korean) and several articles.

Evelyne Huber (formerly Evelyne Huber Stephens) is Morehead Alumni Distinguished Professor of Political Science at the University of North Carolina at Chapel

Hill. Her interests center on the politics of reform, ranging from installation of formal political democracy and widening of political inclusion to establishment and adaptation of generous and redistributive social policy. She has written on these topics comparing cases within and across Latin America and western Europe. Among her recent publications are *Models of Capitalism: Lessons for Latin America* (as editor, 2002), and *Development and Crisis of the Welfare State: Parties and Policies in Global Markets* (with John D. Stephens, 2001).

David Nickerson is a graduate student in political science at Yale University. His major research interests lie in voter mobilization and interpersonal communication. His articles have appeared in the *Journal of Politics*, the *Journal of Political Marketing*, and *Political Analysis*.

Mitchell A. Orenstein is associate professor of political science and director of the Center for European Studies at the Maxwell School of Syracuse University. He is the author of *Out of the Red: Building Capitalism and Democracy in Postcommunist Europe* (2001) and has published widely on the political economy of post-Communist welfare states. He has recently co-authored *Roma in an Expanding Europe: Breaking the Poverty Cycle* (World Bank, 2005). Orenstein's current research examines pension privatization as an instance of global public policy development and diffusion.

Dietrich Rueschemeyer is a professor of sociology and the Charles C. Tillinghast Jr. Professor of International Studies Emeritus at Brown University. He is currently a research professor at Brown's Watson Institute for International Studies. His publications include *Bringing the State Back In* (co-edited with Peter B. Evans and Theda Skocpol, 1985), *Power and the Division of Labour* (1986), *Capitalist Development and Democracy* (co-authored with John D. Stephens and Evelyne Huber Stephens, 1992), and *Comparative Historical Analysis in the Social Sciences* (co-edited with James Mahoney, 2003). He currently works on a monograph in social theory tentatively titled "Usable Theory: Analytic Tools for Social Research."

Ho Keun Song is professor of sociology at Seoul National University. He has written widely on democratization, labor politics, industrial restructuring, and social policy in Korea. Recent work in English includes the chapter on Korea in *Worlds of Work: Building an International Sociology of Work*, edited by Daniel B. Cornfield and Randy Hodson.

John D. Stephens is the Gerhard E. Lenski Jr. Distinguished Professor of Political Science and Sociology at the University of North Carolina, Chapel Hill. His main interests are comparative politics and political economy, with area foci on Europe and the Caribbean. He is the author of *The Transition from Capitalism to Socialism* (1979) and co-author of *Democratic Socialism in Jamaica* (with Evelyne Huber, 1986), *Capitalist Development and Democracy* (with Evelyne Huber and Dietrich Rueschemeyer, 1992), and *Development and Crisis of the Welfare State* (with Evelyne Huber, 2001). He is also author or co-author of a number of book chapters and journal articles, most recently (2003) publishing articles on poverty and income distribution in the *American Sociological Review* and *World Politics*. He is currently working on a study of the impact of neoliberal economic reform of social policy in Latin America, Iberia, and the Antipodes.

Index